The Four Gospels

The Four Gospels

A Translation in Verse

By Kalmia Bittleston

Floris Books

First published in single volumes by Floris Books
The Gospel of Matthew in 1988
The Gospel of Mark in 1986
The Gospel of Luke in 1990
The Gospel of John in 1984

This edition first published in 2007 by Floris Books
© 2007 The Christian Community

All rights reserved. No part of this publication may be reproduced without the prior permission of Floris Books, 15 Harrison Gardens Edinburgh.
www.florisbooks.co.uk

British Library CIP Data available

ISBN 978-086315-570-3

Printed by Cromwell Press, Trowbridge

Contents

Kalmia Bittleston	7
Introduction	9
Synopses	33
The Gospel of Matthew	45
The Gospel of Mark	201
The Gospel of Luke	299
The Gospel of John	467
References to the Old Testament	587

This edition of Kalmia Bittleston's translation of the four Gospels brings together the original four separate publications into a single volume. Some minor editing has been done on the text by Arie Boogert. Kalmia Bittleston's original Preface and Translator's Note have been abridged and combined into the present Preface. Adam Bittleston's two Gospel Introductions are retained as also Michael Tapp's Introduction to Mark.

Kalmia Bittleston

Kalmia Bittleston was born in South Africa in 1909. Her father was an officer in the British Army, later a teacher. Her mother was a niece of Lord Halifax, an erstwhile Viceroy of India. The family returned to England some months after she was born. A brother, Adam, was born in 1911. Kalmia was largely educated at home by her mother. This was followed by a Montessori training. She began work at Sunfield Children's Home for handicapped children, based on the principles of Rudolf Steiner, whose work had been introduced to her when she was 18. Later she worked at a similar home in Switzerland. She returned to England at the outbreak of war. During this time she made a strong connection to the Christian Community and was ordained into the priesthood in 1944. She worked in Leeds and the London area until her retirement in 1979. It was in her remaining ten years that she worked on these translations. It was a real labour of love. They were completed shortly before her death. Her brother, Adam, was ordained in The Christian Community in 1935. They were both unique personalities and remained closely connected throughout their lives. It is fitting that he contributed two of the Gospel introductions to his sister's work. They died within ten days of each other in 1989.

Kalmia Bittleston was in every respect a modest person. Her outer needs were minimal. She cultivated wide and ever new interests which she pursued alongside the constancy of her religious life. Her social awareness extended into her regular practice of the inner life through her cultivation of the remembrance of the dead. This greater dimension was ever present in her life. It was not something she talked about, but in knowing her one could sense how real it was. Her Gospel translations, particularly in the way they are presented, are a witness to a life dedicated, unassumingly but with constancy, to the Christian life.

Her intention with this translation, which may at first suggest verse, was in support of clarity. The narrative was separated from direct speech; whether it is Jesus himself speaking or one of his disciples, or perhaps another actor in the drama. The Gospels are indeed dramatic, and because the short lines of this translation carry the reader forward, it should be read *slowly*, no faster than reading aloud. In early Christian centuries congregations gathered together to hear the Gospel read. Very few would have been able to own a copy of even part of one of the Gospels. They were intended to be heard and have the rhythms and repetitions of speech so that they can be remembered.

Michael Tapp

Introduction

Why another translation?
There is no single way of approaching the Gospels. Like all spiritual documents they open up according to the eye of the beholder. None of us has a totally objective eye which would enable us to see directly into the life and substance of the Gospel. If we know and accept this fact we shall not be tempted to think that what we have discovered is anything like the whole truth. We must be satisfied with just the little insight that we can manage, knowing that further efforts will add to this in time. As the eye opens, so more can be seen.

All the Gospels are history. They describe events which happened at a certain time and at a certain place. But they are also spiritual documents whose substance transcends particular times and places. Several issues arise out of this. One is the establishment of the correct original Greek texts. The earliest texts, which are all copies of earlier texts, go back to the fourth century, though there are earlier fragments. While there is widespread agreement deduced from the manuscripts as to the Greek text to be used, there are nevertheless considerable variations possible, though mainly minor. The second issue concerns the translations of the original Greek into other languages. The Greek text remains the same, but all other languages will be in a constant process of change. The third is the question of interpretation which will inevitably colour the translation. Interpretation is governed by what lives in the mind of the translator. Any documents which are of a spiritual nature will be multi-layered and open up according to the inner disposition of the reader and indeed to that of the translator. The fundamentalist and the mystic, for instance, will live in quite different ways with such documents. Out of all this it is clear that there will always be new attempts to render the scriptures afresh. Kalmia Bittleston describes in her Preface her own approach to this task. Her aim is to encourage readers to live with these texts in a meditative way, for only then will the hidden layers come to the surface.

The Evangelists in their time
The Christ Jesus was born in Palestine and except for a few excursions beyond its borders he lived his whole life there. His physical inheritance was purely Jewish. With it came the religious practices, inaugurated through Moses and cultivated in the sacrificial ceremonies in the Temple and in obedience to the commandments. Unique to the Jews was the worship of the one God, Yahweh, in contrast to the otherwise universal worship of many gods. The Jews stood out as a people whose lives were governed by

a religious practice which did not fit comfortably into the world of that time. But it provided the religious soil into which the Christian seed could be planted.

Palestine was part of the Roman province of Syria. Those were the early years of the Roman Empire, a power which embraced the whole Mediterranean world and which was just establishing a political stability that was to hold for some two hundred years before the migrations from the East began to disturb it. The ancient world had seen a succession of empires, but none of them had consisted of such a variety of cultures. The Roman genius was able to embrace them all — once they had been politically subdued — by including all their deities in the Roman Pantheon and by extending Roman citizenship to all those it considered worthy of this status. It meant that such people had the right to travel throughout the Empire (which the Romans made relatively easy through their road building) and to have accusations against them tried in Rome where they could escape local prejudice. Once a family had citizenship the status was passed on to descendents. There was therefore a certain universality in this setting. Holding this vast administrative organism together was the power of the emperor who was not only the political ruler and military commander but also the highest dignitary of the Roman religion, the Pontifex Maximus. In addition he was granted or assumed the title of 'son of God.' In the world of that time there was a widespread expectation of a saviour or messiah and Rome was no exception. Had not the Roman poet, Virgil, greeted the elevation of Octavian as Augustus as the expected Saviour? He was the one who incorporated into his being the central power of the Empire.

The third important element of the world into which Christ Jesus was born was the Hellenistic culture, the legacy of the conquests of Alexander the Great in the fourth century BC. Though his empire did not survive intact after his death (it was divided into three parts) Greek culture and the Greek language took root in large parts of the original empire including most of those that bordered on the Mediterranean. The Jews kept their language at home, but their many settlements elsewhere were largely Greek speaking. It was to this Greek speaking world that Paul addressed his mission. It was the Hellenistic culture, with its language which had developed the capacity to express the subtle mental processes of its thinkers, that provided Christianity with its original means of expression and formulations of thought. In its own sphere this culture had also its version of 'the One,' the Neoplatonic concept of the ultimate oneness of creation expressed in an all-embracing being.

The fourth element is much more elusive and only in more recent times, with the discovery of manuscripts belonging to those times, has it come into prominence: the mysteries, with their schools of spiritual training and knowledge. They were largely discredited by the nascent Church because of their perceived connection to Gnosticism which, although it accepted Christ, did not accept that he was crucified. This was tantamount to a denial of a true incarnation. The main centres of the mysteries lay beyond the boundaries of the Roman Empire.

When we look at the characters of the four gospels we can venture to relate them to these four elements of the world at that time.

Matthew clearly wrote his gospel with his Jewish home background in mind. Before his calling he was a civil servant, 'sitting at the seat of custom.' Here he would have been part of the government framework, administering the law in the sphere of finance. In Palestine the Jews applied their own laws, though appeal on political grounds to the higher Roman law was possible. Matthew's aim was to point to the transition from Yahweh to Christ, expressed on the one hand by showing how the prophesies were fulfilled in Christ and on the other by making clear, as in the Sermon on the Mount, that this involved a radical change from laws imposed to finding right responses out of one's own free will. Or as Paul put it, when writing about the Gentiles, 'they show that what the law requires is written on their hearts, to which their own conscience bears witness' (Rom.2:15). For Matthew, who more than the other Evangelists uses the phrase, 'this was to fulfil ...,' as for Paul, the true fulfilment of the law was its replacement by an inner freedom governed by the heart.

Mark in reliable Christian tradition was said to have been closely connected with Peter, his main source for his Gospel. Temperamentally they were clearly very similar: Peter comes across in all the Gospels as a man of will, often even acting somewhat recklessly, learning bitter lessons before he could live up to the name which Christ had given him, Peter, the rock. It was in Rome that they worked together and presumably where his Gospel was written. The character of his Gospel is established in its very first statement which implicitly sets the Sonship of Christ over against the claimed divine status of the emperor. Mark's temperament is indicated in the way he writes. He moves along at a brisk rate, punctuated by the word 'immediately.' There is the will to move forward and the feeling of an abundance of life radiating out from his engaged heart. The end of the Gospel is as magnificently concentrated as its beginning as we take leave of the disciples in holy awe of the power of the Resurrection. True power is the *gift* of the One who overcame death. Mark's ending leads into an open future.

Luke provides a moving contrast. A physician, traditionally also an artist, the friend of Paul, accompanying him on part of his journeys, is altogether a more gentle and sensitive soul. He was not brought up in Palestine, but in Antioch, the third city of the Empire and the first important Christian centre outside the Holy Land. Greek would have been his native language which as a writer he used with great artistry. In literary terms he was the most gifted of the Gospel writers. There lived in him something of the feminine soul which we find reflected throughout his gospel, particularly in those passages which are not found in the other gospels. Here we find the sensitivity and compassion of the feeling heart, and in his use of language we can detect the subtlety of description which the Greek language provided as its gift to the nascent Church.

With John we move on to another level. The other three Gospels are known collectively as the synoptics; that is, they see the Incarnation 'with the same eye.' This is an overstatement! They are of course also very different. Yet by and large they bring the same basic material, though details of structure and of some of the material vary. John writes quite differently. Whereas the synoptics live strongly in the sphere of pictures through their concentration on Christ's healing and teaching amongst the people, John's is a Gospel of the Word. Behind all stands the being of Christ, the Logos, the creating Word. We enter into the mysteries of his being, indeed into the fulfilment in him of the ancient mysteries. In his last days, almost a hundred years old, John's message was 'Little children, love one another' and it was with these words that he lay himself down into his grave and died. He had fully absorbed into his own heart what radiates from the heart of Christ, the power of love that transforms.

Today we live in a different world. But we can surely say that the approach to the gospels in relation to the four aspects which we can see as gifts from the world in which Christ lived, can be transferred into pictures which have a general validity, because they are reflected in the Gospels themselves: the heart which guides our freedom, the heart as source of life, the compassionate heart, and the heart which radiates the love that transforms.

Structure of the Gospel
The basic structure of *the* Gospel, which includes all four Gospels, is the chronological sequence of events of the Incarnation. The individual Gospels have their own structures arising out of what each includes in its account, but the chronological sequence underlies all of them. However, putting dates on events has proved difficult, involving as it does harmonizing the various calendars that were in use at that time. Here, we rely on the results of Ormond Edwards' exhaustive researches which are to be found in his book, *The Time of Christ* (Floris Books 1986). The ministry of Christ lasted $2\,1/4$ years, beginning with the Baptism in the Jordan on January 6, AD 31 and ending with the Crucifixion on April 3, AD 33.

This time can be divided into three periods of ten sidereal (moon) months, each lasting roughly forty weeks. Only John records the first of these periods, the so-called silent ministry (Chapters 1–5). The second period begins following the arrest and imprisonment of John the Baptist, when Christ begins his open ministry in Galilee on October 6, AD 31. It

INTRODUCTION

		Matthew	Mark	Luke	John
1 Beginning of the first forty-week period					
AD 31 Jan	Baptism	Judea[1] 3:13	1:9	3:21	1:29
AD 31 Feb	Calling of disciples	Judea			1:35
AD 31 Feb	Cana	Judea			2:1
AD 31 Mar	Temple cleansing	Judea			2:14
	Nicodemus	Judea			3:1
AD 31 May	Samaritan woman	Samaria			4:1
AD 31 Sep	Paralytic	Judea			5:1
AD 31 Sep	Arrest of John	Judea 4:12	1:14		
2 Beginning of the second forty week period					
AD 31 Oct	Public ministry	Galilee[2] 4:12	1:14	4:14	
	Sermon on Mount	Galilee 5:1			
AD 32 Apr	Death of John	14:3	6:17	9:7	
AD 32 Apr	Five Thousand	Galilee 14:13	6:32	9:10	6:1
AD 32 July	Peter's confession	Galilee 16:13	8:27	9:18	
3 Beginning of the third forty-week period					
AD 32 July	Transfiguration	Galilee 17:1	9:2	9:28	
AD 32 Oct	Tabernacles	Judea			8–9
	Luke's journey	Galilee		9:51–19:27	
	Beyond Jordan	Judea 19:1	10:1	to	
	Towards Jerusalem			19.27	
AD 32 Dec	Dedication	Judea			10:22
	Beyond Jordan	Judea			10:40
AD 33 Feb	Lazarus	Judea			11:1
AD 33 Mar	Palm Sunday	Judea 21:1	11:1	19:28	12:12
AD 33 Apr 3	Crucifixion	Judea 27:32	15:21	23:26	19:26

Chronological Table

[1] Judea includes Jerusalem and beyond the Jordan
[2] Galilee includes parts beyond

is at this point that Matthew (4:12), Mark (1:14) and Luke (4:14) take up the story. This period, full of parables and teaching, includes the Feeding of the Five Thousand, and culminates in Peter's confession and the Transfiguration in July 32 (Matthew 16–17, Mark 8–9, Luke 9). This is the turning point into the third period. Christ now begins to prepare his disciples for what lies before him with his prophecies of the Passion. Luke adds further earnest words: '... he set his face towards Jerusalem.' The first two Gospels describe a short transitional phase which leads to Judea, while Luke expands this transition to Jerusalem over some ten chapters as a special journey in itself. It has much material that is to be found only in Luke. Meanwhile John has described the feeding of the 5 000 but then immediately moves to Judea. He differs from the other Evangelists in relating that during what they describe as a continuing ministry in Galilee Christ makes journeys to Jerusalem where his presence is described first at the festival of Tabernacles in October AD 32 and then at the feast of Dedication in December AD 32. He also describes the raising of Lazarus (February AD 33). All four Gospels then come together with the entry of Christ into Jerusalem and the Easter events, albeit each with their own details.

These three periods are quite distinct in their character: the first in which Christ has to establish his divine being in the human constitution before he can, in the second, publicly bestow his healing power on the sick and speak to the people about what his incarnation means, and then, in the third, move on towards fulfilment of his task through death to the Resurrection. For Christ, incarnation means passing through these three embryonic phases of penetrating the soul, life and bodily spheres of the human vessel.

This structure is summarized in the accompanying table above.

Bible scholars have discussed endlessly the differences between the texts of the four Gospels and their sources. We certainly need to have the correct texts as far as this is possible. But then another approach is also needed which goes beyond textual criticism. The words of the Gospels need to resonate in our souls and the many pictures be inwardly brought to life. The Gospels speak to each person as he or she is, where they are on their path of becoming as human beings. They are guides for our inner direction and sources for the nourishment that we need on this path.

Michael Tapp
November 2006

INTRODUCTION

The Gospel of Matthew

The writers of all four Gospels had a devoted, living knowledge of the Old Testament. It was present in their souls like the breath in their bodies. In everything they wrote, its words echoed. This is most clearly evident in the Gospel of Matthew — and sometimes in ways that a reader in the present time can find disconcerting. From the first chapter onwards, passages from the Old Testament are directly quoted; and it is said that events in the life of Jesus fulfilled what these passages prophesied, even that these events happened in order to fulfil them. The present-day reader may know that the learning of the last two centuries has often interpreted these passages in the Old Testament quite differently, as referring to events in the history of Israel much nearer to the time of the original writers. Even if he does not, he may feel that Matthew is straining the interpretation of such passages to make them fit. And in other ways too, the present-day reader may feel that while all the Evangelists are at home in the history of Israel, Matthew is almost its prisoner. Is he writing only for the Jews, to the Jews?

They are indeed intensely concerned with their own destiny as a people. But there is always an underlying theme in the writings, the Psalms, and the prophets: what the people of Israel suffer and achieve is not only for themselves, but it is significant for all mankind; it is a kind of parable of what every human being endures on the path towards spiritual maturity. A parable can be interpreted on many different levels, and has many applications to events in the course of history. The Old Testament is not simply a chronicle of events; its greatest figures — Moses, David, the prophets — are inspired with a poetry reaching far beyond the circumstances of their own lives and times. Such poetry is written down — but the written words are like a tomb, unless their meaning reawakens in living hearts.

Matthew's Gospel distinguishes very clearly three ways of receiving inspired words. The 'scribes and Pharisees' take them only as if they were statements about the physical world and explicit rules of conduct. For 'the crowds' they live indeed in the heart, but like a shared dream to waken and be interpreted only at a later time. But there are some who have begun what is often a lonely struggle to understand the world and themselves; and they want to grasp what they hear with their whole being — with questioning minds, warm hearts, and strong wills. The Apostles are human individualities of this kind.

The distinction between these three groups is one of the themes which Matthew has woven into the whole composition of his Gospel, which contains five discourses, beginning with the Sermon on the Mount (Chapters 5–7) and ending with a great discourse about the future of the world (Chapters 23–25 or 24–25). Careful distinctions are made about the hearers of these discourses, and some indications are given of where they were spoken which can be supplemented by ancient traditions.

Before the Sermon on the Mount, some of the Apostles have been named, and have been told what their task is to be: 'I will make you fishers of men.' And the kinds of people are described, who come in crowds to Jesus; the many illnesses, the many regions of the Holy Land, which are represented among them. But when Jesus, having ascended the mountain, begins to speak, it is in the first place to the disciples. 'There he sat down, and his disciples came to him. Then opening his mouth he taught them, and said ...'

Much in the Sermon on the Mount can come nearer to the reader, if he remembers that it is spoken primarily to people who are already committed to the chief task of their lives, and is about the consequences of this commitment. Yet the fact that he speaks to the disciples in this way has a great impact on the crowds as well, as is described at the end; it is something utterly different from the way of speaking practised by the Scribes.

The second discourse (10:5–42) is quite specifically directed towards the twelve Apostles, who have all just been named; they are sent out to all the regions of Israel, and told how they are to bear themselves, both when they are accepted and when they are rejected.

The third (Chapter 13) begins with teaching given to the crowds, with Jesus sitting in a boat on the lake and the crowds standing on the shore. Later (13:36) Jesus 'sent away the crowds and went into the house.' The whole discourse is concerned with parables and their interpretation. The crowds listen to the parables, but do not understand them, though they make a deep impression — rather as a dream can be impressive, without being interpreted. But the disciples are to understand — and are given some special parables, not given to the crowds.

Between the third and fourth discourses there are several very significant events, through which the disciples can learn more intimately about the quality of their own community; among them the Feeding of the Five Thousand, and the Transfiguration. In the last only Peter, James and John share, from among the twelve. It is again a mountain; traditionally Mount Tabor, no longer looking over the lake, but a mountain among mountains. The minds of the disciples are now directed more explicitly to the Passion and Resurrection.

Chapter 18 is about childhood and forgiveness, closely connected themes; for children forgive most thoroughly, both adults and each other.

After this discourse, Jesus leaves Galilee. All that follows is set in the stern environment of Judea and the desert beyond the Jordan. And here Matthew's narrative joins, in its sequence of events, the other three Evangelists, particularly during the last week leading up to Easter Day. During this week comes the 'little Apocalypse,' the description of the future of the world, which is found in Mark and Luke, but not in John. In

Matthew this is part of the last, the fifth discourse. It is not unmistakably clear where this begins. If we reckon in the 'Woes' as balancing the eight Beatitudes, it can be regarded as beginning with Chapter 23, 'Then Jesus spoke to the crowds and his disciples ...', and as spoken in the Temple at Jerusalem; Chapter 24, says 'Jesus went out of the Temple ...' And there follows the enigmatic indication that at this moment the disciples came to *show* him the buildings of the Temple. Were these not very familiar to him from years past?

John's Gospel bears witness that at a much earlier time Jesus had said 'Destroy this Temple, and I will build it up in three days.' The false witness reported by Matthew at the trial before Caiaphas seems to refer to this saying, which John makes clear referred to Christ's own body. This helps with all the references to the Temple and indeed to the 'house' in the Gospels. What man builds on earth, whether as dwelling-place for the divine or for his own kind, is always an image and parable of the physical body, fashioned in God's likeness. And if the true Spirit no longer indwells it, it is left 'forsaken and desolate,' as Jerusalem is, in spite of the vast crowds moving through its narrow streets. From among these crowds many people can be found prepared to join in the cries of hatred and condemnation against Jesus, which go with him until his death upon the cross. Very few among those who had followed him during the years of his ministry, and had heard his teaching, are able to stand near him underneath the cross, and accompany his body to the grave. And at first it is very few who are able to look at Easter on the new body, the Temple built afresh, in which Christ's Spirit dwells from then onwards.

In the accounts given by the four Evangelists of the events following the Resurrection there are many differences of detail, though the substantial fact is the same. Matthew alone describes two scenes which form a deeply moving contrast. In the first, the soldiers who have been set to guard the tomb see the angel who has rolled back the stone from the entrance to the sepulchre; 'And from fear of him the guards were shaken and became as if they were dead' (28:4). Some of the guards go to the chief priests and tell what has happened; and are bribed to say that disciples of Jesus came while the guards were sleeping and stole away his body. And thus this lie becomes widespread in the years that follow. The second scene, with which the Gospel of Matthew ends, is a meeting of the Risen Christ with the Apostles, not described in the other Gospels, upon a mountain in Galilee. Here they are entrusted with great, living truths, which are to spread through all humanity over millennia.

> Go therefore
> And make disciples of all the nations
> Baptizing them
> In the name of the Father

And of the Son
And of the Holy Spirit

Teaching them to obey everything
That I have commanded you
And how
I
I am with you
Every day
Until the ending of the age

Adam Bittleston
September 1987

The Gospel of Mark

Mark's Gospel is the shortest and most dramatic of the four. This concentration gives strength and tension to what is being portrayed. The strokes are bold, the colours vivid, the actions clear-cut and the whole story is set within a disciplined structure.

The quality of Mark's writing is immediately apparent in the way he opens his Gospel. Both Matthew and Luke spend a lot of time describing the human background to the Incarnation while John in his Prologue sets the story in its eternal context. Mark has no introduction of any kind beyond announcing 'The Gospel of Jesus Christ' and proceeds straight into the story of the ministry. Likewise at the end of the Gospel, having come to the Resurrection as the culmination of the story, Mark simply ends his narrative there and then, eschewing the obvious literary need for a rounding off, which the other three Evangelists provide. Yet by ending with '... because they were afraid' we are left not only with the mystery but with the very real question as to how humanity will respond to this overwhelming event. Mark indicates that this is for us where the story begins. It was only natural that the other possible endings were provided later, but they all lack just the kind of conviction that is so evident throughout Mark's work. There is also a clear form to the Gospel. It consists of a short prelude and three main movements, each of which has its own structure.

The prelude (1:1–13) concerns the work of John. He appears characteristically without any explanation about his background as the one who prepares the inner and outer scene for the Christ. Much of what is described about him in the other Gospels is left out: the focus is on the coming of the Christ and his entry into his earthly task.

INTRODUCTION

The first movement (1:14–8:26) describes the ministry in Galilee. It is the time when Christ pours out his power in healing and in teaching. Mark stresses the immediate impact of Christ's life on mankind by placing the healings in the forefront of this part of the Gospel. Only in Chapter 4 do we have concentrated teaching. The structure of this section is quite complex. We can see three different elements:

The first concerns the stages of Christ's relationship to the disciples: their calling (1:14), their appointment (3:13), their sending out (6:7). The inner thread of the story can be seen linking these events together as the beginning of a path of discipleship.

Following this there is a second structural element: a section of the Gospel appears to repeat itself in a sequence of parallel events (6:35–7:37 and 8:1–26) each of which begins with a feeding (the five thousand and the four thousand), then continues with a journey over the lake, a controversy with the Pharisees, a conversation on bread or leaven and concludes with a healing (the man with a speech impediment, and a blind man). An examination is being described here of the different important steps in the path of discipleship. The passage is an example as to how structural elements can lead to an appreciation of what the Gospel is really trying to convey.

The third structural element in this first movement is the division into chapters. Although they were not created by the Evangelist (in fact they were made in medieval times) they are coherent sections, each of which again has its own form. Chapters 2 and 3 both open with healings which embody the substance of each chapter. The healing of the paralytic is followed by an altercation with the Jews whose rules paralyse the unfolding of new creative gifts. The healing in the synagogue of the man with the withered hand is followed by the appointment of the new community which will be committed to the renewal of the spiritual life of humanity. These two chapters, describing the transition from the old to the new then make possible the teaching of Chapter 4 in which the new is described in the three parables of the seed: not the old, fixed word, but one which grows and bears new fruit. This teaching leads to the first crisis for the disciples (storm on the lake), showing their need for more training to cope with the implications of this new life. In the three healings of Chapter 5 content is provided to meet this need, where we enter into the deeper mysteries of Christ's power. Here Mark uncharacteristically takes his time. In Chapter 6 the disciples are sent out and begin to assist the Christ in his work. There are six scenes which are related: the first and the sixth show Christ with the crowd (6:1, 6:53); the second and fifth have Christ with the disciples (6:7, 6:47); the third and fourth tell of the supersensory community, the beheading of John and the Feeding of the Five Thousand (6:14 and 6:30). Again, the inner implications of all this have to be worked through (indicated by the second crisis on the water, at the end of the chapter) and so Chapter 7 once again has to build on the foundations, summed up in the healing at the end where the ears are opened and the tongue is released. There is the constant challenge to throw off the old tutelage of the law and discover that the source of life has to be found within. The final section of this movement repeats this cycle of events in another key, raising the story to the moment when the disciples reach through to a realization, though perhaps not yet on a fully conscious level, of what it is that they are following.

The second movement (8:27–10:52) has one great theme which Christ himself utters three times: the prophecy of the Passion, Death and Resurrection. The great moment of Peter's confession is immediately clouded by the reality of the Messiah's task, and indeed by the task which follows from it for humanity. Each time Christ brings these stern words the disciples are plunged into the abyss, yet each time there is a step forwards. The pain is not suffered in vain. The movement, which even though not lacking in inner drama may be described as the slow one, ends with the final healing in the Gospel: of the blind man at Jericho whose hymnlike first public proclamation of the Messiah not only brings the movement to a majestic close but also mirrors its opening theme, the first personal confession of the Christ by Peter.

The last movement (11–16) then opens with the triumphant fanfare of Christ's entry into Jerusalem, setting the tone and the direction of the final drama. The disciples now recede into the background and Christ stands alone in the face of the powers of this world. When he is nevertheless with his disciples it is only to emphasize the magnitude of their future task and to prepare them for his own death. Mark describes these events without a hint of emotion. He simply conveys the power that lives in the events themselves.

There is also a form to this whole last part of the Gospel which is similar to the one we saw in Chapter 6. Chapters 11 and 16 have an inner relationship (entry into Jerusalem, and the Resurrection) as do Chapters 12 and 15 (parable of the killing of the heir to the vineyard, and the Crucifixion) and Chapters 13 and 14 (apocalyptic teaching of Christ to his disciples, and the promise in the Last Supper of his abiding presence).

Form in a painting, in music, in architecture, indeed in anything in this world, is an orientation but not yet the substance. But in providing us with such an orientation, form offers us a means of penetrating towards the substance. In the Gospel, too, it can be an orientation which helps to direct our perception towards the ultimate reality that lies at the heart of Christ's work and being.

What then is the underlying approach in Mark? We may think of Christ's work in differing ways: as a moral teaching, as the supreme example of love and sacrifice, as the revelation of the deepest wisdom. It was all these things and many more. Each Gospel has its own background and purpose, each tends to see a particular aspect or dimension of Christ's work. Thus Matthew sees it in relation to the history of his own people and shows how the particular is transformed by Christ into the universal. Luke sees the aspects of human concern, care, and love, and shows how these are raised to the highest level by the Christ. John penetrates to the sphere, in Christ, where wisdom and love become one. The uniqueness of Mark is his experience of Christ's power of life: not the wisdom, nor the love, nor the moral teaching, but quite simply that source of life in Christ which worked outwardly into his surroundings as the power of healing and which worked inwardly into himself as the power that overcame death. It was in meeting and experiencing this extraordinary power of life that the disciples were confronted by the mystery of the Christ. Mark shows how each step in comprehension had to be gained through profound and, in some cases, unnerving experiences and how even when Christ's glorious power of life had won through to its final fulfilment on earth the disciples had still to start on their own conscious realization of that power in themselves. That, too, is where we stand and that is why the Gospel of Mark can speak to us today.

Michael Tapp
February 1986

The Gospel of Luke

The New Testament gives a particularly clear picture of Luke, writer both of the Gospel and its sequel the Acts of the Apostles.

He accompanied Paul on some of his great journeys and voyages, and was his friend and physician as well as his disciple. He learned from Paul, profoundly, and he was recognized from the earliest times as writing in the spirit of Paul's teaching, although there is a marked difference of mood.

In his letters Paul is vigorous and often choleric; Luke shows, in general, a mood of gentleness and restraint, even where severe criticism of the words and actions of the people he is describing is implied.

In the Middle Ages, Luke was sometimes represented as a painter, at work on a portrait of the Mother of Jesus. He may well have learned, before writing his Gospel, from personal meetings at Ephesus with Mary and the beloved disciple, John the Evangelist, as well as earlier from Paul. Luke's writings are indeed different in style from the works attributed to John: the Fourth Gospel, the three Epistles, and the Revelation which ends the New Testament — which are also very different from each other.

It is generally assumed that Luke wrote *before* any of these came into being, and before the fiercest times of persecution of the Christians by the Romans.

INTRODUCTION

For all the Evangelists, and for Paul, the central fact of which they write is the Resurrection of Christ. But it is characteristic of Luke that he alone describes in detail (24:13–35), among the events of the first Easter Sunday, a *journey,* though not a very long one — the walk of Emmaus, on which two disciples, not members of the twelve, are joined by a stranger, whom they do not recognize as Christ, until at supper, he vanishes from their sight. And, although all four Gospels make it clear that during the seven weeks between Easter and Pentecost the Apostles were given their mission to bring their witness to the Resurrection to all peoples, it is Luke who has the most remarkable phrase to describe the greatness of these journeys. The Apostles are to be witness up to the *'eschatou tês gês'* (Acts 1:8). *Eschatos* describes what comes *last* in time (as in eschatology) or in space. They are to go to where the world ends. Luke is very much aware that when we truly go on a journey, we change not only our position in space, but our relation to time. We go to meet the future. It is described in Matthew, Mark and John that during the years between the Baptism and the Crucifixion, Christ alternated between Galilee, where many people lived still in something of a dreamlike consciousness (a heritage from the past), and Judea, where men's minds — in fear or hope — were more strongly turned to the future. But much of Luke is occupied with the journey of Christ from Galilee to Jerusalem through Samaria, a last great journey which leads to the cross and the Resurrection.

Luke is very much aware that these events are the beginning of a great new journey to be undertaken by humanity as a whole, led by Christ Jesus; for only in Luke's Gospel is it said that on the mountain of the Transfiguration the spiritual forms of Moses and Elijah speak with Christ Jesus about his 'going forth' — for this is the literal meaning of the Greek word *exodus* — to be accomplished from Jerusalem, as Moses led out the Israelites on the long journey to the Promised Land (Luke 9:31).

But the counterpart of a journey leading upwards is a journey down which has preceded it. And two of the parables told only in Luke's Gospel, *The Good Samaritan* and *The Prodigal Son,* contain pictures of such downward journeys (10:25–37, 15:11–32).

These stories have had immeasurable moral influence upon human beings, taken quite simply, but they can also be taken as parables of the fate of humanity after the Fall from Paradise, of which Luke is naturally also very much aware. Mankind, going downwards, fell among thieves, was stripped of the robes which expressed his spiritual dignity, beaten, and left half dead. Luke, like Paul, has no doubt at all about the existence of mighty spiritual beings who tempt and rob mankind. This has befallen us; it was not simply our own choice. And yet, from another aspect, humanity has gone willingly on the downward journey, and has been prepared to waste the heritage given from above. We have as a kind of adventure taken the path which leads eventually to hunger and the swine. In the New Testament, swine are a picture of materialism, of a condition of soul in which it is greedily attached to physical things as objects themselves, and not as revelations of the beings who have created them.

It is in the Gospels of Matthew and Luke that an abundance of parables, in the form of detailed stories, can be found. Mark has very few parables; John, in this sense, none at all. Comparing Matthew and Luke, it is directly apparent that the parables told in Luke are rich in mercy and forgiveness while those of Matthew have often a mood of severity and judgment.

But both Evangelists indicate that the Parables have, for the disciples, the character of *riddles*. They cannot be taken, *by them,* simply as moral teaching. They challenge them to think actively about their meaning, and above all, about their relation to the Deed of Christ. So it is to be expected that somewhere in each parable, though perhaps deeply hidden, the being of Christ himself is to be found.

For example — who is the Good Samaritan? Some of the medieval artists gave a remarkable answer to this question. They painted the Good Samaritan with the halo containing the red cross about his head, the halo with which Christ himself is painted, particularly after the Resurrection; but also, as by Fra Angelico, the Christ as child. The stranger who comes to the aid of the man who fell among thieves is a bearer of the spirit of Christ — and truly a neighbour.

In the ancient world, for the great majority of mankind, 'neighbours' were people who spent their lives nearby, with similar racial characteristics and with shared traditions and customs inherited from the past. But through the centuries up to the present, the trend has been for more and more people in a great part of the world to have increasingly significant encounters with others whose inherited qualities and customs are different from their own. Love, and healing, and wisdom come to us from strangers, people encountered on journeys. In Luke, this is described in the teaching given by Jesus in the synagogue at Bethlehem, which ends with the words: 'And there were many lepers in Israel when Elisha was a prophet, but not one of them was cleansed except Naaman, the Syrian.'

This teaching arouses so bitter an anger in the hearers that they have the intention of killing Jesus (Luke 4:29). Some of those who heard the story of the Good Samaritan may well have felt a similar anger; it is the stranger who is the true neighbour.

An encounter on a journey may well prove to be among the most important in the lives of one or both of the participants. Luke gives a striking example in the Acts, with the meeting of Philip the Deacon, and the Ethiopian Minister, who is actually going along in his chariot at the time. An encounter which leads to the Minister's baptism (Acts 8:26–39).

The story of the Good Samaritan is told in the context of a question about eternal life. To recognize in the stranger the true neighbour and treat him accordingly, may prove, together with the great fourfold love of God (with all your heart, and with all your soul, and with all your strength, and with all your mind), the gateway to eternity in the midst of transitory existence. (Far away, this was expressed in the Zen story *The Gates of Heaven and Hell.*) Humanity as a whole is on a journey and on its way it has encountered robbers. For humanity, as a whole, the Christ is the great stranger met on the way; a stranger coming into earthly existence from the realms of eternity, fully known only by the Father who sent him.

In a passage in which Luke's words (10:22) very much resemble passages from the later chapters of John, Jesus says:

>All things
>Were handed over to me
>By my Father
>And no one understands
>Who the Son is
>Except the Father
>And who the Father is
>Except the Son
>And those to whom
>It is the will of the Son
>To reveal him.

In all the Gospel parables, every detail is significant, so we can ask why the Good Samaritan speaks of his return to the inn later? Would not the story have been complete without this? But if we try to enter into the human experience of the man who fell in with robbers, this detail becomes significant. When the Good Samaritan continues on his journey, the injured man is hardly conscious of what has happened to him, or who has helped him. But when the Samaritan returns, they will meet in full consciousness. 'To return' has a deep meaning for Luke. It is he who records one of the most specific statements about the 'Second Coming' of the Christ. At the Ascension, the two men in white robes who appear to the assembly of disciples on the Mount of Olives say: 'This Jesus, who was taken up from you into heaven, will come in the same way as you saw him go into heaven' (Acts 1:11).

When does Jesus return, and reveal himself to the full consciousness of mankind? In Matthew, Mark and Luke, we find accounts of the Sermon on the Mount of Olives, given to a small number of disciples not long before the Passion. They all (with slight variations in detail) describe a time of great trouble for mankind, in which it is not difficult to recognize many characteristics of the present age (Matt.24–25; Mark 13; Luke 21). And in this time, the whole of mankind — not only traditional Christians — is challenged to find a conscious relationship to the Christ: each single individual, wherever he may have been brought up among the varied faiths and world-conceptions of the present.

As it is said in the Apocalypse of John (3:20): 'Behold, I stand at the door and knock.'

Quite particularly, the time of trouble brings distress to mothers of small children (Matt.24:19, Mark 13:17, Luke 21:23):

> Alas for the woman
> In those days
> Who carries a child in her womb
> Or has one at her breast.

In our day, civilization over a great part of the world has taken shape which is harmful to children. And countless women are torn between the claims of a household with one or more small children, and the task of keeping up with a professional or similar career.

In many old pictures of the Mother of Jesus, one hand is given to her child, and the other holds a book. It is clearly meant that this is a holy book, and a source of wisdom and a giver of strength for the inner life.

A book can only do these things for its readers if it is brought to life. The Greek word for reading, *anagnôsis,* in Greek, is very close to the word for resurrection, *anastasis.* The letter kills; if words are taken only into the head, they are inert: they can be brought to life only in the heart, with ever renewed discovery of their meaning. Then they awaken us, and prepare us to meet the Christ — in the conscious understanding of his deed — through the grace of God.

The Gospels, themselves, are such books. For this reason there is such a longing in our time for renewed understanding of the Gospels and the Bible as a whole, and all the ancient holy books: and for a renewed sense of the presence and work of the Holy Spirit.

May this new translation of Luke do its part in meeting these needs.

Adam Bittleston
May 1989

The Gospel of John

John's Gospel differs from the other Gospels in a number of significant ways. It was the last to be written, at the end of a very long life, well over sixty years after the events they describe. This distance of time does not affect the immediacy of what is described. We might have expected less historical accuracy. But in fact the opposite is the case. For only in John's Gospel can we reconstruct the main outline of the chronology of the

Incarnation as described in the Introduction. As mentioned there, John includes the years of the silent ministry, while for the period of the Galilean ministry which forms the central part of the synoptic Gospels, John instead records visits of Christ to Jerusalem during this time.

These differences have the effect of placing the accent of John's Gospel firmly in Judea and Jerusalem, for it is here that Christ is challenged by the Jews and Pharisees and here that he challenges them with his words of self-revelation. Indeed, the weight of John's Gospel lies in the words of Christ, in what he says about himself, beginning already during the silent ministry in private settings, in his teaching to the disciples as preparation for their later task, but then also in the disputes with the Jews.

With the so-called silent ministry we are in the first of the three forty-week periods. By 'silent' is meant that Christ did not specifically enter the public domain. To begin with he is alone in the wilderness and faces the Tempter (not recorded by John). Then there is the first calling of some of the disciples. During the course of this he meets Nathanael, who does not become one of the twelve. But there is an immediate mutual recognition, by Christ of one with great spiritual awareness and knowledge, by Nathanael of the Son of God. At the marriage at Cana (Chapter 2) there is the brief conversation between Christ and Mary, when she tells him that there is no wine, and he replies:

> This is between me and you
> Woman
> My hour has still to come

We may deduce from these words that the Incarnation, as for all human incarnations, is not a completed act at its beginning, but is a process of taking hold and penetrating the earthly vehicle. His words here suggest he is not yet ready to launch out on his own. There are forty weeks from conception to birth. The Incarnation goes through three such periods as the Logos, the Word, penetrates and spiritualizes the vehicle consisting of the spheres of soul, life, and finally in the resurrection, of the physical body. This process of transformation has to be established first in the sphere of the soul where he needs the cooperation of Mary. The Son of God has still to establish and contain himself fully within a human framework.

So during this time Christ works quietly mainly in private settings. The next meeting (Chapter 3) occurs when the Pharisee, Nicodemus, comes to him at night to ask basic questions, which we might well also ask, about being born anew out of the spirit. Again, this is a human being to whom Christ can give profound answers. At this time John the Baptist is giving witness to the Christ, reminding us that he is still the public figure while Christ works in the background. But then we move on to Christ's meeting with the Samaritan woman at the well (Chapter 4). She too asks questions. The subject, in the setting of the well, is the living water that flows from Christ himself. He meets her, one could say, on her own ground and in her he finds a person to whom he can reveal his identity.

Shortly after this meeting at the well John is imprisoned. Chapter 5 marks the transition to the second period. But what John describes here is still before the opening of the Galilean ministry. It describes the healing of the man who had been paralysed for thirty eight-years, following which comes the first real altercation with the Jews. During the course of this he says:

> My Father is still working now
> And I myself am working

This signals an important moment in the Incarnation. A new relationship of God to humanity is coming into being.

John had opened his Gospel with the Prologue in which the Incarnation is placed in its widest context. It stands before us wherever we are in the Gospel, a statement to be pondered ever anew of the relationship of the creating Word to the created world. And indeed his Gospel is a Gospel of the Word, largely expressed in Christ's words. Now, with John's imprisonment he moves out onto the public stage. Outwardly his work is increasingly contested, inwardly the self-revelation becomes ever more the core of his teaching. At the heart of this self-revelation are the seven I AM sayings which form the nodal points around which the substance of the teaching moves forward.

The first saying (in Chapter 6) comes when the disciples have had sufficient preparation to become active helpers in Christ's work: they had been called, formed into the group of twelve and sent out to stand on their own feet. Now they have returned. All this is described in the other Gospels. It is at this point that John joins up with the other Gospels for an account of the Feeding of the Five Thousand, albeit for only the one chapter. For the first time the disciples become active helpers in Christ's work. Some time later those who had been fed seek out Christ to question him. He responds with:

> I
> I AM the bread of life
> He who comes to me
> Will not hunger
> He who believes in me
> Will never thirst

In all these sayings Christ is talking about his relationship to human beings and their relationship to him. He is speaking for all time. The foundation for these relationships, however, had to be established through the course of his life on earth. What he expressed at particular moments during this life belonged to the establishment of this foundation. The fulfilment for human beings could only begin to come about after that life was completed. So the puzzlement of the people and the anger of the Jewish teachers are understandable, yet both led to responses from Christ which are vital for a deeper understanding of the nature of his work.

The second saying (in Chapter 8) follows the story of the woman taken in adultery in which he declines to condemn her. In place of such a condemnation he says:

> I
> I AM the light of the world
> He who follows me
> Will not walk in darkness
> But will have the light of life

This is nothing less than a future alternative to the Law, a new basis for morality and inner enlightenment. Once again an altercation ensues. It becomes the opportunity for Christ to make far-reaching statements about himself. He is uncompromising. To be otherwise would be to deny himself. The scene ends with the Jews threatening to stone him.

Chapter 9 brings us the healing of the man born blind: one on whom Christ bestows the light of sight. As in the case of the healing of the paralytic (Chapter 5) the blind man is cross-examined by the Jews afterwards. Both avoid arguments by sticking to the facts of their healings and particularly in the case of the man born blind we meet a strong sense of self who is fully capable of defending himself without making any comment on Christ beyond what he did to heal him. He was a person in whom we can imagine the dawning of the light of life.

The next two sayings follow immediately (Chapter 10). Christ uses a setting very familiar to his hearers: the shepherd and his flock, stressing the importance of the sheepfold where the sheep are safe. The shepherd leads them in and out. They have to be led out of the sheepfold in order to eat, but then the shepherd has to protect them from predators. Here we have a double picture. The first is

> I
> I AM the door for the sheep
> Anyone who comes through me
> Will be saved
> And will go in
> And go out
> And find pasture

A door or a gate is a threshold. The accent here is on leaving the sheepfold, the threshold from the enclosure into the pasture which provides nourishment. Christ describes himself as that threshold, as the one in whom we find the threshold to the pasture. But he is also the shepherd:

> I
> I AM the shepherd
> The rightful one
> The real shepherd
> Who lays down his soul-bearing life
> For the sheep

In him we find the opening to the other world. Through his shepherding we can access the new life brought to humanity through the sacrifice of his human life. This is the central saying of the seven. It can be seen as an inner parallel to the beginning of the third period, mentioned in the General Introduction, when the focus of the Incarnation turns towards Golgotha. It forms the turning point which will link Christ's Crucifixion and Resurrection to the human path towards redemption.

Next we come to the raising of Lazarus (Chapter 11):

> I
> I AM the Resurrection
> And the life
> He who believes in me
> Will live
> Even if he dies
> And all those who live
> And believe in me
> They will not die

Christ knows his own time is approaching. There are just forty days to pass before Golgotha. Lazarus is initiated into this mystery through which he himself will have the strength and the inner perception for the events that follow.

The sixth and seventh sayings are spoken at the Last Supper (Chapters 14 and 15). These discourses are Christ's final gift to the disciples before his arrest, trial and Crucifixion, but they look forward to a new era when his power will be available for all human beings:

> I
> I AM the way
> And the truth
> And the life
> No one comes to the Father

> Except through me
> If you had recognized me
> You would also have known my Father

Here all the disputes about his being are left behind. The disciples are free to ask questions and in return they receive the gospel of compassion and love, a reciprocal love between Christ and disciple. He has trodden the way and made it his own. He has revealed the truth of his own being. He gives his life for the life of the world.

Finally, the human community is embraced in Christ:

> I
> I AM the true vine
> And my Father cultivates the ground ...
> You are the branches
> He who remains in me
> And I in him
> Bears plentiful fruit
> Because separated from me
> You have no power to do anything

These revelations are expanded and filled out with compassion and love for the disciples as they face their great challenges ahead. The discourses end in the High Priestly Prayer, in which Christ prays to the Father (Chapter 17) for those who have been entrusted to him:

> So that the love
> With which thou hast loved me
> May be in them
> And I
> In them

Just as the opening Prologue to the Gospel opens up what is to come through the actual Incarnation, so this prayer sums up what the sending of Christ is to bring for the future of humanity.

John's very full description of the Easter events follows, concluding with some of the Risen Christ's appearances and John's own testimony to the truth of his Gospel.

One particular event stands out in John's Gospel, not recorded by the others: the raising of Lazarus, which occupies the middle chapter of the Gospel. It clearly is a particularly special event. Yet it concerns a human being whose identity has been shrouded in mystery. One could say the same about all the others who were healed, but none of the others was close to Christ himself.

INTRODUCTION

Of none of the others do we hear that Jesus loved them. This was the one whom Jesus loved. The only mention in the Gospel of such a person otherwise is in the final chapter (21:20) following Christ's questions to Peter as to whether he loved him. At the end of this conversation Peter turns round and sees the disciple whom Jesus loved following them, the one who had leaned on his breast at the supper. A little later we read:

> This is the disciple
> Who bears witness to these events
> And who has recorded them
> And we know
> That what he says is true

Thus Lazarus is identified as the writer of the Gospel. That this has not been generally accepted is because it raises questions about John the son of Zebedee, who has widely been held to be the one next to Christ at the Last Supper and the writer of the Gospel. There is in fact no absolute consensus as to who wrote the Gospel. But if we add to what the Gospel itself implies, the profundity of the Gospel's substance and also that of the Apocalypse, we surely have to accept that the author of these works must have been spiritually a quite exceptionally mature person. This would be confirmed by the fact of his being raised from the dead, which we may surmise to be an initiation experience, forty days before Christ's own Death and Resurrection. Lazarus John underwent the final preparation for his task in this moment for conveying in his later work the true substance of Christ's deed. His experience gave him the strength to stand beneath the cross and the inner perception to be able to write the Gospel.

Michael Tapp
October 2006

Synopses

The Gospel of Matthew

The Birth, Baptism, and Temptation

1	1	*The genealogy*
	18	*The birth of Jesus Christ*
2	1	*The visit of the magi*
	13	*The flight into Egypt*
	16	*The massacre of the innocents*
	19	*The return from Egypt*
3	1	*The preaching of John the Baptist*
	13	*Jesus is baptized*
4	1	*The Temptation*
	12	*Jesus returns to Galilee*
	18	*The calling of four disciples*
	23	*Jesus preaches and heals in Galilee*

The Sermon on the Mount

5	1	*The Beatitudes*
	13	*Salt and light*
	17	*The old Law and new demands*
6	1	*Almsgiving and prayer and fasting*
	19	*Serving the light*
	25	*Trust in God*
7	1	*Do not criticize others*
	6	*Giving and receiving*
	13	*The narrow gate*
	15	*False prophets*
	24	*The two builders*

Healings in Galilee

8	1	*A leper is cleansed*
	5	*The healing of the centurion's servant*
	14	*Jesus heals Peter's mother-in-law and many sufferers*
	18	*The difficulties of discipleship*

	23	*Jesus calms the storm*
	28	*Two demoniacs are healed*
9	1	*A paralytic is healed*
	9	*The calling of Matthew*
	14	*A question about fasting*
	18	*The cure of a woman and the raising of a young girl*
	27	*Two blind men are healed*
	32	*A dumb demoniac is healed*

Teachings for the disciples

10	1	*The sending out of the twelve*
	17	*The disciples will be persecuted*
	26	*The disciples should have courage*
	32	*The disciples should follow Christ*

The rejection of John the Baptist and of Jesus

11	1	*Jesus answers John the Baptist*
	7	*Jesus talks to the people about John*
	20	*Jesus reproves the lakeside towns*
	25	*Jesus prays to the Father*
	27	*The weary will find rest*
12	1	*In the cornfields on the sabbath*
	9	*Healing of a man with a withered hand*
	15	*Many people are healed*
	22	*Jesus heals a demoniac and reproves the Pharisees*
	38	*The scribes and Pharisees ask for a sign*
	46	*The family of Jesus*

Parables and teachings of the kingdom of the heavens

13	1	*Parable of the sower*
	10	*Seeing and hearing*
	18	*The meaning of the sower*
	24	*Parable of the field of the world*
	31	*Parable of the mustard seed*
	33	*Parable of the yeast*
	36	*The meaning of the field of the world*
	44	*Parable of the treasure*
	45	*Parable of the pearl*
	47	*Parable of the net*
	53	*Jesus is not accepted in his native place*

The Feedings and the Transfiguration

14	1	*The death of John the Baptist*
	13	*Feeding of the five thousand*

	22	*Jesus is seen walking on the sea*
	34	*Jesus heals many who are sick*
15	1	*Clean and unclean*
	21	*Healing of the daughter of the Canaanite woman*
	29	*Feeding of the four thousand*
16	1	*The Pharisees and Sadducees ask for a sign*
	5	*Jesus warns against the teaching of the Pharisees*
	13	*Christ's charge to Peter*
	21	*First prophecy of the Passion*
17	1	*The Transfiguration*
	14	*Healing of the demoniac boy*
	22	*Second prophecy of the Passion*
	24	*The tax money*

Discourse on childhood and forgiveness

18	1	*The disciples' question*
	12	*Parable of the lost sheep*
	15	*Teaching for the disciples*
	21	*Parable of the unforgiving servant*

The journey to Jerusalem

19	1	*A discussion about marriage*
	13	*Children are brought to Jesus*
	16	*The rich young man*
20	1	*Parable of the workers in the vineyard*
	17	*Third prophecy of the Passion*
	20	*The mother of James and John asks a favour*
	29	*Two blind men healed*
21	1	*The entry into Jerusalem*
	12	*Jesus clears the Temple*
	17	*The fig tree*
	23	*Jesus questions the chief priests about John*
	28	*Parable of the two sons*
	33	*Parable of the wicked farmers*
22	1	*Parable of the marriage of the king's son*
	15	*The Pharisees' question*
	23	*The Sadducees' question*
	34	*The lawyer's question*
	41	*Jesus questions the Pharisees*

Discourse on entering the kingdom of the heavens

23	1	*Condemnation of the scribes and the Pharisees*
24	1	*Prophecies of war and persecution*
	26	*The advent of the Son of Man*

25	1	*Parable of the ten virgins*
	14	*Parable of the talents*
	31	*Prophecy of the sheep and the goats*

The Passion, Death and Resurrection

26	1	*The anointing in Bethany*
	14	*Judas betrays Jesus*
	17	*Preparations for the Passover*
	20	*The Last Supper*
	31	*Jesus foretells Peter's denial*
	36	*Gethsemane*
	57	*Jesus before Caiaphas*
	69	*Peter's denial*
27	1	*The death of Judas*
	11	*Jesus before Pilate*
	27	*Jesus is mocked by the soldiers*
	32	*The Crucifixion*
	57	*The burial*
	62	*A guard is set on the tomb*
28	1	*The Resurrection*
	11	*The soldiers go to the chief priests*
	16	*Jesus sends the disciples out into the world*

The Gospel of Mark

In Galilee

1	1	*Prologue*
	2	*John the Baptist*
	9	*Jesus is baptized*
	12	*The Temptation*
	14	*Calling of four disciples*
	21	*The healing of a demoniac*
	29	*The healing of Simon's mother-in-law*
	32	*Healing and teaching in Galilee*
	40	*The healing of a leper*
2	1	*The healing of a paralytic*
	13	*The calling of Levi*
	15	*Eating with outcasts*
	18	*A question about fasting*
	23	*In the cornfields on the sabbath*
3	1	*The healing of a man with a useless hand*
	7	*Crowds come to Jesus for help*
	13	*The calling of the twelve*
	22	*The scribes accuse him*
	31	*The family of Jesus*
4	1	*The parable of the sower*
	21	*Jesus teaches in parables*
	35	*The calming of the storm*
5	1	*The healing of the man with legion*
	21	*The cure of a woman and raising Jairus' daughter*
6	1	*Jesus is not accepted in his native place*
	7	*The mission of the twelve*
	14	*The death of John the Baptist*
	30	*The feeding of the five thousand*
	47	*Jesus comes to the disciples on the sea*
	53	*Healings at Gennesaret*
7	1	*A discussion about tradition*
	14	*Clean and unclean*
	24	*The healing of the Syrophoenician woman's daughter*
	31	*The healing of the deaf man*
8	1	*The feeding of the four thousand*
	10	*The Pharisees seek for a sign*
	13	*The disciples fail to understand the signs*
	22	*The healing of a blind man*

Prophecy of the Passion, Death and Resurrection

	27	*Peter declares Jesus to be the Christ*
	34	*Following Christ*
9	2	*The Transfiguration*
	14	*The healing of a boy with a dumb spirit*
	30	*Teaching the disciples in Galilee and Capernaum*
10	1	*A discussion about divorce*
	13	*Children are brought to Jesus*
	17	*The rich man*
	32	*The last prophecy of the Passion*
	35	*The request of James and John*
	46	*The healing of blind Bartimaeus*

Jerusalem

11	1	*The entry into Jerusalem*
	12	*The fig tree and the clearing of the Temple*
	22	*Teaching about prayer*
12	1	*The parable of the cruel farmers*
	13	*The Pharisees ask a question about taxes*
	18	*The Sadducees ask a question about resurrection*
	28	*A scribe asks about the commandments*
	35	*A warning about the scribes*
	41	*The widow's gift*
13	1	*Jesus prophesies war and persecution*
	24	*The coming of the Son of Man*
14	1	*The anointing at Bethany*
	10	*The betrayal*
	12	*Preparations for the Passover*
	17	*The Last Supper*
	27	*Jesus foretells Peter's denial*
	32	*Jesus prays at Gethsemane*
	43	*The arrest*
	53	*Jesus before the council*
	66	*Peter's denial*
15	1	*Jesus before Pilate*
	16	*Jesus mocked by the soldiers*
	21	*The Crucifixion*
	42	*The burial*
16	1	*The women at the tomb*
	8	*The shorter ending*
	9	*The longer ending*

The Gospel of Luke

The Birth, Baptism, and Temptation

1
  1 *Prologue*
  5 *The Angel comes to Zechariah*
  26 *The Angel Gabriel comes to Mary*
  39 *Mary visits her cousin Elizabeth*
  57 *The birth of John the Baptist*

2
  1 *The birth of Jesus in Bethlehem*
  21 *Jesus is circumcised*
  22 *Jesus is presented in the Temple*
  41 *The twelve year old Jesus in the temple*

3
  1 *The preaching of John the Baptist*
  19 *Herod puts John in prison*
  21 *The Baptism of Jesus Christ*
  23 *The ancestry of Jesus*

4
  1 *The Temptation*

Healings and teachings in Galilee

  14 *Jesus preaches in Nazareth*
  31 *A demoniac is healed in Capernaum*
  38 *The healing of Simon's mother-in-law*
  40 *Jesus heals at sunset*
  42 *Jesus preaches throughout the land*

5
  1 *Simon's great catch of fish*
  12 *The healing of a leper*
  17 *The healing of a paralytic*
  27 *The calling of Levi*
  29 *Jesus teaches in Levi's house*

6
  1 *In the cornfields on the sabbath*
  6 *The healing of a man with a useless hand*
  12 *Jesus chooses the twelve apostles*
  17 *The sermon on the plain*

7
  1 *The healing of the centurion's servant*
  11 *The widow's son is restored to life*
  18 *John sends his disciples to Jesus*
  24 *Jesus talks to the people about John*
  36 *The woman who anointed Jesus*

8
  1 *The parable of the sower*
  19 *The mother and the brothers of Jesus*
  22 *Jesus calms the storm*

	26	*The healing of the Gadarene demoniac*
	40	*Cure of a woman and Jairus' daughter is raised*
9	1	*The mission of the twelve*
	7	*Herod wishes to see Jesus*
	10	*The feeding of the five thousand*
	18	*Peter's confession of faith*
	22	*First prophecy of the Passion*
	28	*The Transfiguration*
	37	*The healing of the demoniac boy*
	44	*Second prophecy of the Passion*
	46	*Who is the greatest?*

The journey to Jerusalem

	51	*On the road to Jerusalem*
10	1	*The mission of the seventy*
	17	*Return of the seventy*
	21	*Jesus prays to the Father*
	25	*The good Samaritan*
	38	*Martha and Mary*
11	1	*The Lord's Prayer*
	5	*Teaching about prayer*
	14	*Casting out demons*
	29	*The sign of Jonah*
	37	*Woe to the Pharisees and the lawyers*
12	1	*Jesus warns his disciples*
	13	*Parable of the rich landowner*
	22	*Trust in God*
	35	*Be watchful*
	54	*Right judgment*
13	1	*The death of the Galileans*
	6	*Parable of the fig tree*
	10	*Healing of a woman who was disabled*
	22	*Teaching on the road to Jerusalem*
14	1	*Healing of a man suffering from water retention*
	7	*Humility and care for the poor*
	15	*Parable of the great feast*
	25	*Following Christ*
15	1	*The lost sheep*
	8	*The lost coin*
	11	*The lost son*
16	1	*The untrustworthy agent*
	14	*Christ answers the Pharisees*
	19	*The rich man and Lazarus*
17	1	*Christ teaches the disciples*

	11	*Ten lepers are healed*
	22	*The coming of the Son of Man*
18	1	*Parable of the determined widow*
	9	*The parable of the Pharisee and the tax-collector*
	15	*Children are brought to Jesus*
	18	*The problem of riches*
	31	*Third prophecy of the Passion*
	35	*Healing of a blind man*
19	1	*Jesus and Zacchaeus*
	11	*Parable of the ten servants*

Holy Week

	28	*The entry into Jerusalem*
	41	*Jesus weeps over Jerusalem*
	45	*Jesus clears the Temple*
20	1	*Jesus questions the elders about John*
	9	*Parable of the wicked farmers*
	19	*A question about taxes*
	27	*The Sadducees' question*
	41	*Jesus questions the scribes*
21	1	*The widow's offering*
	5	*Jesus prophesies disasters and persecution*
	25	*The coming of the Son of Man*

The Passion, Death and Resurrection

22	1	*The betrayal*
	7	*Preparation for the Passover*
	14	*The Last Supper*
	24	*Rivalry among the disciples*
	31	*Jesus foretells Peter's denial*
	39	*Jesus prays on the Mount of Olives*
	47	*The arrest*
	54	*Peter's denial*
	63	*Jesus is mocked and beaten*
	66	*Jesus before the Council*
23	1	*Jesus is brought before Pilate*
	6	*Jesus is sent to Herod*
	13	*Pilate fails to release Jesus*
	26	*The Crucifixion*
	50	*The burial*
24	1	*The Resurrection*
	13	*The road to Emmaus*
	36	*Jesus appears to the disciples*
	50	*The Ascension*

The Gospel of John

Jesus makes the journey from the Jordan Valley to Galilee, and back to the Jordan

- **1** 1 *Prologue*
  - 19 *The witness of John the Baptist*
  - 35 *The calling of the first disciples*
- **2** 1 *The wedding at Cana*
  - 13 *Traders expelled from the Temple in Jerusalem*
- **3** 1 *The conversation with Nicodemus*
  - 22 *The confession of John the Baptist*

Jesus journeys to Galilee and then returns to Jerusalem

- **4** 1 *The conversation with a Samaritan woman*
  - 43 *The healing of a courtier's son*
- **5** 1 *The healing at the Pool of Bethesda*
  - 19 *Jesus answers the Jews*

Jesus in Galilee

- **6** 1 *The feeding of the five thousand*
  - 16 *The disciples see Jesus walking on the water*
  - 22 *The sermon in Capernaum on the bread of life*
  - 60 *The difficulties of the disciples*

Jesus in Jerusalem

- **7** 1 *The feast of Tabernacles*
  - 14 *Jesus teaches the crowds in the Temple*
  - 32 *The attempt to arrest Jesus*
  - 45 *The Pharisees and Nicodemus*
  - [53 *The adulterous woman*]
- **8** 12 *The light of the world*
  - 21 *A warning to the Jews*
  - 31 *Jesus and Abraham*
- **9** 1 *The healing of the man born blind*
- **10** 1 *The shepherd of the sheep*
  - 22 *The feast of the Dedication of the Temple*
  - 40 *Jesus returns to the Jordan Valley*

Jesus in Bethany and Ephraim

- **11** 1 *The raising of Lazarus*
  - 45 *The chief priests and Pharisees hold a council*
  - 55 *The last Passover is near*

Jesus returns to Bethany and Jerusalem

12	1	*The anointing at Bethany*
	12	*The entry into Jerusalem*
	20	*Jesus foretells his death*
	37	*The Jews are unable to believe*
13	1	*Jesus washes his disciples' feet*
	21	*Judas leaves the upper room*
	31	*Jesus begins his farewell talks*
14	1	*The way, the truth, and the life*
15	1	*The true vine*
	18	*Hatred and persecution*
16	4	*The sending of the Holy Spirit*
17	1	*The high priestly prayer of Christ*

The Passion

18	1	*Jesus is arrested*
	12	*Jesus before Annas and Caiaphas*
	28	*Jesus before Pilate*
19	12	*Jesus is condemned to death*
	17	*The Crucifixion*
	32	*The burial*

The Resurrection

20	1	*Mary Magdalene and two disciples find the tomb empty*
	11	*Jesus appears to Mary Magdalene*
	19	*Jesus appears to the disciples in the upper room*
21	1	*The appearance by the Sea of Tiberias*
	15	*The charge to Peter*
	24	*Conclusion*

The Gospel of Matthew

1 *The genealogy*

1 The record of the genesis
Of Jesus Christ
The son of David
The son of Abraham

2 Abraham was the father of Isaac
And Isaac of Jacob
And Jacob of Judah and his brothers

3 Judah was the father of Perez
And of Zerah
Their mother was Tamar

Perez was the father of Hezron
And Hezron of Ram
4 And Ram of Amminadab
And Amminadab of Nahshon
And Nahshon of Salmon

5 Salmon was the father of Boaz
Whose mother was Rahab
And Boaz was the father of Obed
Whose mother was Ruth

And Obed was the father of Jesse
6 Who was the father of David the King

David was the father of Solomon
Whose mother had been the wife of Uriah

7 Solomon was the father of Rehoboam
And Rehoboam of Abijah
And Abijah of Asa

8 Asa was the father of Jehoshaphat
And Jehoshaphat of Joram
And Joram of Uzziah

9   Uzziah was the father of Jotham
       And Jotham of Ahaz
       And Ahaz of Hezekiah

10   Hezekiah was the father of Manasseh
       And Manasseh of Amos
       And Amos of Josiah
11   And Josiah of Jechoniah and his brothers
       At the deportation to Babylon

12   After the deportation to Babylon
       Jechoniah was the father of Shealtiel
       And Shealtiel of Zerubbabel
13   And Zerubbabel of Abiud
       And Abiud of Eliakim
       And Eliakim of Azor

14   Azor was the father of Zadok
       And Zadok of Achim
       And Achim of Eliud
15   And Eliud of Eleazar
       And Eleazar of Matthan
       And Matthan of Jacob

16   Jacob was the father of Joseph
       The husband of Mary
       Of whom was born Jesus
       Who is called Christ

17   Therefore all the generations
       From Abraham to David
       Were fourteen generations
       And from David
       Until the deportation to Babylon
       Were fourteen generations
       And from the deportation to Babylon
       Until the Christ
       Were fourteen generations

The birth of Jesus Christ

18   Now the birth of Jesus Christ
       Happened in this way

His mother Mary
Was promised in marriage to Joseph
But before they came together
She was found to have conceived
By the Holy Spirit

19   As her husband Joseph
Was an upright man
And did not wish
To make an example of her
He resolved to dismiss her secretly

20   But while he was thinking of this
An angel of the Lord
Appeared to him in a dream
   And said
      Joseph son of David
      Do not be afraid
      To take your wife Mary
      As her conception
      Is of the Holy Spirit

21   She will give birth to a son
      And you shall give him
      The name Jesus
      Because he will save his people
      From their sins

22   All this happened
So that might be fulfilled
What was spoken by the Lord
Through the prophet
Saying
23   *Now the Virgin will conceive*
And will give birth to a son
And they will call his name
Emmanuel
Which is translated
God with us

24   When Joseph rose up from sleep
He did what the angel of the Lord
Had commanded him
And took his wife

25 He did not know her
Until she had borne a son
And he gave him
The name Jesus

2

The visit of the magi

1 Now when Jesus was born
In Bethlehem of Judea
During the reign of King Herod
Magi from the East
Arrived in Jerusalem
2   And they said
        Where is the one
        Who is born King of the Jews?
        We have seen his star
        In the East
        And have come to worship him

3 When he heard this
King Herod was disturbed
And with him
The whole of Jerusalem

4 Having assembled
All the chief priests
And scribes of the people
He asked them
Where the Christ should be born

5   And they told him
        In Bethlehem of Judea
        As the prophet has written
6   *And you Bethlehem*
In the land of Judah
Are not in any way the least
Among the leaders of Judah
Because from you
Will come a leader
Who will shepherd my people Israel

7 Then Herod
Called the Magi secretly
And made careful enquiries

About the time
When the star appeared

8 He sent them to Bethlehem
  And said
   Make searching enquiries
   About the child
   And when you have found him
   Bring me the news
   So that I myself
   May also come and worship him

9 When they had heard the King
They continued on their way
And now the star
Which they saw in the East
Led them
Until it came to stand
Over where the child was

10 On seeing the star
They rejoiced with the greatest joy

11 When they came into the house
They saw the child
With his mother Mary
And they fell down
And worshipped him

They opened their treasures
And offered him gifts
Gold
Frankincense
And myrrh

12 As they had been warned
In a dream
Not to return to Herod
They took another road
And departed to their country

The flight into Egypt

13 When they had gone
An angel of the Lord
Appeared to Joseph in a dream
    And said
        Get up
        Take the child and his mother
        And go away into Egypt
        Stay there until I tell you
        As Herod
        Is now going to search for the child
        To destroy him

14 So he got up
And took the child
And his mother
At night
And went away into Egypt

15 He was there until Herod's death
To fulfil what the Lord
Had spoken through the prophet
Saying
Out of Egypt I called my son

The massacre of the innocents

16 When Herod
Saw that the Magi had scorned him
He was full of fury

He sent out
And killed all the boys in Bethlehem
And in the surrounding districts
Who were two years old
Or less
According to the time
Which he had carefully enquired
From the Magi

17 Then what was said
Through Jeremiah the prophet
Was fulfilled

18 *A voice was heard in Ramah*
Weeping and sorrowing
Rachel weeping for her children
And would not be comforted
Because they are no more

The return from Egypt
19 When Herod had died
An angel of the Lord
Appeared in a dream
To Joseph in Egypt
20   And said
        Get up
        Take the child and his mother
        And go into the land of Israel
        Because the people are dead
        Who wished to take the child's life

21 So he got up
And taking the child
And his mother
He went into the land of Israel

22 But when he heard that Archelaus
Was ruling over Judea
In place of his father Herod
He was afraid to go there

And being warned in a dream
He turned away
Into the region of Galilee
23 And went to live
In a town called Nazareth
So that what was spoken
Through the prophets
Was fulfilled
He shall be called a Nazarene

3

The preaching of John the Baptist
1 Now in those days
John the Baptist appeared
Preaching in the desert of Judea

2   And saying
        Change your hearts and minds
        As the kingdom of the heavens
        Has come close

3   This is the one
    Who is spoken of
    Through Isaiah the prophet
    When he says
    A voice is calling in the desert
    Prepare the road for the Lord
    Make his paths straight

4   John himself
    Wore a garment of camel hair
    With a leather belt round his waist
    His food was locusts and wild honey

5   Then all Jerusalem
    Went out to him
    And all Judea
    And all the neighbourhood
    Of the Jordan
6   And they were baptized by him
    In the River Jordan
    Acknowledging their sins

7   When he saw many of the Pharisees
    And Sadducees
    Coming to the baptism
        He said to them
            Offspring of vipers
            Who warned you to escape
            From the anger which is to come?

8   Therefore bear fruit
        Worthy of your change of heart
9   And do not think to yourselves
        We have Abraham as our father
        Because I say to you
        That from these stones
        God has the power
        To raise up children to Abraham

10   The axe is already laid
　　At the root of the trees
　　Therefore every tree
　　That does not bear sound fruit
　　Is cut down
　　And thrown into the fire

11   I myself
　　Baptize you in water
　　For a change of heart and mind
　　But the one
　　Who comes after me
　　Who is stronger than I am
　　And of whom I am not worthy
　　To carry the sandals
　　He will baptize you
　　In Holy Spirit and fire

12   The winnowing fan
　　Is in his hand
　　And he will sweep clean
　　His threshing floor
　　He will gather his wheat
　　Into the barn
　　But the chaff
　　He will burn with a fire
　　That cannot be put out

Jesus is baptized

13   Then Jesus appeared from Galilee
　　Coming to John at the Jordan
　　To be baptized by him

14   But John
　　Was determined to prevent it
　　　　Saying to him
　　　　　　I myself
　　　　　　Need to be baptized by you
　　　　　　And yet you come to me?

15   Jesus answered him
　　　　Allow it now
　　　　As it is proper for us
　　　　To complete all that is needed

    Then he allowed him

16   Jesus
    Having been baptized
    Came up at once
    Out of the water
    Then
    The heavens opened
    And he saw the Spirit of God
    Descending like a dove
    And coming down upon him

17   And now
       A voice out of the heavens said
          This is my son
          My beloved
          In whom I rejoice

4 *The Temptation*

1   Then Jesus
    Was led by the Spirit
    Into the desert
    To be tempted by the devil

2   He fasted forty days
    And forty nights
    And afterwards he was hungry

3   Then the tempter came to him
       And said
          If you are God's son
          Speak to these stones
          That they may become
          Loaves of bread

4   But he answered him
       It has been written
          Mankind
          Shall not only live on bread
          But on every word
          That comes from the mouth of God

5   Then the devil
Took him into the holy city
And stood him
On the parapet of the Temple
6   And said to him
            If you are God's son
            Throw yourself down

            As it has been written
            He will command his angels
            To be concerned with you
            And on their hands
            They will carry you
            Lest you strike your foot
            Against a stone

7   Jesus said to him
            Again it has been written
            You shall not
            Put the Lord your God
            To the test

8   Again the devil
Took him to a very high mountain
And showed him
All the kingdoms of the world
And their magnificence
9   And said to him
            I will give all this
            To you
            If you will fall down
            And worship me

10   Then Jesus said to him
            Go
            Satan
            As it has been written
            You shall worship
            The Lord your God
            And you shall serve him only

11   Then the devil left him
And now angels
Came to bring him aid

Jesus returns to Galilee
12 When he heard
That John had been arrested
He went away into Galilee

13 He left Nazareth
And came to live in Capernaum
By the sea
In the district of Zebulun and Naphtali

14 So that what was said
Through Isaiah the prophet
Might be fulfilled
15 *Land of Zebulun*
And land of Naphtali
The sea road
Beyond the Jordan
Galilee of the Gentiles

16 *The people who dwelt in darkness*
Have seen a great light
And for those
Who dwelt in the region
And shadow of death
Light has dawned

17 From then on
Jesus began to preach
    And said
        Change your hearts and minds
        As the kingdom of the heavens
        Has come close

The calling of four disciples
18 As he walked
Beside the Sea of Galilee
He saw two brothers
Simon called Peter
And his brother Andrew
Casting a net into the sea
Because they were fishers
19   And he said to them
        Come with me

                    And I will make you
                    Fishers of men

20   Immediately
                They left their nets
                And followed him

21   Going farther on
                He saw two other brothers
                James the son of Zebedee
                And his brother John
                In the boat
                With Zebedee their father
                Mending their nets

                He called them
22   Then at once
                They left the boat
                And their father
                And followed him

                Jesus preaches and heals in Galilee
23   He went round
                The whole of Galilee
                Teaching in their synagogues
                Preaching the Gospel of the kingdom
                And healing all diseases
                And all disabilities
                Among the people

24   News of him
                Spread into the whole of Syria
                And they brought to him all those
                Who were suffering from various diseases
                Or were in pain
                Also those who were possessed by demons
                Or were lunatics
                Or paralysed
                And he healed them

25   Large crowds followed him
                From Galilee
                And the Decapolis

And Jerusalem
And from Judea and beyond the Jordan

The Sermon on the Mount

5   *The Beatitudes*

1   When he saw the crowds
He went up on to the mountain
There he sat down
And his disciples came to him

2   The opening his mouth
He taught them
   And said

3   Blessed
      Are the beggars in the spirit
      As theirs
      Is the kingdom of the heavens

4   Blessed
      Are those who mourn
      As they will be comforted

5   Blessed
      Are the gentle
      As they will inherit the earth

6   Blessed
      Are those who hunger and thirst
      For what is right
      As they will be satisfied

7   Blessed
      Are the merciful
      As they will have mercy
      Shown to them

8   Blessed
      Are those with pure hearts
      As they will see God

9   Blessed
    Are the peacemakers
    As they will be called
    Sons of God

10 Blessed
    Are those who are persecuted
    For the sake of what is right
    As theirs
    Is the kingdom of the heavens

11 Blessed
    Are you when they reproach you
    And persecute you
    For my sake
    And say many evil things
    Against you
    Which are untrue

12 Rejoice and be glad
    Because you have a great reward
    In the heavens
    As this is how they persecuted
    The prophets who came before you

Salt and light

13 You are the salt of the earth
    But how shall it be salted
    If the salt is useless?

    It is no longer worth anything
    Except to be thrown outside
    Where people will tread on it

14 You are the light of the world
    A city built on a mountain
    Cannot be hidden
15 Nor do people light a lamp
    And put it under the corn-measure
    But on the lampstand
    Where it gives light
    To everyone in the house

16   Let your light
      Shine out to your fellow men
      So that they see
      The nobility of your deeds
      And praise
      Your Father in the heavens

The old Law and new demands

17   Do not think
      That I came to destroy
      The Law and the prophets
      I did not come to destroy
      But to complete them
18   Certainly I say to you
      Until heaven and earth pass away
      By no means
      Will one letter
      Or one comma
      Pass away from the Law
      Until everything has happened

19   Therefore
      Whoever breaks one
      Of the very least
      Of these commandments
      And teaches his fellow men
      To do so
      Will be called least
      In the kingdom of the heavens
      But whoever keeps
      And teaches them
      Will be called great
      In the kingdom of the heavens

20   Because I say to you
      That unless your virtue
      Is more
      Than that of the scribes and Pharisees
      Certainly
      You will not enter
      The kingdom of the heavens

21 You heard
    That in the past
    The people were told
    You shall not kill
    And whoever kills
    Will be judged responsible

22 But I
    I say to you
    That everyone
    Who is angry with his brother
    Will be judged responsible

    And whoever
    Says to his brother
    Worthless fellow
    Must answer to the council

    And whoever says
    You fool
    Will be in danger
    Of the fire of retribution

23 Therefore
    If you bring your gift
    To the altar of sacrifice
    And then remember
    That your brother
    Has something against you

24 Leave your gift there
    In front of the altar
    And first
    Go and be reconciled
    With your brother
    And then come
    And offer your gift

25 Come to terms
    With your opponent
    While you are with him
    On the road
    Or your opponent
    Will hand you over

To the judge
And the judge
To the officer
And you
May be thrown into prison

26 Certainly I say to you
By no means
Will you come out of there
Until you have repaid
The last copper

27 You heard
That it was said
You shall not commit adultery

28 But I
I say to you
That everyone
Who looks at a woman
With desire
Has already committed adultery
With her
In his heart

29 So if your right eye
Causes your downfall
Pluck it out
And throw it away from you
It is to your advantage
That one of your members
Should perish
Rather
Than that your whole body
Is thrown into the fire of retribution

30 And if your right hand
Causes your downfall
Cut it off
And throw it away from you
It is to your advantage
That one of your members
Should perish
Rather

Than that your whole body
Go into the fire of retribution

31 And it was said
Whoever releases his wife
Let him give her a divorce

32 But I
I say to you
That everyone
Who releases his wife
Except for immorality
Causes her to commit adultery
And whoever
Marries a divorced woman
Commits adultery

33 Again
You heard that in the past
The people were told
You shall not swear falsely
But shall keep your vows
To the Lord

34 But I
I say to you
Do not swear at all
Either by heaven
Because it is the throne of God
35 Or by the earth
Because it is the stool
For his feet
Or by Jerusalem
Because it is the city
Of the great King
36 Or by your head
Because you cannot make one hair
White or black

37 Let your words be
Yes yes
No no
Because what is more than this
Is evil

38 You heard that it was said
An eye for an eye
And a tooth for a tooth

39 But I
I say to you
Do not oppose evil
But if anyone
Strikes you on the right cheek
Turn the other also
Towards him
40 And whoever
Would sue you
For your tunic
Allow him also
To take your cloak
41 And if anyone
Would impress you into service
To go one mile
Go with him two

42 Give to whoever asks you
And do not turn away anyone
Who wishes to borrow from you

43 You heard that it was said
You shall love your neighbour
And hate your enemy

44 But I
I say to you
Love your enemies
And pray
For those who persecute you
45 So that you may be the sons
Of your Father in the heavens
He causes his sun to rise
On those who are wicked
And on those who are good
And he sends rain
On the just and the unjust

46 If you love those who love you
What reward should you have?

                    Surely even the tax collectors
                    Do the same

47   And if you only greet your brothers
                    What more are you doing
                    Than the Gentiles
                    Who do the same?

48   Therefore
                    Become perfect
                    As your heavenly Father
                    Is perfect

6   *Almsgiving and prayer and fasting*
1   Take care
                    That you do not perform
                    Your virtuous deeds
                    In the sight of your fellow men
                    Intending them to notice you
                    For then
                    You will not be rewarded
                    By your Father in the heavens

2   Therefore
                    When you give to those in need
                    Do not sound a trumpet
                    In front of you
                    In the synagogues
                    And in the streets
                    Like the hypocrites
                    Who want to be praised
                    By their fellow men
                    Certainly I say to you
                    They have their reward

3   But when you give to the needy
                    Do not allow your left hand
                    To be aware
                    Of what your right hand does
4   So that your gift
                    May be kept secret
                    And your Father
                    Who sees what is kept secret
                    Will repay you

5 When you pray
Do not imitate the hypocrites
Because they like to pray
In the synagogues
And standing at the corners
Of the open streets
Where they are noticed
By their fellow men
Certainly I say to you
They have their reward

6 But when you pray
Go into your inner room
And when you have shut the door
Pray to your Father
Who is there in secret
And your Father
Who sees what is kept secret
Will repay you

7 In your prayers
Do not use meaningless words
Like the Gentiles
Who think
That they will be heard
Because they talk so much

8 So do not be like them
As your Father
Knows what you need
Before you ask him

9 Therefore
You should pray like this
OUR FATHER
IN THE HEAVENS
MAY YOUR NAME
BE KEPT HOLY
10 YOUR KINGDOM COME
YOUR WILL BE DONE
AS IN HEAVEN
SO ALSO ON EARTH
11 THE BREAD WE NEED EVERY DAY
GIVE US TODAY

12   AND FORGIVE US OUR DEBTS
      AS WE FORGIVE OUR DEBTORS
13   DO NOT BRING US TO THE TEST
      BUT RESCUE US FROM THE EVIL ONE

14   Because if you forgive
      Your fellow men
      Their shortcomings
      Your heavenly Father
      Will also forgive you

15   But if you do not forgive
      Your fellow men
      Neither will your Father
      Forgive your shortcomings

16   When you fast
      Do not appear depressed
      Like the hypocrites
      Because they disfigure their faces
      So that their fasting
      May be visible
      To their fellow men
      Certainly I say to you
      They have their reward

17   But when you fast
      Anoint your head
      And wash your face
18   So that your fasting
      Is not visible
      To your fellow men
      But to your Father
      Who is there in secret
      And your Father
      Who sees what is kept secret
      Will repay you

Serving the light

19   Do not
      Store up treasure for yourselves
      On the earth
      Where moths and worms

MATTHEW 6

        Eat it away
        And where thieves
        Break in and steal
20   But store up treasure for yourselves
        In heaven
        Where neither moths nor worms
        Eat it away
        And where thieves
        Do not break in and steal

21   Because where your treasure is
        There your heart
        Will be also

22   The lamp of the body
        Is the eye
        So if your eye sees clearly
        The whole of your body
        Will shine
23   But if your eye sees falsely
        The whole of your body
        Will be dark

        If therefore
        The light in you
        Is darkness
        How great is the darkness

24   No-one can serve two overlords
        For either he will hate the one
        And love the other
        Or he will hold firmly to the one
        And scorn the other
        You are not able
        To serve God and riches

Trust in God

25   Therefore I say to you
        Do not be too concerned
        About your soul-bearing life
        About what you should eat
        Or what you should drink

MATTHEW 6

    Or about your body
    What you should wear

    Is not the soul-bearing life
    More than food
    And the body
    More than dress?

26   You should look
    At the birds of heaven
    They do not sow
    Neither do they reap
    Nor store in barns
    And your heavenly Father
    Feeds them
    Are you
    Not worth more than they are?

27   But which of you
    By his concern
    Can alter the way he is made?

28   And why are you concerned
    About dress
    Observe the lilies
    How they grow in the fields
    They do not labour or spin
29   But I say to you
    That Solomon
    In all his glory
    Was not robed
    Like one of them

30   If the grass in the fields
    Which is there today
    And tomorrow
    Is thrown into the oven
    Is so clothed by God
    Will he not do much more
    For you?
    You that have little faith

31   Therefore do not be concerned
    And say

What are we going to eat?
Or what
Are we going to drink?
Or what
Are we going to put on?

32 The Gentiles
Search for all these things
And your heavenly Father
Knows that you need them all

33 But first
Seek his kingdom
And his justice
And all these things
Will be given to you

34 Therefore do not be concerned
About tomorrow
As tomorrow
Will take care of itself
Enough for today
Are its difficulties

7 *Do not criticize others*

1 Do not judge
So that you are not judged
2 As with the judgment
With which you judge
You will be judged yourselves
And the measure
With which you measure
Will be the measure
Which is given to you

3 And why
Do you see the splinter
In your brother's eye
And do not pay attention
To the beam
In your own eye?
4 Or how will you say
To your brother

MATTHEW 7

Allow me
To take the splinter
Out of your eye
When just look
What a beam
Is in your own eye?

5 Hypocrite
First take the beam
Out of your own eye
Then you will see clearly
To take the splinter
Out of your brother's eye

Giving and receiving

6 Do not give anything holy
To the dogs
Or throw down your pearls
In front of pigs
Because they may tread on them
With their feet
And then turn round
And tear you

7 Ask
And it will be given to you
Seek
And you will find
Knock
And it will be opened for you

8 As everyone who asks
Receives
And whoever seeks
Finds
And for the one who knocks
It will be opened

9 Or which man of you
When his son
Asks him for a loaf of bread
Will give him a stone?
10 Or if he asks for a fish
Will give him a snake?

11   So if you
      Who are evil
      Know how to give good gifts
      To your children
      How much more
      Will your Father in the heavens
      Give good things
      To those who ask him

12   Therefore
      Everything that you wish others
      Would do for you
      Do the same to them
      As this is the Law
      And the prophets

The narrow gate

13   Go in through the narrow gate
      Because the gate is wide
      And the road is broad
      Which leads on to destruction
      And there are many
      Who enter that way

14   But because the gate is narrow
      And the road made troublesome
      Which leads on to life
      There are few
      Who find it

False prophets

15   Watch out for false prophets
      Who come to you
      In sheep's clothing
      But inwardly
      Are thieving wolves

16   You will recognize them
      By their fruits
      Are grapes gathered from thorns
      Or figs from thistles?

17 So every good tree
Produces sound fruit
But the rotten tree
Produces evil fruit
18 A good tree
Is not able to bear evil fruit
Nor a rotten tree
To bear sound fruit

19 Every tree
That does not bear sound fruit
Is cut down
And thrown into the fire

20 So you will recognize them
By their fruit

21 Not everyone who says to me
Lord
Lord
Will enter
The kingdom of the heavens
But whoever
Does the will of my Father
In the heavens

22 In that day
Many will say to me
Lord
Lord
Have we not prophesied
In your name?
And cast out demons
In your name?
And done many powerful deeds
In your name?

23 Then I will declare to them
I never recognized you
Depart from me
You law-breakers

The two builders

24 So everyone who hears
These words of mine
And does them
Will be like a thoughtful man
Who built his house
On a rock

25 Then the rain poured down
The rivers rose
The winds blew
And beat upon that house
But it did not fall
Because the foundations
Were on the rock

26 But everyone who hears
These words of mine
And does not do them
Will be like a foolish man
Who built his house
On the sand

27 Then the rain poured down
The rivers rose
The winds blew
And struck against that house
And it fell
With a mighty fall

28 And it happened
That when Jesus
Had ended these words
The crowds
Were astonished at his teaching
29 Because he was teaching them
As someone who had authority
And not like their scribes

8

A leper is cleansed

1 As he came down from the mountain
Large crowds followed him

2 Now a leper came to him
   And bowing down
      He said
         Lord
         If it is your will
         You have the power
         To make me clean

3 He stretched out his hand
   And touched him
      Saying
         I will
         You are clean

   At once
   He was cleared of his leprosy

4   Jesus said to him
         See that you tell no one
         But go
         Show yourself to the priest
         And offer the gift
         Which Moses commanded
         As evidence to the people

   The healing of the centurion's servant
5 When he entered Capernaum
   A centurion came to him
   With an urgent request
6   And said
         Sir
         My personal attendant
         Is lying at home
         Paralysed and in terrible pain

7   He said to him
         I
         I will come
         And heal him

8   But the centurion said
         Sir
         I am not worthy

To receive you under my roof
Only speak the word
And my attendant will be healed

9   As I myself
Am also a man under authority
With soldiers under me
And I say to one
Go
And he goes
And to another
Come
And he comes
And to my slave
Do this
And he does it

10 When he heard this
Jesus was astonished
   And said to those who were following
      Certainly I say to you
      I have not found such great faith
      From any one in Israel

11   And I say to you
That many will come
From the east
And from the west
And will sit at the table
With Abraham
Isaac
And Jacob
In the kingdom of the heavens
12   But the sons of the kingdom
Will be cast out
Into the outer darkness

There will be weeping
And gnashing of teeth

13   Then Jesus said to the centurion
   Go
   As you believe
   So may it be for you

And in that hour
The boy was healed

Jesus heals Peter's mother-in-law and many sufferers
14 Jesus went into Peter's house
And saw his mother-in-law
Laid low and suffering from fever
15 He touched her hand
The fever left her
And she got up and served them

16 When evening came
They brought to him
Many people possessed by demons
He cast out the spirits
With a word
And all who suffered
He healed

17 So that what was said
Through the prophet Isaiah
Was fulfilled
He took our disabilities
And bore our diseases

The difficulties of discipleship
18 Jesus saw that a crowd
Was gathering round him
So he gave the order to go away
To the other side

19   Then one of the scribes
    Came to him and said
        Teacher
        I will follow you
        Wherever you go

20   Jesus said to him
        The foxes have holes
        And the birds of heaven
        Have their dwellings

>   But the Son of Man
>   Has nowhere to lay his head

21   And another of the disciples
>   Said to him
>>   Lord
>>   First let me go away
>>   And bury my father

22   But Jesus said to him
>>   You follow me
>>   And leave the dead
>>   To bury their dead

Jesus calms the storm

23   As he embarked on to the boat
>   His disciples followed him

24   Now a great disturbance
>   Took place in the sea
>   So that the boat
>   Was covered by the waves

>   But he was asleep
25   And they went to him
>   And woke him
>>   Saying
>>>   Lord
>>>   Save us
>>>   We are lost

26   But he said to them
>>   Why are you such cowards
>>   You that have little faith?

>   Then he got up
>   And spoke sternly
>   To the winds
>   And to the sea
>   And there was a great calm

27   The men were astonished
>   And said

What sort is he
That even the winds
And the sea
Obey him?

Two demoniacs are healed

28 When he came to the other side
Into the country of the Gadarenes
Two demoniacs met him
Coming out of the tombs

They were exceedingly hostile
So that no-one was strong enough
To pass along that road

29 Now they called out
And said
What is there between us and you
Son of God?
Have you come here
To torment us
Before the moment has come?

30 At a distance from them
A large herd of pigs were feeding

31 And the demons begged him
If you cast us out
Send us into the herd of pigs

32 He said to them
Go

So those who came out
Went away into the pigs

Then the whole herd
Rushed down the steep incline
Into the sea
And died in the water

33 The herdsmen fled
And went away into the town

      Where they reported everything
      Also what had happened to the demoniacs

34   All the townspeople came out
      In order to meet Jesus
      When they saw him
      They begged him to leave their district

9

A paralytic is healed

1   Embarking on to a boat
      He crossed over
      And came to his home town

2   And now
      They brought a paralytic to him
      Lying on a mattress

      When Jesus saw their faith
          He said to the paralytic
              Take courage
              Child
              Your sins are forgiven

3   Some of the scribes
        Said among themselves
           He blasphemes

4   As he knew their thoughts
        Jesus said
           Why do you think evil
           In your hearts?
5   For which is easier
           To say
           Your sins are forgiven
           Or to say
           Rise up and walk?

6   Only that you may know
           That the Son of Man
           Has authority on the earth
           To forgive sins

>   Then he said to the paralytic
>> Get up
>> Take your mattress
>> And go home

7 He got up
And went away to his house

8 But when they saw it
The people were afraid
And praised God
Who had given such authority to men

The calling of Matthew
9 He left there
And as he passed by
Jesus saw a man
Whose name was Matthew
Sitting in the custom house

>   He said to him
>> Follow me

He rose up
And followed him

10 It happened
That he was having a meal
In the house
And many tax-collectors
And outcasts
Came to sit at the table
With Jesus and his disciples

11 When they saw it
>   The Pharisees said to his disciples
>> Why does your teacher
>> Eat with tax-collectors
>> And with outcasts?

12 But when Jesus heard it
>   He said

Those who have good health
Do not need a doctor
But those who are suffering

13   Go and learn what that is
I wish mercy
And not sacrifice
As I did not come
To call the just
But the outcasts

A question about fasting
14   Then John's disciples
Came to him
   And said
      Why do we fast
      And the Pharisees fast
      But your disciples do not fast?

15   Jesus said to them
      Can the bridegroom's attendants mourn
      As long as the bridegroom
      Is with them?
      The day will come
      When the bridegroom
      Is taken away from them
      And then they will fast

16   No one puts a patch
      Of untreated cloth
      On to an old cloak
      As its quality
      Will pull away from the cloak
      And the tear
      Will be made worse

17   Neither do they put new wine
      Into old wineskins
      Otherwise
      The wineskins burst
      The wine pours out
      And the wineskins are destroyed

> But they put new wine
> Into fresh wineskins
> And both are saved

The cure of a woman and the raising of a young girl

18 Now while he was still speaking
An official came up to him
And bowing down
>   He said
>   > My daughter has just died
>   > But if you come
>   > And lay your hand on her
>   > She will live

19 Jesus got up
And followed him with his disciples

20 Then a woman came behind him
Who for twelve years
Had suffered from a flow of blood

She touched the fringe of his cloak
21 As she said within herself
If only
I am able to touch his cloak
I shall be saved

22 Jesus turned
And when he saw her
>   He said
>   > Courage
>   > Daughter
>   > Your faith has healed you

And from that hour
The woman was healed

23 When Jesus came into the official's house
And saw the flute players
And the crowd
All making a noise
24   He said

> Leave here
> The young girl has not died
> She is asleep

But they laughed at him

25 However
When the people had been put outside
He went in
And took hold of her hand
And the young girl was raised up

26 Then this report
Went out all over the country

Two blind men are healed

27 As Jesus went on from there
Two blind men followed
> Calling out
>> Pity us
>> Son of David

28 When he entered the house
The blind men came up to him
> And Jesus said to them
>> Do you believe
>> That I have the power
>> To do this?

> They said
>> Yes
>> Lord

29 Then he touched their eyes
> And said
>> As is your faith
>> So it shall be for you

30 Their eyes were opened
And Jesus spoke to them sternly
Saying
>> See that no one
>> Becomes aware of this

31 But they went out
And talked of him
In all the countryside

A dumb demoniac is healed
32 Just as those were leaving
They brought to him
A dumb demoniac

33 And when the demon
Was cast out
The dumb man spoke

The crowds were amazed
And said
Such a thing
Has never been seen in Israel

34 But the Pharisees said
Through the ruler of the demons
He casts out the demons

35 Jesus went about the towns and villages
Teaching in the synagogues

Preaching the Gospel of the kingdom
And healing all diseases
And all disabilities

36 When he saw the crowds
He was full of concern for them
Because they were faint
And scattered
Like sheep without a shepherd

37 Then he said to his disciples
Indeed there is a great harvest
But there are few labourers
38 Therefore pray the lord of the harvest
To speed labourers into his harvest

10 *The sending out of the twelve*

1   He called to him
His twelve disciples
And gave them authority
Over unclean spirits
So that they could cast them out
And could heal all diseases
And all disabilities

2   These are the names
Of the twelve apostles

First Simon called Peter
And his brother Andrew
James the son of Zebedee
And his brother John
3   Philip and Bartholomew
Thomas and Matthew the tax-collector
James the son of Alphaeus
And Thaddaeus
4   Simon the Canaanaean
And Judas Iscariot who betrayed him

5   Jesus sent out these twelve
And giving them their instructions
   He said
      Do not take the road
      To the Gentiles
      Or enter a Samaritan town
6   But go rather to the lost sheep
      Of the house of Israel

7   And preach on your way
      Saying
      The kingdom of the heavens
      Has come close

8   Heal the sick
      Raise the dead
      Cleanse the lepers
      Cast out demons

      What you received as a free gift
      Give as a free gift

9	Do not possess gold or silver
	Or have small coins
	In your belts
10	Or a bag for the road
	Two tunics
	Sandals
	Or a staff
	As the worker
	Deserves his food
11	When you enter a town
	Or a village
	Make careful enquiries
	As to who in it is deserving
	And stay there until you leave
12	When you enter a house
	Greet them
13	And if the house
	Is indeed deserving
	Let your peace come to it
	But if it is not deserving
	Let your peace
	Return to you
14	And whoever does not receive you
	Or hear your words
	When you come outside that house
	Or that town
	Shake off the dust from your feet
15	Certainly I say to you
	It will be more bearable
	For the land of Sodom and Gomorrah
	In the day of judgment
	Than for that town
16	See how I
	I send you out
	As sheep among wolves
	Therefore have the sense of serpents
	And the simplicity of doves

MATTHEW 10

The disciples will be persecuted

17 Guard against men
As they will hand you over
To councils
And they will scourge you
In their synagogues

18 You will be brought before
Governors and kings
For my sake
As a witness to them
And to the nations

19 But when they arrest you
Do not be anxious
About what you should say
Or how you should say it
Whatever you should say
Will be given to you
20 As it is not you who speak
But the spirit of your Father
Who is speaking in you

21 And a brother
Will betray a brother to death
And a father a child
And children
Will rise against parents
And will put them to death

22 Everyone will hate you
Because of my name
But whoever
Remains steadfast to the end
Will be saved

23 But when they persecute you
In one town
Escape to another
As certainly I say to you
By no means
Will you have passed through
All the towns of Israel
Before the Son of Man comes

24 A disciple
Is not above his teacher
Or a servant
Above his master
25 It is enough for the disciple
To be like his teacher
And the servant
Like his master

If they called the householder
Beelzebub
How much more
Those who belong to his house

The disciples should have courage

26 Therefore
You should not be afraid of them
As nothing has been covered
Which will not be revealed
Or is secret
Which will not be known

27 What I say to you
In darkness
You should tell in the light
And what you hear in your ear
Preach from the housetops

28 And do not be afraid
Of those who kill the body
But have no power
To kill the living soul

But rather be afraid
Of those who have the power
To destroy both soul and body
In the valley of burning

29 Are not two sparrows
Sold for a small copper coin
And not one of them
Will fall to earth
Without your Father

30   Even the hairs on your head
     Are all counted

31   So do not be afraid
     You are worth more
     Than many sparrows

The disciples should follow Christ

32   Everyone who acknowledges me
     In the presence of men
     I myself
     Will also acknowledge him
     In the presence of my Father
     In the heavens

33   And whoever disowns me
     In the presence of men
     I myself
     Will also disown him
     In the presence of my Father
     In the heavens

34   Do not suppose
     That I came to bring peace
     On the earth
     I did not come to bring peace
     But a sword

35   As I came to cause disagreement
     Between a man and his father
     A daughter and her mother
     A bride and her mother-in-law
36   And a man's enemies
     Will be those in his house

37   The one
     Who cares for father or mother
     More than for me
     Is not worthy of me
     And the one
     Who cares for son or daughter
     More than for me
     Is not worthy of me

38   The one
Who does not take his cross
And follow after me
Is not worthy of me

39   The one
Who finds his soul-bearing life
Will lose it
And the one
Who loses his soul-bearing life
For my sake
Will find it

40   The one
Who receives you
Receives me
And the one
Who receives me
Receives the one who sent me out

41   The one
Who receives a prophet
Because he is a prophet
Will obtain a prophet's reward
And the one
Who receives a just person
Because he is a just person
Will obtain a just person's reward

42   And whoever
Gives one of these little ones
Even a cup of cold water
Because he is a disciple
Certainly I say to you
By no means
Will he lose his reward

11 *Jesus answers John the Baptist*

1   And it happened
That when Jesus had finished
Giving his instructions
To his twelve disciples
He left there

To teach and to preach
In their towns

2 But when John heard in prison
About the deeds of the Christ
He sent his disciples to him
3   Who said
           Are you the one who is coming
           Or may we expect someone else?

4   Jesus answered them
           Go and give the news to John
           About what you hear and see

5   The blind have sight again
           And the lame walk
           Lepers are cleansed
           The deaf hear
           The dead are raised up
           The poor receive the Gospel
6   And all who do not reject me
           Are blessed

Jesus talks to the people about John
7 As they were leaving
Jesus began to talk to the crowds
About John
       And said
           What did you go out
           Into the desert
           To behold?
           A reed shaken by the wind?

8   But what did you go out
           To see?
           A man wearing fine clothes?
           Look how those who wear fine clothes
           Are in kings' houses

9   But why did you go out?
           Was it to see a prophet?
           I say to you

MATTHEW 11

      Yes
      And more than a prophet

10   This is he
      Of whom it has been written
      See how I myself
      Send out my messenger
      Before thy face
      Who will make ready
      Thy road in front of thee

11   Certainly I say to you
      There has not risen up
      Among those born of women
      Anyone greater than John the Baptist
      But the least
      In the kingdom of the heavens
      Is greater than he is

12   From the days of John the Baptist
      Until now
      The kingdom of the heavens
      Gathers force
      And the forceful take hold of it

13   Because all the prophets
      And the Law
      Prophesied until John
14   And if you are willing to receive him
      He is Elijah
      Who is about to come

15   Whoever has ears
      Should hear

16   But to whom
      Shall I compare this generation?

      It is like children
      Sitting in the market
      Who call to the others
17   And say
      We piped to you
      And you did not dance

We mourned
And you did not beat your breasts

18 Because John
Came neither eating nor drinking
And they say
He has a demon

19 The Son of Man
Came eating and drinking
And they say
Look
This is a man who is greedy
And drinks wine
A friend of tax-collectors
And of outcasts

But wisdom
Is justified by her deeds

Jesus reproves the lakeside towns
20 Then he began to reproach the towns
In which he had done
Very many of his powerful deeds
Because they did not change
Their hearts and minds

21 Woe to you
Chorazin
Woe to you
Bethsaida
Because if the powerful deeds
Had been done in Tyre and Sidon
Which have been done in you
They would have altered long ago
Putting on sackcloth and ashes

22 However
I say to you
It will be more bearable
For Tyre and Sidon
At the day of judgment
Than for you

23   And you
                Capernaum
                Were you lifted up
                As far as heaven?
                You shall go down
                As far as Hades
                Because if the powerful deeds
                Had been done in Sodom
                Which have been done in you
                It would have remained
                Until today

24   However
                I say to you
                It will be more bearable
                For the land of Sodom
                At the day of judgment
                Than for you

Jesus prays to the Father

25   At that moment
        Jesus responded by saying
                I give praise to you
                Father
                Lord of heaven
                And of earth
                Because you have hidden these things
                From the wise and the able
                And have revealed them to babes

26   Yes
                Father
                As thus it was pleasing to you

The weary will find rest

27   Everything was handed over to me
                By my Father
                And no one really knows the Son
                Except the Father
                Nor does anyone really know the Father
                Except the Son
                And the one to whom

It is the will of the Son
To reveal him

28 Come to me
All who are growing weary
And on whom
Burdens have been laid
And I myself
Will rest you

29 Take my yoke on you
And learn from me
Because I am gentle
And humble in heart
And you will find rest
For the life of your souls

30 As my yoke is easy
And my burden is light

12 *In the cornfields on the sabbath*

1 At that season
Jesus was passing through the cornfields
On the sabbath

As his disciples were hungry
They began to pick ears of corn
And to eat them

2 But when the Pharisees saw this
They said to him
Look how your disciples
Are doing something
Which it is not lawful
To do on the sabbath

3 And he said to them
Have you not read
What David did
When he was hungry
As were those with him?

4   How he entered the house of God
And ate the loaves of offering
Which it was not lawful
For him to eat
Nor for those with him
But only for the priests?

5   Or have you not read
In the Law
That on the sabbath
The priests in the Temple
Profane the sabbath
And are not to blame?

6   But I say to you
That here
There is something greater
Than the Temple

7   If you had been aware
What this is
I wish mercy
And not sacrifice
You would not have condemned
Those who are blameless
8   As the Son of Man
Is also lord of the sabbath

Healing of a man with a withered hand

9   Then he left
And went into their synagogue

10   And now there was a man
Whose hand had wasted away

    So that they could accuse him
They asked him
    Is it lawful
    To heal on the sabbath?

11   He said to them
    Is there a man among you
    Who has one sheep

And if it falls into a pit
On the sabbath
Will not take hold of it
And pull it out?

12 How much more is a man worth
Than a sheep?

Therefore it is lawful
To do what is right
On the sabbath

13 Then he said to the man
Stretch out your hand

He stretched it out
And it was made good
As healthy as was the other

14 When they went outside
The Pharisees
Considered how to proceed against him
So that they could destroy him

15 But Jesus was aware of this
And went away from there

Many people are healed
Many people followed him
And he healed them all
16 Telling them sternly
Not to make him known

17 So that what was said
Through the prophet Isaiah
Might be fulfilled

18 *See my servant*
Whom I have chosen
My beloved
In whom my living soul rejoiced

I will put my spirit upon him
And he will announce judgment
To the nations

19 *He will not quarrel*
Or cry out
Nor will anyone in the street
Hear his voice

20 *He will not break a reed*
Which has been bruised
Nor put out
The smoking wick
Until he brings judgment to victory

21 *And in his name*
Will the nations hope

Jesus heals a demoniac and reproves the Pharisees
22 A man was brought to him
Possessed by a demon
Who was both blind and dumb

And he healed him
So that the dumb man
Could both speak and see

23 All the people were astonished
    And said
        Is not he
        The Son of David?

24 But when the Pharisees heard it
    They said
        He does not cast out demons
        Except through Beelzebub
        The ruler of the demons

25 As he knew what they were thinking
    Jesus said to them
        Every kingdom
        Divided against itself
        Is made a desert

And every city or house
Divided against itself
Will not stand

26 And if Satan
Casts out Satan
He is divided against himself
So how will his kingdom stand?

27 And if I
I cast out the demons
Through Beelzebub
By whom do your sons
Cast them out?
Therefore
They shall be your judges

28 But if by the Spirit of God
I
I cast out the demons
Then the kingdom of God
Has come upon you

29 Or how has any one the power
To enter a strong man's house
And seize his equipment
Unless he first ties up
The strong man?
And then he will plunder his house

30 He that is not with me
Is against me
And he
Who does not gather with me
Scatters

31 Therefore I say to you
All sin and blasphemy
Will be forgiven to men
But the blasphemy of the spirit
Will not be forgiven

32 And whoever speaks a word
Against the Son of Man

        It will be forgiven him
        But whoever speaks
        Against the Holy Spirit
        It will not be forgiven him
        Neither in this age
        Nor in the one which is coming

33   Either make the tree sound
        And its fruit sound
        Or make the tree rotten
        And its fruit rotten
        Because the tree
        Is recognized by its fruits

34   Offspring of vipers
        How have you the ability
        To say something good
        When you are evil?
        Because the mouth speaks
        Out of the overflowing heart

35   The good man
        Out of good treasure
        Brings out good things
        And the evil man
        Out of evil treasure
        Brings out evil things

36   But I say to you
        That every idle word
        Which men speak
        Must be accounted for
        In the day of judgment
37   As by your words
        You will be justified
        Or by your words
        You will be condemned

The scribes and Pharisees ask for a sign
38   Then some of the scribes and Pharisees
        Said to him
            Teacher
            It is our wish
            To see a sign from you

39 But he answered them
    An evil and adulterous generation
    Looks for a sign
    And no sign
    Shall be given to it
    Except the sign
    Of the prophet Jonah

40 Just as Jonah
    Was three days
    And three nights
    In the belly of the whale
    So the Son of Man
    Will be three days
    And three nights
    In the heart of the earth

41 The population of Nineveh
    Will rise up at the judgment
    And condemn this generation
    Because they changed
    Their hearts and minds
    At the preaching of Jonah
    And now
    Something greater than Jonah
    Is here

42 The queen of the South
    Will be raised at the judgment
    And condemn this generation
    Because she came
    From the bounds of the earth
    To hear the wisdom of Solomon
    And now
    Something greater than Solomon
    Is here

43 Now when the unclean spirit
    Goes out of a man
    He passes through waterless places
    Looking for rest
    But he does not find it

44	Then he says
	I will go back into my house
	Which is where I came from
	And when he returns
	He finds it unoccupied
	Having been swept and put in order
45	Then he enters in there to stay
	Taking with him
	Seven other spirits
	More evil than himself
	And the last state of that man
	Is worse than the first
	It will also be so
	With this evil generation

The family of Jesus

46	While he was still speaking
	To the people
	His mother and his brothers
	Were standing outside
	Trying to speak to him
48	When he had been told this
	He answered
	Who is my mother
	And who are my brothers?
49	Then he stretched out his hand
	Towards his disciples
	And said
	See here is my mother
	And here are my brothers
50	As whoever does the will
	Of my Father in the heavens
	Is my brother
	And my sister
	And my mother

13 *Parable of the sower*

1 On that day
   Jesus went out of the house
   And sat beside the sea

2 Large crowds gathered round him
   So that he embarked on to a boat
   And sat there
   While all the people
   Stood on the shore

3 He told them many things
   In parables
      And said
         See how the sower
         Went out to sow

4   As he sowed
            Some seeds fell by the wayside
            And the birds
            Came and ate them

5   But others fell on rocky places
            Where they did not have much earth
            And they sprouted at once
            Because they had no depth of earth
6   When the sun rose
            They were scorched
            And as they had no root
            They dried out

7   Others fell among thorn bushes
            And the thorns came up
            And choked them

8   Others fell on cultivated ground
            And yielded fruit
            Some increased a hundred
            Some sixty
            And some thirty times

9   Whoever has ears to hear
            Should hear

Seeing and hearing

10   The disciples
          Came and said to him
              Why do you speak to them
              In parables?

11   And he answered them
              Because it has been given
              To you
              To become aware of the mysteries
              Of the kingdom of the heavens
              But it has not been given
              To them

12   Whoever has
              To him will be given
              More than he needs
              But whoever has not
              From him will be taken
              Even what he has

13   Therefore
              I speak to them in parables
              Because seeing
              They do not see
              And hearing
              They do not hear
              Neither do they understand

14   In them the prophecy of Isaiah
              Is indeed fulfilled
              Which says
              Hearing
              You will hear
              But in no way understand
              And seeing
              You will see
              But in no way perceive
15   *For the heart of this people*
              Has become insensitive
              And their ears
              Are hard of hearing
              And their eyes
              They have closed

Lest they should perceive
With the eyes
And hear
With the ears
And understand
With the heart
But should they come to themselves
I will heal them

16 But blessed are your eyes
Because they see
And your ears
Because they hear

17 Certainly I say to you
That many prophets
And upright men
Longed to perceive what you see
And did not perceive it
And to hear what your hear
But did not hear it

The meaning of the sower
18 Therefore listen
To the parable of the sower

19 When anyone hears
The word of the kingdom
And does not understand it
Then the evil one comes
And takes possession
Of what was sown in his heart
This is the seed
Sown by the wayside

20 The seed sown in the rocky places
Is the one who hears the word
And at once
Receives it with joy
21 But having no root in himself
It is short-lived
And when difficulties come about
Or there is persecution

Because of the word
He gives up at once

22 The seed sown among thorn bushes
Is the one who hears the word
And the problems of the present age
And the deceit of riches
Choke the word
And it becomes unfruitful

23 The seed sown on cultivated ground
Is the one who hears the word
And understands it
He indeed yields fruit
Some increased a hundred
Some sixty
And some thirty times

Parable of the field of the world
24 He set before them
Another parable
   And said
      The kingdom of the heavens
      Is like a man
      Who sowed the proper seed
      In his field
25   But while everybody was sleeping
      His enemy came
      Sowed darnel between the wheat
      And went away

26 When the green blade sprouted
And produced fruit
The darnel also appeared

27 The householder's servants
Came to him and said
Sir
Did you not sow the proper seed
In your field
Then where has the darnel come from?

28 And he said to them
A man who is my enemy
Has done this

So the servants said to him
Do you wish us
To go and collect them?

29 But he said to them
No
As in collecting the darnel
You might root up the wheat
With it
30 Leave them both to grow together
Until the harvest

At the harvest season
I will say to the reapers
First collect the darnel
And bind it in bundles
To be burnt
But gather the wheat
Into my barn

Parable of the mustard seed
31 He set before them
Another parable
   And said
      The kingdom of the heavens
      Is like a mustard seed
      Which a man took
      And sowed in his field

32 It is the smallest
Of all the seeds
But when it has grown
It is larger than other vegetables
Becoming a tree
So that the birds of heaven
Come and nest in the branches

Parable of the yeast
33   He told them
    Another parable
        The kingdom of the heavens
        Is like yeast
        Which a woman took
        And hid in three large measures
        Of fine flour
        Until it was all leavened

34 Jesus said all this to the people
In parables
And he said nothing to them
Except in a parable
35 Thus fulfilling
What was spoken through the prophet
When he said
I will open my mouth in parables
I will speak of things kept secret
From the foundation of the world

36 Then he sent away the crowds
And went into the house

The meaning of the field of the world
    His disciples came to him
    And said
        Explain to us the parable
        Of the darnel in the field

37   And he answered
        The one sowing the proper seed
        Is the Son of Man
38   The field is the world
        And the proper seed
        That is the sons of the kingdom
        The darnel
        That is the sons of the evil one

39   The enemy sowing it
    Is the devil
    The harvest
    Is the end of the age

And the reapers
Are the angels

40   Therefore
As the darnel is collected
And burnt in the fire
That is how it will be
At the end of the age
41   When the Son of Man
Will send out his angels
And they will collect
From out of his kingdom
All offences
And all who break the Law
42   And will throw them
Into the furnace of fire

There will be weeping
And gnashing of teeth

43   Then those who did what was right
Will shine out like the sun
In the kingdom of their Father

Whoever has ears
Should hear

Parable of the treasure
44   The kingdom of the heavens
Is like treasure hidden in a field
Which when a man found
He hid it
And in his joy
He went and sold everything he had
And bought that field

Parable of the pearl
45   Again
The kingdom of the heavens
Is like a merchant
Searching for fine pearls

46 When he found one pearl
Of great value
He went away
And sold everything he had
And bought it

Parable of the net
47 Again
The kingdom of the heavens
Is like a fishing net
Which was cast into the sea
Gathering all kinds
48 When it was filled
And brought up on to the beach
The fishermen sat down
And the wholesome fish
Were sorted into buckets
But the worthless were thrown away

49 That is how it will be
At the end of the age
The angels will go out
And will separate the evil doers
From among those who do right
50 And will throw them
Into the furnace of fire

There will be weeping
And gnashing of teeth

51 Have you understood
All these things?

They said to him
Yes

52 So he said to them
Therefore every scribe
Who is made a disciple
In the kingdom of the heavens
Is like a man
Who is a householder
And who brings out of his treasure

Both the new
And the old

Jesus is not accepted in his native place

53 And it happened
That when Jesus
Had reached the end
Of these parables
He went away from there

54 When he came to his native place
He taught them in their synagogues
So that they were astonished
    And said
        From where has he the wisdom
        And the powerful deeds?

55   Is he not the carpenter's son
        And is not his mother called Mary
        And are not his brothers
        James and Joseph
        Simon and Judas
        And are not his sisters
        All here with us?

56   From where has he
        All these things?

57 And they would not accept him

    But Jesus said to them
        A prophet
    Is not without honour
    Except in his native place
    And in his own house

58 There
He did not perform
Many powerful deeds
Because of their lack of faith

14 *The death of John the Baptist*

1   It was at that season
    When Herod the Tetrarch
    Heard reports about Jesus
2   And said to his attendants
            This is John the Baptist
            He has risen from the dead
            And therefore these powerful deeds
            Are active in him

3   Herod had taken John
    And bound him captive in prison
    Because of Herodias
    The wife of his brother Philip

4   As John had said to him
    It is not lawful
    For you to have her

5   Although he wanted to kill him
    He was afraid of the people
    Because they held him
    To be a prophet

6   When Herod's birthday came
    Herodias' daughter
    Danced in front of them
    And pleased Herod
7   So that with an oath
    He promised to give her
    Whatever she would ask

8   So being led on
    By her mother
            Give me
        She said
            Here on a dish
            The head of John the Baptist

9   The King was distressed
    But because of his oath
    And those at the table with him
    He ordered that it should be given

10 And sent and beheaded John
In the prison

11 His head
Was brought on a dish
And given to the young girl
Who brought it to her mother

12 His disciples came up
And took the corpse
Which they buried

Then they came and brought the news
To Jesus

Feeding of the five thousand
13 When Jesus heard it
He went away on his own
By boat
And came to a desert place

Hearing of this
The people followed him on foot
From out of the towns
14 So that on landing
He saw a large crowd
And he had compassion on them
And healed their sick

15 As the evening drew on
The disciples came to him
    And said
        This is a desert place
        And the hour is late
        Send the crowds away
        Into the villages
        To buy for themselves

16   But Jesus said to them
        It is not necessary
        For them to go away
        You give them something to eat

17   They answered him
        We have nothing here
        Except five loaves
        And two fishes

18   And he said
        Bring them here to me

19   When he had ordered the crowds
    To sit down on the grass
    He took the five loaves
    And the two fishes
    And looking up to heaven
    He blessed
    And broke them

    Then he gave the loaves
    To the disciples
    And the disciples
    Gave them to the people

20   They all ate
    And were satisfied
    And they collected the fragments left over
    Twelve wicker baskets full

21   Those who had eaten
    Were about five thousand men
    Apart from the women and children

Jesus is seen walking on the sea
22   Then he demanded that his disciples
    Should embark on to the boat
    And go ahead of him
    To the other side
    While he sent away the crowds

23   When he had sent the people away
    He went up by himself
    On the mountain
    To pray
    And when the evening came
    He was there alone

24 But the boat
Was now far away from the land
Tossed by the waves
As the wind was contrary

25 In the fourth watch of the night
He came towards them
Walking on the sea

26 When the disciples saw him
Walking on the sea
They were troubled
   And said
      It is a phantom

And they cried out in fear

27 But Jesus spoke to them at once
   And said
      Be brave
      I
      I AM
      Do not be afraid

28 Peter said to him
   Lord
   If it is you
   Order me to come to you
   On the water

29 And he said
   Come

Lowering himself out of the boat
Peter walked on the water
And came close to Jesus

30 But when he saw
The strength of the wind
He was afraid
And beginning to sink
   He cried out
      Lord
      Save me

31 At once
Jesus stretched out his hand
And taking hold of him
He said
You have little faith
Why did you doubt?

32 As they got into the boat
The wind dropped

33 Those who were in the boat
Bowed down before him
Saying
It is true
You are God's son

Jesus heals many who are sick
34 They crossed over
And came to Gennesaret

35 When they recognized him
The inhabitants of the place
Sent out into the whole surroundings
And brought to him
All those who had fallen ill
36 And asked him to allow them
Only to touch the fringe of his cloak
And all who touched it
Recovered

15 *Clean and unclean*
1 Then Pharisees and scribes from Jerusalem
Came to Jesus
And said
2 Why do your disciples
Not keep the tradition of the elders
As they do not wash their hands
Whenever they eat bread?

3 And he answered them
Why do you yourselves

Not keep the commandment of God
Because of your tradition?

4 As God said
Honour your father and your mother
And
Whoever speaks evil
Of father or mother
Let him die the death

5 But you say
Whoever says to his father or mother
What might be due to you
From me
Is offered to the Temple
6 Certainly he does not honour
His father or his mother

You have set aside
The word of God
Because of your tradition

7 Hypocrites
It was right what Isaiah
Prophesied about you
When he said
8 *This people*
Honour me with their lips
But their heart
Is far from me
9 *They worship me in vain*
Teaching as doctrine
The commandments of men

10 He called the crowd to him
And said to them
You should listen
And understand

11 It is not what enters the mouth
Which makes a man unclean
But what comes out of the mouth

12 The disciples came to him

MATTHEW 15

    And said
        Do you know
        That the Pharisees
        Heard your words
        And were offended?

13   And he answered
        Every plantation
        Which my heavenly Father
        Has not planted
        Will be uprooted

14   Leave them
        They are blind leaders of the blind
        And if a blind man
        Leads a blind man
        Both will fall into a pit

15   Peter said to him
        Make this parable
        Clear to us

16   So he said
        Are you also
        Without understanding?
17   Do you not grasp
        That everything entering the mouth
        Goes into the stomach
        And is cast out into the drain?

18   But what comes out of the mouth
        Comes from the heart
        And that
        Is what makes a man unclean

19   Out of the heart
        Come forth
        Evil thoughts
        And murders and adulteries
        Fornications and thefts
        False witness and blasphemies

20   These are the things
        Which make a man unclean

>   But eating with unwashed hands
>   Does not make a man unclean
>
> *Healing of the daughter of the Canaanite woman*
>
> 21 Jesus left there
>   And went to the region
>   Of Tyre and Sidon
>
> 22 And now
>   There came a Canaanite woman
>   From that district
>   Who cried out
>   Pity me
>   Lord
>   Son of David
>   My daughter is possessed of a demon
>   And has it badly
>
> 23 But he did not answer a word
>
>   And his disciples came
>   And begged him
>   Saying
>   Send her away
>   Because she is calling out behind us
>
> 24 He replied to them
>   I have only been sent
>   To the lost sheep
>   Of the house of Israel
>
> 25 She came however
>   And bowing down
>   She said
>   Lord
>   Help me
>
> 26 He answered
>   It is not right
>   To take the children's bread
>   And throw it to the household dogs
>
> 27 And she said
>   Yes

          Lord
          But even the household dogs
          Eat the crumbs
          Which fall from their master's table

28   Then Jesus replied to her
        O woman
        You have great faith
        It shall be as you wish

    And at that hour
    Her daughter was healed

Feeding of the four thousand

29   Jesus went away from there
    And passing the sea of Galilee
    He went up into a mountain
    Where he sat down

30   And large crowds came to him
    Bringing with them
    The lame
    The maimed
    The blind
    The dumb
    And many others

    They laid them at his feet
    And he healed them

31   So that the people were astonished
    When they saw
    The dumb speaking
    The maimed whole
    The lame walking
    The blind seeing
    And they praised the God of Israel

32   Then Jesus
    Called his disciples to him
        And said
            I have compassion on the crowd
            Because they have been with me
            Three days

            And have nothing to eat
            I am unwilling
            To send them away hungry
            As they might faint on the road

33   His disciples said to him
            We are here in a wilderness
            From where
            Could we get enough bread
            To satisfy so many people?

34   Jesus said to them
            How many loaves
            Have you?

      And they said
          Seven
          And a few little fish

35   Then he ordered the crowd
      To sit down on the ground

36   Taking the seven loaves
      And the fish
      He gave thanks
      And broke them

      Then he gave them to the disciples
      And the disciples
      Gave them to the people

37   They all ate
      And were satisfied
      Then they filled seven reed baskets
      With the fragments left over
      Which they took up

38   Those who had eaten
      Were about four thousand men
      Besides women and children

39   When he had sent away the crowds
      He embarked on to a boat
      And came to the district of Magadan

16 *The Pharisees and Sadducees ask for a sign*

1 The Pharisees and Sadducees
Came to him to tempt him
And asked him to show them
A sign from heaven

2 But he answered them
When evening comes
You say
It will be fair weather
As the sky is red
3 But in the morning
It will be stormy today
As the sky is red and overcast

You are able to interpret
The face of heaven
But not the signs
Of the moment in time

4 An evil and adulterous generation
Looks for a sign
But no sign
Shall be given to it
Except the sign of Jonah

Then he left them
And went away

Jesus warns against the teaching of the Pharisees

5 When the disciples
Came to the other side
They had forgotten to take any bread

And Jesus said to them
6 Watch out
And guard against the yeast
Of the Pharisees and Sadducees

7 But they discussed it
Among themselves
Saying
We did not bring any bread

8   As he was aware of this
         Jesus said
               You that have little faith
               Why do you discuss among yourselves
               That it is
               Because you have no bread?

9   Do you not understand
               Neither remember
               The five loaves
               Of the five thousand
               And how many wicker baskets
               You took up?

10   Nor the seven loaves
               Of the four thousand
               And how many reed baskets
               You took up?

11   Why do you not understand
               That I was not speaking to you
               About bread
               But to guard against the yeast
               Of the Pharisees and Sadducees

12   Then they understood
      That he did not say
      They should guard against the yeast
      But against the teaching
      Of the Pharisees and Sadducees

      Christ's charge to Peter
13   When Jesus
      Came into the region of Caesarea Philippi
         He asked his disciples
               Whom do men believe
               The Son of Man
               To be?

14   And they said
               Some indeed
               John the Baptist
               Others Elijah

      And others Jeremiah
      Or one of the prophets

15 He said to them
      But you
      Whom do you believe
      Me to be?

16 Simon Peter answered
      You are the Christ
      The Son of the living God

17 Jesus answered him
      You are blessed
      Simon Bar-Jona
      Because flesh and blood
      Have not revealed it to you
      But my Father in the heavens

18   And I tell you myself
      That you are Peter
      And on this rock
      I will build my community
      And the gates of the underworld
      Will not hold out against it

19   I will give you the keys
      Of the kingdom of the heavens
      And whatever you bind on earth
      It shall be
      As having been bound in the heavens
      And whatever you release on earth
      It shall be
      As having been released in the heavens

20 Then he warned his disciples
That they should not tell anyone
That he is the Christ

First prophecy of the Passion
21 From then on
Jesus Christ
Began to show to his disciples
That it would be necessary for him

To go to Jerusalem
And to endure much suffering
From the elders
And chief priests and scribes
To be killed
And to be raised
On the third day

22 Taking him aside
Peter began to speak sternly to him
    And said
        May mercy be on you
        Lord
        This must not happen to you

23 But he turned
    And said to Peter
        Go behind me
        Satan
        You would cause my downfall
        Because you are not thinking
        Of the concerns of God
        But of the concerns of men

24 Then Jesus
Said to his disciples
    If any one
    Is willing to come after me
    He should not consider himself
    But take his cross
    And follow me

25   For whoever wishes to save
    His soul-bearing life
    Will lose it
    And whoever loses
    His soul-bearing life
    For my sake
    Will find it

26   What use is it to a man
    To gain the whole world
    And suffer the loss
    Of his living soul?

        Or what will a man give
        As the price
        Of his living soul?

27   When the Son of Man comes
        Revealing the glory of his Father
        And his angels
        Then he will reward each one
        According to what he has done

28   Certainly I say to you
        That there are some standing here
        Who will surely not taste death
        Until they see the Son of Man
        Coming in his kingdom

17   *The Transfiguration*

1   After six days
Jesus
Took Peter
With James and his brother John
And brought them by themselves
Up on to a high mountain

2   He was transformed
In their presence
His face shone like the sun
And his clothing
Became white as the light

3   And now
Moses and Elijah
Were seen by them
Talking with him

4   Peter said to Jesus
      Lord
      It is right
      For us to be here
      If you wish
      I will put up three tents here

　　　　　One for you
　　　　　One for Moses
　　　　　And one for Elijah

5　　While he was speaking
　　　A bright cloud overshadowed them
　　　　　And a voice out of the cloud said
　　　　　　　This is my son
　　　　　　　The beloved
　　　　　　　In whom I rejoice
　　　　　　　Listen to him

6　　On hearing this
　　　The disciples fell on their faces
　　　And were very much afraid

7　　Jesus came and touched them
　　　　　And said
　　　　　　　Get up
　　　　　　　And do not be afraid

8　　As they lifted up their eyes
　　　They saw no one
　　　Except Jesus himself

9　　And coming down from the mountain
　　　　　Jesus instructed them
　　　　　　　Do not tell anyone
　　　　　　　About the vision
　　　　　　　Until the Son of Man
　　　　　　　Has been raised from the dead

10　　Then the disciples asked him
　　　　　Why do the scribes
　　　　　Say that Elijah must come first?

11　　And he answered
　　　　　Indeed Elijah does come
　　　　　And will restore everything
12　　　　But I say to you
　　　　　That Elijah has come already
　　　　　And they failed to recognize him
　　　　　But did to him
　　　　　Whatever they wanted

        So also the Son of Man
        Is about to suffer from them

13 Then the disciples understood
    That he spoke to them
    About John the Baptist

Healing of the demoniac boy

14 When they reached the crowd
    A man came to him
    And kneeling in front of him
15   He said
        Lord
        Have pity on my son
        Because he is lunatic
        And has it badly
        As often he falls into the fire
        And often into the water

16   I brought him to your disciples
        And they were not able
        To heal him

17 Jesus answered
        O faithless and perverse generation
        How long
        Shall I be with you?
        How long
        Shall I endure you?
        Bring him here to me

18 When Jesus spoke to it sternly
    The demon came out of him
    And from that hour
    The boy was healed

19 The disciples
    Came to Jesus on their own
        And said
            Why were we not able
            To cast it out?

20   And he said to them
        Because of your little faith
        Certainly I say to you
        If your faith is as much
        As a mustard seed
        You will say to this mountain
        Move over to there
        And it will be removed
        And nothing
        Will be impossible for you

Second prophecy of the Passion
22   As they remained in Galilee
        Jesus said to them
            The Son of Man
            Is about to be betrayed
            Into the hands of men
23   They will kill him
            And on the third day
            He will be raised

    They were very much distressed

The tax money
24   When they came to Capernaum
    Those who collected
    The half drachma Temple tax
        Went up to Peter
        And said
            Does not your teacher
            Pay the tax?

25   He said
        Yes he does

    He came into the house
        And Jesus spoke to him at once
        And said
            How does it seem to you
            Simon?
            From whom
            Do the kings of the earth

	Take toll or tax?
	From their sons
	Or from strangers?

26　　So he said
　　　　From strangers

　　　And Jesus said to him
　　　　Then the sons are free

27　　　　But so as not to offend them
　　　　Go to the sea
　　　　Cast a hook
　　　　And take the first fish
　　　　That comes up
　　　　On opening its mouth
　　　　You will find a silver shekel
　　　　Take that
　　　　And give it to them
　　　　For me and for you

18 *The disciples' question*

1　In that hour
　The disciples came to Jesus
　　　And said
　　　　　Then who is the greatest
　　　　　In the kingdom of the heavens?

2　And calling a little child
　To come to them
　He placed it in their midst
3　　　And said
　　　　　Certainly I say to you
　　　　　Unless you turn
　　　　　And become like the children
　　　　　By no means will you enter
　　　　　The kingdom of the heavens

4　　　Therefore
　　　Whoever humbles himself
　　　Like this child
　　　Is the greatest
　　　In the kingdom of the heavens

5   And whoever receives
    One such child
    In my name
    Receives me

6   But whoever causes the downfall
    Of one of these little ones
    Who believe in me
    It would be to his advantage
    If a great mill-stone
    Were hung round his neck
    And he was drowned
    In an ocean of sea

7   Woe to the world
    On account of its pitfalls
    It is necessary that temptations come
    But woe to that man
    Through whom the temptation comes

8   If your hand or your foot
    Causes your downfall
    Cut it off
    And throw it away from you
    It is right for you
    To enter into Life
    Maimed or lame
    Rather than having two hands
    Or two feet
    To be thrown into the fire
    That burns throughout the ages

9   If your eye
    Causes your downfall
    Pluck it out
    And throw it away from you
    It is right for you
    To enter one-eyed into Life
    Rather than having two eyes
    To be thrown
    Into the retribution of fire

10 Make sure
    That you do not despise

　　　　　　　One of these little ones
　　　　　　　For I say to you
　　　　　　　That in the heavens
　　　　　　　Their angels
　　　　　　　Always see the face of my Father
　　　　　　　In the heavens

11　　　　　　For the Son of Man
　　　　　　　Came to save the lost

　　　　　Parable of the lost sheep
12　　　　　　How does it seem to you?
　　　　　　　If any man
　　　　　　　Has a hundred sheep
　　　　　　　And one of them strays away
　　　　　　　Will he not leave
　　　　　　　The ninety-nine in the mountains
　　　　　　　And go to look for the wanderer?

13　　　　　　And if it happens
　　　　　　　That he finds it
　　　　　　　Certainly I say to you
　　　　　　　That he rejoices more
　　　　　　　Over that one
　　　　　　　Than over the ninety-nine
　　　　　　　That did not stray

14　　　　　　So before the face of your Father
　　　　　　　In the heavens
　　　　　　　It is not the intention
　　　　　　　That one of these little ones
　　　　　　　Should be lost

　　　　　Teaching for the disciples
15　　　　　　If your brother does wrong
　　　　　　　Go and tell him
　　　　　　　When you are alone with him
　　　　　　　If he listens to you
　　　　　　　You have gained your brother

16　　　　　　But if he does not listen
　　　　　　　Take one or two people with you

That on the evidence
Of two or three witnesses
All that is said
May be confirmed

17   And if he refuses
To listen to them
Tell the assembly
Then let him be to you
As a Gentile and a tax-collector

18   Certainly I say to you
Whatever you bind on earth
Shall be
As having been bound in heaven
And what ever you release on earth
Shall be
As having been released in heaven

19   Again I say to you
That if two of you agree
On the earth
About any concern
For which you ask
So it shall be for you
From my Father in the heavens

20   For when two or three
Have come together
In my name
There
I am in the midst of them

Parable of the unforgiving servant
21   Then Peter
Came to him and said
Lord
If my brother wrongs me
How often should I forgive him?
As often as seven times?

22   Jesus said to him
I do not tell you

As often as seven times
But as often as seventy times seven

23   Therefore the kingdom of the heavens
Is like a man
Who was a king
And who wished to settle accounts
With his servants

24   And as he began the reckoning
Someone was brought to him
Who owed him
Ten thousand talents weight
Of silver pieces

25   As he could not pay
The lord gave orders
That he should be sold
Together with his wife
And his children
And everything that he had
So that the debt should be repaid

26   Then the servant
Fell down and implored him
Saying
Wait with your fury against me
And I will repay you everything

27   Filled with compassion
The lord of that servant
Released him
And forgave him the debt

28   But when he went out
That servant
Found one of his fellow servants
Who owed him a hundred denarii
And choking him
He said
Repay what you owe

29 Then his fellow servant
    Fell down and begged him
    Saying
    Wait with your fury against me
    And I will repay you

30 He would not wait
    But went away
    And threw him into prison
    Until he should repay what was owing

31 When his fellow servants
    Saw what took place
    They were much distressed
    And went to their lord
    To make clear to him
    Everything that had happened

32 Summoning him
    His lord said
    You wicked servant
    I forgave you your debt
    Because you begged me

33 Should you not have had pity
    On your fellow servant
    As I myself pitied you?

34 His lord was angry
    And handed him over
    To the tormentors
    Until he should repay
    Everything that he owed

35 This my heavenly Father
    Will also do to you
    Unless each one of you
    Forgives his brother
    From his heart

19 *A discussion about marriage*

1   Now it happened
    That when Jesus

MATTHEW 19

    Had finished speaking these words
    He left Galilee
    And came into the district of Judea
    Across the Jordan
2   Large crowds followed him
    And he healed them there

3   Pharisees came to him
    To test him
        And said
            Are there any grounds
            On which it is lawful
            For a man to release his wife?

4   He answered
            Have you not read
            That from the beginning
            The Creator
            Made them male and female?

5   And he said
            Because of this
            A man should leave
            His father and his mother
            And be joined to his wife
            The two
            Shall be one flesh
6   So that they are no longer two
            But one flesh

            Therefore
            What God joined together
            Man should not separate

7   They said to him
        Then why did Moses
        Command us
        To provide a document of divorce
        For her release

8   He said to them
        It was because
        Of your unyielding hearts
        That Moses

Allowed you to release your wives
But from the beginning
It was not so

9 Now I say to you
That whoever releases his wife
Except for immorality
And marries another
Commits adultery

10 The disciples said to him
If this is the relationship
Between a man and his wife
It is not an advantage
To marry

11 And he said to them
Not everyone
Can accept these words
But only those
To whom it has been given

12 Some
Were born from a mother's womb
Incapable of marriage
And some
Were made incapable by men
And some
Made themselves incapable
For the sake
Of the kingdom of the heavens

Whoever can accept this
Let him accept it

Children are brought to Jesus

13 Then children were brought to him
So that he
Might put his hands on them
And pray
But the disciples reproved them

14   So Jesus said
>   Allow the children
>   To come to me
>   And do not hinder them
>   For of such as they are
>   Is the kingdom of the heavens

15   He put his hands on them
And went away from there

The rich young man

16   Then
Someone came up to him
>   And said
>   >   Teacher
>   >   What good that I do
>   >   Would enable me to have life
>   >   Throughout the ages?

>   Jesus said to him
17
>   >   Why do you ask me
>   >   What is good?
>   >   There is one who is good
>   >   But if you wish
>   >   To enter into life
>   >   Keep the commandments

18
>   He said to him
>   >   Which?

>   And Jesus said
>   >   You shall not kill
>   >   You shall not commit adultery
>   >   You shall not steal
>   >   You shall not witness falsely
>   >   Honour your father and your mother
19
>   >   And you shall love your neighbour
>   >   As yourself

20
>   The young man said to him
>   >   I have kept all these things
>   >   How do I fall short?

21 Jesus said to him
> If you wish to be perfect
> Go and sell what belongs to you
> To give to the poor
> You will have treasure in heaven
> Then come and follow me

22 When the young man
Heard these words
He went sadly away
As he had extensive possessions

23 So Jesus said to his disciples
> Certainly I say to you
> That a rich man
> Will have difficulty
> In entering the kingdom of the heavens

24 > And again I say to you
> It is easier for a camel
> To pass
> Through the eye of a needle
> Than for a rich man
> To enter the kingdom of God

25 When the disciples heard this
They were absolutely astonished
> And said
>> Who then
>> Is able to be saved?

26 Gazing into them
Jesus said
> With men
> This is impossible
> But with God
> Everything is possible

27 Peter said to him
> Look how we have left everything
> And followed you
> Then what shall we have?

28   And Jesus said to them
> Certainly I say to you
> That at the rebirth
> When the Son of Man
> Sits on his throne of glory
> You who have followed me
> Will yourselves
> Also sit on twelve thrones
> Judging the twelve tribes of Israel

29   And everyone
Who has left houses
Or brothers or sisters
Or father or mother
Or children or lands
For the sake of my name
Will receive many times more
And will inherit life
Throughout the ages
30   But many first
Will be last
And the last first

20 *Parable of the workers in the vineyard*

1   As the kingdom of the heavens
Is like a man
Who was a householder
And went out
Early in the morning
To hire workers for his vineyard

2   He agreed with the workers
For a denarius a day
And sent them into his vineyard

3   At about the third hour
He went out
And saw others
Standing in the market
Doing nothing

4   He said to them
You also
Should go into the vineyard
And I will pay you
Whatever is just

So they went

5   Again
He went out
At about the sixth
And the ninth hour
And did the same

6   Going out
At about the eleventh hour
He found others standing there
And said to them
Why do you stand here all day
Doing nothing?

7   They said
Because no-one has hired us

He said to them
You also
Should go into the vineyard

8   When it was evening
The lord of the vineyard
Said to his bailiff
Call the workers
And pay their wages
Beginning with the last
Up to the first

9   When those came
Who had been hired
At about the eleventh hour
They each received a denarius

10   When the first came
They thought
That they would receive more

	But they also
	Each received a denarius

11	On receiving it
	They grumbled about the householder
	And said
12	Those who came last
	Worked for one hour
	And you
	Have made them equal to us
	Who have borne the burden
	And the searing heat
	Of the day

13	But he answered one of them
	Companion
	I am not unjust to you
	Did you not agree with me
	For a denarius?

14	Take what is yours
	And go
	I wish to give to this last one
	The same
	As I have given to you

15	Is it not lawful
	For me to do what I wish
	With what is mine?
	Or is your eye evil
	Because I
	I am good?

16	Thus the last will be first
	And the first last

Third prophecy of the Passion

17	When Jesus
	Was about to go up to Jerusalem
	He took the twelve disciples
	On their own
	And on the road
	He said to them

18	See how we are going up
	To Jerusalem
	And the Son of Man
	Will be handed over
	To the chief priests and scribes
	And they
	Will condemn him to death
19	They will deliver him
	To the Gentiles
	To be mocked
	And scourged
	And crucified
	And on the third day
	He will be raised

The mother of James and John asks a favour

20 Then the mother of Zebedee's sons
Came to him
With her sons

She bowed down
And asked him for something

21   He said to her
        What do you want?

    She said to him
        Say that these my two sons
        May sit
        One on your right
        And one on your left
        In your kingdom

22   Jesus answered
        You do not know
        What you ask
        Are you able to drink the cup
        Which I myself
        Am about to drink?

    They said to him
        We are able

23 He said to them
    Indeed you shall drink my cup
    But to sit on my right
    And on my left
    This is not mine to give
    But is for those
    For whom it has been prepared
    By my Father

24 When the ten heard this
They were indignant
About the two brothers

25 So Jesus called them to him
And said
    You know
    That those who rule the Gentiles
    Dominate them
    And their great ones
    Have authority over them

26 It is not so among you
But whoever among you
Wishes to become great
Will be the one who serves you

27 And whoever wishes
To be first among you
Will be your servant

28 As the Son of Man
Did not come to be served
But to serve
And to give his soul-bearing life
As ransom for many

Two blind men healed

29 As they left Jericho
A large crowd followed him

30 And now there were two blind men
Sitting beside the road
When they heard

             That Jesus
             Is passing by
                 They cried out
                     Lord
                     Pity us
                     Son of David

31   The crowd
             Ordered them to be quiet
                 But they cried out
                 All the more
                     Lord
                     Pity us
                     Son of David

32   Jesus stood still
                 And calling them
                 He said
                     What do you want me
                     To do for you?

33   They said to him
                 Lord
                 That our eyes
                 May be opened

34   And filled with compassion
             Jesus touched their eyes
             And immediately
             They could see again
             And followed him

21   *The entry into Jerusalem*
1   When they drew near Jerusalem
         And came to Bethphage
         On the Mount of Olives
         Then Jesus sent out two disciples
2   Saying to them
                 Go into the village
                 That is in front of you
                 And immediately
                 You will find an ass
                 Tied up

And a colt with her
Untie them
And bring them to me

3   And if anyone
Says anything to you
Say
The Lord needs them
And he will send them at once

4   This happened
So that what was spoken
Through the prophet
Might be fulfilled
When he said
5   *Tell the daughter of Zion*
See how your King comes to you
Gentle
And mounted on an ass
On a colt
Foal of a beast of burden

6   The disciples went
And did as Jesus
Had directed them

7   They brought the ass
And the colt
Putting on them their cloaks
On which he sat

8   The large crowd
Spread out their cloaks
On the road
And others cut branches from the trees
And spread them on the road

9   The crowds who went in front
And those who followed
    Cried out
        Hosanna
        To the Son of David
        Blest be the one who comes
        In the name of the Lord

             Hosanna
             In the highest places

10   As he entered Jerusalem
      The whole city was in uproar
          Saying
             Who is this?

11   And the crowds said
             This is the prophet Jesus
             From Nazareth in Galilee

      Jesus clears the Temple
12   Jesus entered the Temple
      And cast out
      All who were selling
      And were buying
      In the Temple
      He overturned
      The tables of the money-changers
      And the seats of those selling doves

13   And he said to them
             My house
             Shall be called
             A house of prayer
             But you
             Are making it
             A robber's cave

14   The blind and the lame
      Came to him in the Temple
      And he healed them

15   The chief priests and the scribes
      Saw the wonders which he did
      And the children in the Temple
          Who were calling out
             Hosanna to the Son of David

          And they were indignant
16   And said to him
             Do you hear
             What they are saying?

Jesus said to them
>Yes
>>Have you never read
>>*Out of the mouths*
>>*Of little children*
>>*And babes in arms*
>>*Thou hast perfected praise*

The fig tree

17 He left there
And went out of the city
To Bethany
And stayed overnight

18 Going up early to the city
He was hungry
19 And when he saw one fig tree
By the road
He went up to it
But found nothing except leaves
>And he said to it
>>May you never bear fruit
>>Throughout the ages

And the fig tree
Was withered up instantly

20 When they saw it
The disciples were astonished
>And said
>>How was the fig tree
>>Withered up in an instant?

21 Jesus answered them
>Certainly I say to you
>If you believe
>And do not waver
>You will not only perform
>The sign of the fig tree
>But if you say to this mountain
>Be taken up
>And thrown into the sea
>It will be so

22   And all that you ask
      In prayer
      If you have faith
      You will receive it

      Jesus questions the chief priests about John
23   He entered the Temple
      And the chief priests
      And the elders of the people
      Came to him
      While he was teaching
        And said
            By what authority
            Are you doing these things?
            And who gave you this authority?

24   Jesus answered them
            I will also ask you one question
            And if you answer me
            I will also tell you
            By what authority
            I do these things

25   Where did John's baptism come from?
            From heaven
            Or from men?

        They discussed it among themselves
            If we say
            From heaven
            He will say to us
            Why then did you not believe him?

26   But if we say
            From men
            We are afraid of the people
            As everyone believes John
            To be a prophet

27   So they answered Jesus
            We do not know

>Then he said to them
>>Neither will I
>>I say to you
>>By what authority
>>I do these things

Parable of the two sons
28   What is your opinion?

>>A man had two children
>>He went to the first
>>And said
>>Child
>>Go and work in the vineyard today
29
>>He answered
>>I am going sir
>>But he did not go

30
>>Then he went to the second
>>And said the same
>>He answered
>>I will not
>>But later he changed his mind
>>And went

31
>>Which of the two
>>Carried out
>>The will of the father?

>They said
>>The second

>Jesus said to them
>>Certainly I say to you
>>Tax-collectors and prostitutes
>>Will go in front of you
>>Into the kingdom of God

32
>>John came to you
>>On a righteous path
>>And you did not believe him
>>But the tax-collectors

And the prostitutes
Believed him
But you
Seeing this
Did not change your minds later
And believe him

Parable of the wicked farmers

33   Hear another parable

        A man who owned property
        Planted a vineyard
        Set a hedge round it
        Dug in it a wine press
        And built a watch tower
        Then let it to farmers
        And went out of the country

34   When it was almost the season
        For the vintage
        He sent his servants to the farmers
        To receive the fruit

35   The farmers took his servants
        And beat this one
        Killed that one
        And stoned another

36   Again
        He sent out more servants
        Than at first
        And they treated them
        In the same way

37   Later
        He sent his son to them
        As he said
        They will respect my son

38   But when those farmers
        Saw the son
        They said to one another

MATTHEW 21

           This is the heir
           Let us kill him
           And take possession of the inheritance

39   They took him
           And throwing him out
           Outside of the vineyard
           They killed him

40   Therefore
           When the lord of the vineyard comes
           What will he do to those farmers?

41   They said to him
           He will utterly destroy those wicked ones
           And will let out the vineyard
           To other farmers
           Who will give up to him
           The fruit in its season

42   Jesus said to them
           Have you never read in the Scriptures
           A stone which the builders rejected
           Became the head of the corner
           This comes from the Lord
           And is wonderful in our eyes

43   I tell you
           That because of this
           The kingdom of God
           Will be taken from you
           And will be given to that nation
           Which produces its fruits

44   Whoever
           Falls on to this stone
           Will be broken in pieces
           But whoever
           It falls on
           Will be crushed to powder

45   When the chief priests and the Pharisees
       Heard the parable

They were aware
That he was speaking about them

46 Then they tried to seize him
But were afraid of the crowds
Because they took him for a prophet

22 *Parable of the marriage of the king's son*
1   Jesus spoke to them again in parables
And said
2   The kingdom of the heavens
Is like a man who was king
And who made a marriage
For his son

3   He sent out his servants
To call those invited to the marriage
But they did not wish to come

4   Again
He sent out other servants
Saying
Tell those who were invited
Look
Now I have prepared my banquet
My oxen
And the fatted cattle
Have been slaughtered
Everything is ready
Come to the marriage

5   But they were unconcerned
And went away
One to his own fields
Another to his warehouse
6   And the rest
Took his servants
Insulted them
And killed them

7   The king became angry
And sent out his soldiers

MATTHEW 22

      To destroy those murderers
      And set their city on fire

8   Then he said to his servants
      Indeed the marriage is ready
      But those who were invited
      Were not worthy

9   Therefore go out to the crossroads
      And call to the marriage
      All whom you find

10   And those servants
      Went out on to the roads
      And gathered all whom they found
      Both the wicked and the good
      And in the wedding hall
      The tables were filled

11   But when the king entered
      To behold those who were feasting
      He saw there a man
      Who had not been dressed
      In a wedding garment

12   And he said to him
      Companion
      How did you come in here
      Without having a wedding garment?

      And he was silenced

13   Then the king
      Said to those who were serving
      Tie his feet
      And his hands
      And throw him out
      Into the outer darkness

      There will be weeping
      And gnashing of teeth

14   For many are called
      But few are chosen

The Pharisees' question

15 Then the Pharisees
Went and considered
How they could trap him
In what he said

16 So they sent their disciples
With the Herodians to him
 And they asked
  Teacher
  We know that you are truthful
  And in truth
  Teach the way of God
  And that no-one's position
  Matters to you
  As you do not look
  At the status of men

17   Therefore tell us
  How it seems to you
  Is it lawful or not
  To pay the tax to Caesar?

18 But Jesus
Was aware of their wickedness
 And said
  Why do you hypocrites
  Tempt me?
19   Show me the tax money

And they brought him
A denarius

20 So he said to them
  Of whom is this portrait?
  And of whom the inscription?

21 They said
  It is Caesar's

 Then he said to them
  Therefore
  Give back to Caesar
  What belongs to Caesar

        And to God
        What belongs to God

22   They were astonished
     At what they heard
     And leaving him
     They went away

The Sadducees' question

23   On that same day
     Sadducees
     Who say that there is no resurrection
     Came to him
        And asked the question

24   Teacher
          Moses said
          If any man dies
          Who has no children
          Then afterwards
          His brother shall marry the wife
          And raise up descendants
          To his brother

25   Now seven brothers
          Were with us
          The first
          Married and died
          As he had no children
          He left his wife to his brother
26   It was the same with the second
          And the third
          Until the seventh

27   Last of all
          The woman died

28   In the resurrection
          Whose wife of the seven
          Will she be?
          Because all of them had her

29   Jesus answered them
           You are wrong
           You neither know the Scriptures
           Nor the power of God

30   Because in the resurrection
      They neither marry
      Nor are given in marriage
      But are like the angels
      In heaven

31   Concerning the resurrection of the dead
      Have you not read
      What was told to you by God
32   When he said
      I
      I AM the God of Abraham
      And the God of Isaac
      And the God of Jacob

      He is not the God
      Of the dead
      But of the living

33 The crowds who heard him
Were astonished at his teaching

The lawyer's question
34 When the Pharisees
Heard that he had silenced
The Sadducees
They met together
35 And one of them
Who was a lawyer
    Put this question to him
    To tempt him
36   Teacher
        Which is the great commandment
        In the Law?

37 And he said to him
    You shall love the Lord your God
    With all your heart

And with all your soul
And with all your mind

38 This is the great
And first
Commandment

39 The second is like it
You shall love your neighbour
As yourself

40 On these two commandments
Hang all the Law
And the prophets

Jesus questions the Pharisees
41 When the Pharisees
Had gathered together
   Jesus
      Asked them a question
42   What is your opinion of Christ
            Of whom is he the son?

They said to him
   Of David

43 He said to them
      Then how is David in spirit
      Able to call him Lord
      Saying
44   *The Lord*
      Said to my Lord
      Sit on my right
      Until I put your enemies
      Under your feet

45   Then if David
         Calls him Lord
         How is he his son?

46 And no-one was able
To answer a word to him
Nor from that day

Did anyone
Dare to question him any more

23 *Condemnation of the scribes and the Pharisees*

1 Then Jesus
Spoke to the crowds and his disciples
2 And said
The scribes and the Pharisees
Sit on Moses' seat
3 Therefore you must obey them
And do whatever they tell you
But do not perform their deeds
For what they say
Is not what they do

4 They bind heavy burdens
Which are hard to bear
And lay them on men's shoulders
But they are not willing
To move them with their finger

5 They do all their deeds
So that men may behold them
They broaden the little leather prayer boxes
Worn on the forehead and the arm
And lengthen the tassels
On their cloaks

6 They like the best places
At meals
And the first seats
In the synagogues
7 And greetings in the public places
And to be called Rabbi
By men

8 But you
Should not be called Rabbi
As you have one teacher
And you are all brothers
9 And call no-one your father
On the earth
As there is one

MATTHEW 23

	Who is your heavenly Father
10	Neither should you
	Be called leader
	Because you have one leader
	The Christ
11	The greatest among you
	Should serve you
12	And whoever exalts himself
	Will be humbled
	Whoever humbles himself
	Will be exalted
13	Woe to you
	Scribes and Pharisees
	Hypocrites
	Because you close
	The kingdom of the heavens
	Against men
	And you do not go in yourselves
	Nor allow those who would enter
	To go in
14	Woe to you
	Scribes and Pharisees
	Hypocrites
	Who eat up the inheritance of widows
	And make pretence of long prayers
	You will receive greater condemnation
15	Woe to you
	Scribes and Pharisees
	Hypocrites
	Because you travel over the sea
	And over dry land
	To make one convert
	And when he has been converted
	You make him twice as much
	A son of retribution
	As yourselves
16	Woe to you
	Blind guides
	As you say

Whoever swears
By the shrine
That is nothing
But whoever swears
By the gold of the shrine
He is bound by his oath

17 Blind fools that you are
As which is greater
The gold
Or the shrine
Which consecrates the gold?

18 And
Whoever swears
By the altar of sacrifice
That is nothing
But whoever swears
By the gift upon it
Is bound by his oath

19 Blind that you are
For which is greater
The gift
Or the altar
Which consecrates the gift?

20 Therefore
Whoever swears
By the altar
Swears by it
And by all that is on it

21 And whoever swears
By the shrine
Swears by it
And by the one
Who dwells in it

22 And whoever swears
By heaven
Swears by the throne of God
And by the one
Who sits upon it

23 Woe to you
Scribes and Pharisees
Hypocrites
For you take a tenth of peppermint
Dill and cumin
And neglect
The weightier aspects of the Law
Judgment
Mercy and faith
You should do these things
While not neglecting the others

24 You blind guides
Who strain out the tiny insect
But swallow the camel

25 Woe to you
Scribes and Pharisees
Hypocrites
Because you clean the outside
Of the cup and the elegant dish
But inside
They are full of grasping
And excess

26 You blind Pharisees
First clean the inside
Of the cup
Then the outside
May also be clean

27 Woe to you
Scribes and Pharisees
Hypocrites
Because you are like graves
Which have been whitened
They indeed appear beautiful
On the outside
But inside
They are full
Of the bones of the dead
And all uncleanness

28   Thus outwardly
You appear to men to do what is right
But inwardly
You are full of hypocrisy
And law-breaking

29   Woe to you
Scribes and Pharisees
Hypocrites
Because you build the graves
Of the prophets
And adorn the tombs
Of the just
30   And say
If we had been present
In the days of our fathers
We would not have shared with them
In the blood of the prophets
31   You yourselves bear witness
That you are the sons
Of those who murdered the prophets
32   And you complete
The measure of your fathers

33   Serpents
Offspring of vipers
How will you flee
From the judgment of retribution

34   Therefore
See how I
I send out to you
Prophets
And learned men
And scribes

Some of them
You will kill and crucify
Some of them
You will scourge in your synagogues
And will pursue
From city to city

35	So that there will come upon you
	All the righteous blood
	Shed on the earth
	From the blood of righteous Abel
	To the blood of Zachariah
	Son of Barachiah
	Whom you murdered
	Between the shrine
	And the altar of sacrifice
36	Certainly I say to you
	All these things
	Will come upon this generation
37	Jerusalem
	Jerusalem
	Who killed the prophets
	And stoned those sent out to her
	How often
	I wished to gather your children
	As a bird gathers her nestlings
	Under her wings
	But you would not
38	Look how your house
	Is left to you
39	Because I say to you
	It is certain that from now on
	You will not see me
	Until you say
	Blest be the one who comes
	In the name of the Lord

24 *Prophecies of war and persecution*

1   As Jesus went out of the Temple
His disciples
Came to show to him
The buildings of the Temple

2   And he said to them
      You see all this

MATTHEW 24

>   Certainly I say to you
>   There will not be left here
>   Stone upon stone
>   Which shall not be thrown down
>
> 3   He sat on the Mount of Olives
>   And the disciples
>   Came to him on their own
>   And said
>   Tell us
>   When will this happen
>   And what will be the sign
>   Of your advent
>   And of the end of the age?
>
> 4   Jesus answered
>   See that no one misleads you
> 5   As many will come in my name
>   Saying
>   I
>   I am the Christ
>   And many will lead you astray
>
> 6   When you hear of wars
>   And reports of battles
>   See that you are not disturbed
>   As they must take place
>   But that is not yet the end
>
> 7   For nation will rise against nation
>   And kingdom against kingdom
>   There will be famine and earthquakes
>   In many places
> 8   All this is the beginning
>   Of the pains of birth
>
> 9   They will hand you over to torture
>   And kill you
>   And you will be hated
>   By all nations
>   Because of my name
>
> 10   Then many will turn away
>   And will betray one another

MATTHEW 24

      And hate one another
11   Many false prophets will rise up
      And will lead many astray
12   Because lawlessness will increase
      Many people's love will grow cold

13   Whoever remains steadfast
      To the end
      Will be saved

14   This Gospel of the kingdom
      Will be preached
      In the whole inhabited world
      As a witness to all nations
      And then will come the end

15   Therefore when you see
      The abomination of desolation
      Of which the prophet Daniel spoke
      Stand in the holy place
      (Let the reader understand)
16   Then those in Judea
      Should flee to the mountains
17   Anyone up on the roof
      Should not come down
      To take the things
      Out of his house

18   Anyone out in the field
      Should not turn back
      To take his cloak
      Which he left behind

19   Alas for the woman
      In those days
      With a child in her womb
      Or one at her breast

20   Pray that your flight
      May not be in winter
      Or on a sabbath
21   As there will be great persecution
      Such as there has not been
      Since the beginning of the world

Until now
And could not be again

22 And if those days
Were not cut short
No-one living would be saved
But for the sake of the elect
Those days will be cut short

23 Then if anyone says to you
See here is the Christ
Or here
Do not believe it

24 False Christs
And false prophets
Will rise up
They will perform great signs
And portents
And if it were possible
They would even mislead the elect

25 Now as you see
I have already told you

The advent of the Son of Man

26 Therefore if they say to you
See he is in the desert
Do not go out
See he is in the store-rooms
Do not believe it

27 Just as the lightning
Comes out of the east
And shines as far as the west
So will be the advent
Of the Son of Man

28 Wherever the carcass is
There the eagles will be gathered

29 Immediately
After those days of persecution

The sun
Will be darkened
And the moon
Will not shed her beams

The stars
Will fall from heaven
And the powers of the heavens
Will be shaken

30 Then the sign of the Son of Man
Will appear in heaven
Then all the tribes of the earth
Will mourn
They will see the Son of Man
Coming in the clouds of heaven
With power and great glory
31 And he will send out his angels
With a loud trumpet
They will assemble the elect
Out of the four winds
From one end of the heavens
To the other

32 Learn this parable
From the fig tree
When the branch becomes tender
And puts out leaves
You are aware
That the summer is near

33 So you also
When you see all these things
Are aware that he is near
At the doors

34 Certainly I say to you
That this generation
Will by no means pass away
Before all this takes place
35 Heaven and earth
Will pass away
But my words
Will never pass away

36   Concerning that day
      Or that hour
      No one knows
      Neither the angels of heaven
      Nor the Son
      But only the Father

37   As it was in the days of Noah
      So will be the advent
      Of the Son of Man

38   As it was in those days
      Before the flood
      When there was eating and drinking
      Marrying and giving in marriage
      Until the day when Noah
      Went into the ark
39   And they were unaware
      Until the flood came
      And took them all

      So will also be the advent
      Of the Son of Man

40   Then two men
      Will be out in the field
      One will be taken
      And one left

41   And of two women
      Grinding at the mill
      One will be taken
      And one left

42   Watch therefore
      Because you do not know
      On what day
      Your Lord is coming

43   But be aware of this
      If the householder had known
      In which part of the night
      The thief was coming
      He would have watched

And would not have allowed
That his house
Should be broken into

44 Therefore you
Must also be ready
Because the Son of Man
Will come at an hour
When you
Do not think of his coming

45 Who then is the trustworthy
And thoughtful servant
Whom the lord appointed
Over his household
To give to them the food
Which is due to them?

46 Blessed is that servant
Whom his lord
Will find doing this
When he comes

47 Certainly I say to you
That he will appoint him
Over all his property

48 But if the bad servant
Says in his heart
My lord is delayed
49 And begins to hit his fellow servants
And eats and drinks with drunkards
50 The lord of that servant
Will come
On a day
Which he did not expect
And in an hour
Of which he was not aware

51 He will cut him off
And his place
Will be among the hypocrites

There will be weeping
And gnashing of teeth

25 *Parable of the ten virgins*

1. Then the kingdom of the heavens
Will be like ten virgins
Who took their lamps with them
And went out
For a meeting with the bridegroom

2. Now five of them were foolish
And five thoughtful

3. Those who were foolish
Took their lamps with them
But did not take oil

4. The thoughtful
Took oil in their flasks
With their lamps

5. But the bridegroom delayed
And they all dropped off to sleep

6. In the middle of the night
There was a cry
Here is the bridegroom
Go out to meet him

7. Then all those virgins got up
And trimmed their lamps

8. So the foolish
Said to the thoughtful
Give us some of your oil
Because our lamps are going out

9. The thoughtful answered
There might not be enough
For us and for you
You should go rather
To those who sell oil
And buy some for yourselves

10 While they went away to buy it
The bridegroom came
Then those who were ready
Went into the marriage with him
And the door was shut

11 Later
Also the other virgins came and said
Lord
Lord
Open to us

12 But he answered
Certainly I say to you
I do not know you

13 Therefore keep watch
Because you do not know
Either the day or the hour

Parable of the talents

14 It is as if a man
Going out of the country
Called his own servants
And handed over to them
His property

15 To one he gave
Five talents weight of silver pieces
To another two
To another one
To each according to his ability
Then he left the country

16 At once
He who had received five
Talents of silver
Went and traded with them
And gained another five

17 So also
He who had received two
Gained another two

18 But he who had received one
    Went away
    And dug in the earth
    And hid his lord's silver

19 After a long time
    The lord of those servants
    Came to take their account

20 He who had received five talents
    Came to him
    Bringing another five
    And said
    Lord
    You handed over to me
    Five talents
    See how I have gained
    Five talents more

21 His lord said to him
    Well done
    Good and faithful servant
    You have been faithful
    Over a few things
    I will appoint you over many
    Enter into the joy of your lord

22 He who had received two talents
    Also came to him
    And said
    Lord
    You handed over to me
    Two talents
    See how I have gained
    Two talents more

23 His lord said to him
    Well done
    Good and faithful servant
    You have been faithful
    Over a few things
    I will appoint you over many
    Enter into the joy of your lord

24 Then he also came
Who had received one talent
And said
Lord
I was aware
That you are a hard man
Reaping
Where you did not sow
And gathering
Where you did not scatter
25 And because I was afraid
I went away
And hid your talent in the earth
See here you have
What is your own

26 His lord answered him
Evil and idle servant
You know that I reap
Where I did not sow
And gather
From where I did not scatter

27 You should therefore
Have taken my silver pieces
To the bankers
So that when I came
I myself
Would have received what was mine
With interest

28 Therefore take the talent
Away from him
And give it to the one
Who has ten talents
29 For to everyone who has
More will be given
And he will have more than enough
But from him who has not
Even what he has
Will be taken away from him

30 And throw the useless servant
Into the outer darkness

There will be weeping
And gnashing of teeth

Prophecy of the sheep and the goats

31 When the Son of Man comes
Revealing his glory
And all the angels with him
He will sit on his glorious throne
32 And all the nations
Will gather before him

He will separate them
From one another
As the shepherd separates
The sheep from the goats
33 And will place the sheep
On his right
And the goats
On the left

34 The king
Will say to those on his right
Come
You who are blessed by my Father
Inherit the kingdom
Which has been made ready for you
From the foundation of the world

35 For I was hungry
And you gave me something to eat
I was thirsty
And you gave me a drink
I was a stranger
And you brought me in
36 Naked
And you clothed me
I was sick
And you visited me
I was in prison
And you came to me

37 Then the righteous will answer him
Lord

When did we see you hungry
And feed you
Or thirsty
And give you a drink?
38 When did we see you a stranger
And bring you in
Or naked
And clothe you?
39 And when did we see you
Sick or in prison and come to you?

40 And the king will answer them
Certainly I say to you
In so far
As you did it
To one of the least of my brothers
You did it to me

41 Then he will say
To those on the left
You who have been cursed
Go away from me
Into the fire
Which has been prepared
Throughout the ages
For the devil and his angels

42 For I was hungry
And you gave me nothing to eat
I was thirsty
And you did not give me a drink
43 A stranger
And you did not bring me in
Naked
And you did not clothe me
Sick and in prison
And you did not visit me

44 Then they will also answer
Lord
When did we see you
Hungry or thirsty
A stranger or naked

| | Sick or in prison |
| | And did not help you? |

45 | He will answer them
   | Certainly I say to you
   | In as far
   | As you did not do it
   | To one of the least of these
   | Neither did you do it to me

46 | And they will go away
   | Into punishment
   | Throughout the ages
   | But the righteous
   | Throughout the ages
   | Into life

26 *The anointing in Bethany*

1 It so happened
That when Jesus had ended his words
    He said to the disciples
2   You know that after two days
        It will be Passover
        And the Son of Man
        Will be handed over to be crucified

3 Then the Chief priests
And the elders of the people
Were gathered together
In the court of the high priest
Whose name was Caiaphas
4 And they considered
How they might take Jesus by stealth
And kill him

5   But they said
        Not at the feast
        As there might be a disturbance
        Among the people

6 Now when Jesus was in Bethany
In the house of Simon the leper
7 A woman came to him

With an alabaster jar of ointment
Worth a great deal
And poured it on his head
As he sat at table

8 When they saw it
Some of the disciples were indignant
   And said
      Why this waste?
9   Could it not have been sold
      For a high price
      To be given to the poor?

10 As he was aware of this
   Jesus said to them
      Why do you trouble the woman?
      For me she has performed
      An honourable deed

11   You always have the poor with you
      But you do not always have me
12   She put this ointment on my body
      To do it for my burial

13   Certainly I say to you
      That wherever this Gospel is preached
      In all the world
      What she did will be related
      In memory of her

Judas betrays Jesus
14 Then one of the twelve
Called Judas Iscariot
Went to the chief priests
   And said
      What are you
      Willing to give to me
      If I myself
      Hand him over to you?

15 And they weighed him out
Thirty pieces of silver

16   From then on
       He looked for the right moment
       To betray him

Preparations for the Passover

17   On the first day of Unleavened Bread
       The disciples came to Jesus
           And said
                Where do you wish us to prepare
                For you to eat the Passover?

18   He said
           Go into the city
           To a certain person
           And say to him
           The Teacher says
           For me
           The moment is near
           I will keep the Passover
           With you
           With my disciples

19   The disciples
       Did as Jesus had instructed them
       And prepared the Passover

The Last Supper

20   When the evening came
       He sat at table
       With the twelve disciples

21   As they were eating
           He said
                Certainly I say to you
                That one of you
                Will betray me

22   And filled with sadness
       Each one began to ask him
           Lord
           It is not I
           Myself?

23   He answered
         It is the one
         Who is dipping his hand
         Into the bowl with me
         Who will betray me

24   Indeed the Son of Man
         Is going
         As it has been written about him
         But woe to that man
         Through whom the Son of Man
         Is betrayed
         It would be better for that man
         If he had not been born

25   Judas
     Who was betraying him
     Answered
         Rabbi
         It is not I
         Myself?

     Jesus said to him
         That is what you say

26   As they were eating
     Jesus took bread
     And blessing it
     He broke it
     And gave it to the disciples
         And said
             Take and eat
             This is my body

27   He took a cup
     And giving thanks
     He gave it to them
         And said
             Drink from this
             All of you
28   For it is my blood
             Of the new covenant
             Which is poured out for many
             For the forgiveness of sins

29   Certainly I say to you
From now on
I will not drink
Of this fruit of the vine
Until that day
When with you I drink it new
In my Father's kingdom

30   When they had sung a hymn
They went out
To the Mount of Olives

Jesus foretells Peter's denial

31   Then Jesus said to them
All of you
Will turn away from me tonight
As it has been written
I will strike the shepherd
And the sheep of the flock
Will be scattered

32   But after I am raised up
I will go before you
To Galilee

33   Peter said to him
If they all turn away from you
Yet I
I will never turn away

34   Jesus answered
Certainly I say to you
Tonight
Before a cock crows
You will disown me three times

35   Peter said to him
Even if I must die with you
By no means
Will I disown you

And all the disciples
Said the same

Gethsemane

36 Jesus came with them
To a place called Gethsemane
    And said to the disciples
        Sit here
        While I go away and pray

37 So taking Peter
And the two sons of Zebedee
He began to be sorrowful and distressed

38   Then he said to them
        My living soul
        Is sorrowful unto death
        Stay here
        And watch with me

39 Going on a little further
He fell on his face
And prayed
    Saying
        My Father
        If it is possible
        Let this cup pass from me
        But not as I
        I will
        But you

40 When he came to the disciples
And found them sleeping
    He said to Peter
        So you had not the strength
        To watch with me
        One hour

41   Watch and pray
        That you do not come into temptation
        Indeed the spirit is eager
        But the flesh is weak

42 Again a second time
He went away and prayed
    Saying

My Father
If it is not possible
For this to pass
Unless I drink it
May your will be done

43 He came back again
And found them sleeping
As their eyes were heavy

44 Again he left them
And went away
And prayed a third time
Saying the same words

45 Then he came to the disciples
   And said to them
      Sleep now and rest
      For see
      The hour is near
      When the Son of Man
      Is to be betrayed
      Into the hands of sinners

46   Get up now
   And let us go
   Look how near is my betrayer

47 Indeed
While he was still speaking
Judas came
One of the twelve
And a large crowd
With swords and clubs
Came with him
From the chief priests
And the elders of the people

48 The betrayer gave them a sign
   Saying
      Whoever I kiss
      He it is
      Take him

49   And at once
He came up to Jesus
    And said
        Greetings
        Rabbi
And kissed him warmly

50   But Jesus said to him
        Companion
        Why are you here?

Then they came up to Jesus
And laid hands on him
To take him away

51   But now
One of those who were with Jesus
Stretched out his hand
And drawing his sword
He struck the high priest's servant
And took off his ear

52   Then Jesus said to him
        Put your sword
        Back into its place
        For all who take the sword
        Will perish by the sword

53   Or do you think
        That I am not able
        To ask of my Father
        And he will bring to me now
        More than twelve legions of angels?
54   But then
        How are the Scriptures fulfilled
        That it must be so?

55   In that hour
Jesus said to the crowds
        Have you come out to take me
        With swords and clubs
        As if against a robber?
        Every day

        I sat teaching in the Temple
        And yet you did not arrest me

56   But all this has happened
        So that what the prophets wrote
        Might be fulfilled

Then all the disciples
Left him and fled

Jesus before Caiaphas

57 Then those who had taken Jesus
     Led him away to Caiaphas
     The high priest
     Where the scribes and the elders
     Had gathered together

58 Peter followed him at a distance
     As far as the courtyard
     Of the high priest
     There he went inside
     And sat with the attendants
     To see the end

59 The chief priests
     And the whole council
     Tried to find false witnesses
     Against Jesus
     That they might put him to death

60 Although many false witnesses came
     They could not find anything

     Finally there came two
61   Who said
        He declared
        I am able to destroy
        The shrine of God
        And build it after three days

62 The high priest stood up
     And said to him
        Do you answer nothing

> To the evidence
> That is given against you?

63 But Jesus was silent

> Then the high priest
> Said to him
> > I put you on oath
> > By the living God
> > That you tell us
> > If you are the Christ
> > The Son of God?

64 Jesus answered him
> > That is what you say
> > Yet I tell you
> > That from now on
> > You will see the Son of Man
> > Sitting on the right of the Power
> > And coming on the clouds of heaven

65 Then the high priest
Rent apart his clothes
> And said
> > He has blasphemed
> > Do we need yet more witnesses?
> > For indeed you heard the blasphemy

66 > > How does it seem to you?

> And they answered
> > He is liable
> > To be put to death

67 Then they spat in his face
And ill-used him
> They also slapped him
68 > Saying
> > Prophesy to us
> > Christ
> > Who was it
> > That hit you?

Peter's denial

69 Peter sat outside in the courtyard
And one of the maid-servants
Came to him and said
You too were with Jesus
The Galilean

70 But he denied it
In front of them all
And said
I do not know
What you are saying

71 Then he went out into the entrance
Where another maid saw him
And said to those who were there
He was with Jesus
The Nazarene

72 Again he denied with an oath
I do not know the man

73 After a little while
Those who were standing there
Came to Peter and said
It is true
That you are one of them
It is clear
From the way you speak

74 Then he began to curse
And to swear
I do not know the man

And immediately
A cock crowed

75 Then Peter
Remembered the words of Jesus
When he had said
Before a cock crows
You will disown me three times
And he went outside
And wept bitterly

27 *The death of Judas*

1   When dawn came
    The chief priests
    And the elders of the people
    Considered how to proceed against Jesus
    So as to put him to death

2   Then they tied him up
    And led him away
    To be handed over to Pilate
    The governor

3   When Judas
    Who had betrayed him
    Saw that he had been condemned
    He changed his mind
    And gave the thirty pieces of silver
    Back to the chief priests and elders
        And said
            I sinned
            I have betrayed innocent blood

4   But they answered
            Does that matter to us?
            Deal with that yourself

5   And he scattered the pieces of silver
    In the shrine
    And left

    Then he went away
    And hanged himself

6   But the chief priests
    Took the silver pieces
        And said
            It is against the Law
            To put them into the offertory
            As they are the price of blood

7   After due consideration
    They bought the potter's field
    In which to bury strangers

8   So to this day

That field is called
The Field of Blood

9 Then the words were fulfilled
Which were spoken
By the prophet Jeremiah
When he said
They took the thirty pieces of silver
The price
At which the one whom they valued
Had been priced by sons of Israel
10 *And gave them for the potter's field*
As the Lord directed me

Jesus before Pilate
11 Jesus
Stood in front of the governor
And the governor asked him
Are you
The King of the Jews?

Jesus said
You say so

12 He was accused
By the chief priests and the elders
But he did not answer

13 Then Pilate said to him
Do you not hear
What they witness against you?

14 To the governor's astonishment
He did not reply to anything

15 Now at a festival
The governor was accustomed
To release to the crowd
One prisoner whom they wanted

16 They had then a well-known prisoner
Called Barabbas
17 So when they were gathered together

MATTHEW 27

> Pilate said to them
>> Whom do you wish me
>> To release for you
>> Jesus Barabbas
>> Or Jesus called Christ?

18 He knew
That it was because of their jealousy
They had handed him over

19 As he sat in judgment
His wife sent to him
> Saying
>> You must do nothing
>> To that just person
>> As today
>> I suffered a great deal
>> In a dream
>> Because of him

20 But the chief priests
And the elders
Convinced the crowds
That they should ask for Barabbas
And destroy Jesus

21 > So the governor asked them
>> Which of the two
>> Do you wish me
>> To release to you?

> And they said
>> Barabbas

22 > Pilate said to them
>> Then what shall I do
>> To Jesus called Christ?

> They all said
>> Let him be crucified

23 > But Pilate said
>> Why
>> What evil has he done?

They cried out all the more
    Let him be crucified

24 When Pilate
Saw that there was nothing
To be gained
But rather
That there might be a disturbance
He took some water
And washed his hands
In front of the crowd
    Saying
        I am innocent
        Of the blood of this man
        Deal with it yourselves

25   All the people answered
        His blood is on us
        And on our children

26 Then he released for them
Barabbas

Having had Jesus scourged
He handed him over
To be crucified

Jesus is mocked by the soldiers
27 The governor's soldiers
Took Jesus into the praetorium
And assembled the whole company
In his presence

28 They stripped him
And put a scarlet mantle on him

29 When they had plaited
A crown of thorns
They placed it on his head
And put a reed
In his right hand

    Bending their knees
    In front of him
    They mocked him
       And said
          Hail
             King of the Jews

30 They spat at him
    And taking the reed
    They struck at his head

31 When they had mocked him
    They took the mantle off him
    And put on him his own clothes

    Then they led him away
    To be crucified

    The Crucifixion
32 As they set out
    They came upon a man
    A Cyrenian
    Whose name was Simon
    And they pressed him into service
    To carry the cross

33 When they had come to a place
    Named Golgotha
    Which is called
    A place of a skull
34 They gave him wine to drink
    Mixed with gall

    Having tasted it
    He did not wish to drink it

35 When he had been crucified
    They threw dice
    And divided his clothing

36 So sitting there
    They kept a watch on him

37   Above his head
       They put the accusation against him
       On which was written
       THIS IS JESUS
       THE KING OF THE JEWS

38   Two bandits were crucified with him
       One on the right
       And one on the left

39   The people passing by
       Blasphemed him
          Shaking their heads
40   And saying
             You
             Who would overthrow the shrine
             And build it in three days
             Save yourself
             If you are the Son of God
             Come down from the cross

41   In the same way
       The chief priests
       With the scribes and the elders
       Also mocked him
          And said
42   He saved others
             He cannot save himself
             He is King of Israel
             So let him now
             Come down from the cross
             And we will believe in him

43   He trusted in God
             Who should deliver him now
             If he wishes to have him
             For he said
             I am God's Son

44   And the bandits crucified with him
       Also reproached him

45 From the sixth hour
There was darkness over all the earth
Until the ninth hour

46 At about the ninth hour
    Jesus
        Called out in a loud voice
            Eli
            Eli
            Lama sabachthani
        Which is
        My God
        My God
        Why hast thou forsaken me?

47 Some of those standing there
When they heard it
    Said
        He is calling Elijah

48 At once
One of them ran
And taking a sponge
Filled it with vinegar
Then put it on a reed
And gave it to him to drink

49   But the rest said
        Leave him
            Let us see if Elijah
            Will come to save him

50 Again Jesus cried out
In a loud voice
And released his spirit

51 But now
The curtain of the shrine
Was rent in two
From top to bottom
The earth was shaken
And the rocks were split

52 The tombs were opened
And many bodies of the holy ones
Who had fallen asleep
Were raised
53 And coming out of the tombs
After he had risen
They entered the Holy City
And appeared to many

54 The centurion
And those who were with him
Guarding Jesus
Saw the earthquake
And everything that happened
And they were very much afraid
   And said
      It is true
         That this was a Son of God

55 There were many women
Watching from a distance
Who had followed him from Galilee
Serving him
56 Among them Mary Magdalene
And the mother
Of James and of Joseph
And the mother
Of the sons of Zebedee

The burial
57 When the evening came
A rich man from Arimathea
Whose name was Joseph
Himself a disciple of Jesus
58 Approached Pilate
And asked for the body of Jesus

Then Pilate ordered
That it should be given to him

59 Joseph took the body
And wrapped it
In a length of clean linen

60   Then placed it in his new tomb
Which he had hewn in the rock

When he had rolled a large stone
To the door of the tomb
He went away

61   Mary Magdalene
And the other Mary
Were sitting opposite the grave

A guard is set on the tomb

62   On the next day
That is
After the day of Preparation
The chief priests and the Pharisees
Assembled in the presence of Pilate

63   And said
> Sir
> We remember how that impostor
> Said while he was still alive
> After three days
> I will rise

64   Therefore
> Give orders that the grave
> Be secured until the third day
> As the disciples
> Might come and steal him
> And say to the people
> That he has been raised
> From the dead
> Then the last deception
> Will be worse than the first

65   Pilate said to them
> You have a watch
> Go and make it as secure
> As you know how

66   They went and made the grave secure
Sealing the stone
And setting a watch

28 *The Resurrection*

1 When the sabbath was over
At daybreak
On the first day after the sabbath
Mary Magdalene
And the other Mary
Came to watch at the grave

2 But now
There was a great earthquake
As an angel of the Lord
Descended out of heaven
And coming close
He rolled away the stone
And sat upon it

3 His form was like lightning
And his garment
Was white as snow

4 And from fear of him
The guards were shaken
And became as if they were dead

5   But the angel
  Said to the women
      You should not be afraid
      I know
      That you are searching for Jesus
      Who was crucified
6   He is not here
      For he was raised
      As he said

      Come
      Look at the place where he lay
7   And go quickly
      To tell his disciples
      That he was raised from the dead
      Now he is going before you
      To Galilee
      There you will have sight of him
      As I have told you

8   And going away quickly
    From the tomb
    With fear and great joy
    They ran to give the news
    To his disciples

9   And then Jesus met them
        And said
            Greetings

    They came close
    And holding his feet
    They worshipped him

10   Then Jesus said to them
            Do not be afraid
            Go and give the news
            To my brothers
            So that they may go away
            Into Galilee
            And there
            They will have sight of me

The soldiers go to the chief priests
11   Now while they were going
    Some of the watch
    Went into the city
    And told the chief priests
    All that had happened

12   When they had met with the elders
    And taken counsel
    The chief priests
    Gave enough silver to the soldiers
13   And told them
            You should say
            That during the night
            His disciples came
            And while we slept
            They stole him away

14   And if the governor hears of this
        We will convince him
        So that you need have no anxiety

15 They took the silver
And did
As they had been instructed

And the story
Has been spread about by the Jews
Even to this day

Jesus sends the disciples out into the world
16 So the eleven disciples
Went to Galilee
To the mountain
To which Jesus had sent them

17 When they saw him
They worshipped him
But some doubted

18   Jesus came up to them
    And spoke to them
    Saying
        All authority
        Has been given to me
        In heaven
        And on earth

19   Go therefore
    And make disciples of all the nations
    Baptizing them
    In the name of the Father
    And of the Son
    And of the Holy Spirit

20   Teaching them to obey everything
    That I have commanded you
    And how
    I
    I am with you
    Every day
    Until the ending of the age

The Gospel of Mark

1   *Prologue*
1   Beginning
    The Gospel of Jesus Christ
    The Son of God

    John the Baptist
2   As Isaiah the prophet
    Has written
    See how I send out my messenger
    Before thy face
    Who will make ready thy road

3   *A voice calling in the desert*
    Prepare the road for the Lord
    Make his paths straight

4   John
    The one baptizing
    Came into the desert
    Preaching a baptism
    To change heart and mind
    For forgiveness of sins

5   All the country of Judea
    And all the people of Jerusalem
    Went out to him
    And when he baptized them
    In the River Jordan
    They acknowledged their sins

6   John
    Was dressed in camel hair
    With a leather belt round his waist
    He ate locusts
    And wild honey

7   And proclaimed
            There is one coming after me
            Who is stronger than myself

I cannot stoop down and untie
The thong of his sandals

8 I
I have baptized you in water
But he will baptize you
In Holy Spirit

Jesus is baptized
9 It happened during those days
That Jesus
Came from Nazareth in Galilee
And was baptized by John
In the Jordan

10 And immediately
As he came up out of the water
He saw the heavens rent apart
And the Spirit as a dove
Coming down upon him

11 And there was a voice
 Out of the heavens
  Thou art my son
  The beloved
  I rejoice in thee

The Temptation
12 Straight away
The Spirit drove him out
Into the desert

13 He was in the desert
For forty days
Being tempted by Satan

He was with the wild creatures
And the angels served him

Calling of four disciples
14 After John was arrested
Jesus came into Galilee
Proclaiming the Gospel of God

15   And saying
> The right moment is here
> The kingdom of God
> Has come close
> Change your hearts and minds
> And believe the Gospel

16   As he passed by the Sea of Galilee
He saw Simon
And his brother Andrew
Casting nets into the sea
As they were fishers

17   Jesus said to them
> Come with me
> And I will make you
> Into fishers of men

18   At once
They left their nets
And followed him

19   Going a little further
He saw James
The son of Zebedee
And his brother John
In their boat mending the nets

20   He called to them immediately
And leaving their father Zebedee
In the boat with the hired servants
They went with him

The healing of a demoniac

21   They came to Capernaum
And on the sabbath
He went straight to the synagogue
And taught

22   The people
Were astonished at his teaching
Because he taught them with authority
And not like the scribes

23   In their synagogue
       Was a man
       Who had an unclean spirit

24   Suddenly he cried out
            What is between us and you
            Jesus Nazarene
            Have you come to destroy us?
            I know you who you are
            The Holy One of God

25   Jesus spoke sternly to him
           And said
                Be silenced
                And come out

26   After throwing him down
       And shouting with a loud voice
       The unclean spirit
       Came forth out of him

27   They were all astounded
       And discussing it among themselves
           They said
                Is this a new teaching?
                He has authority
                    To command the unclean spirits
                    And they obey him

28   His fame soon spread everywhere
       Through all the Galilean countryside

The healing of Simon's mother-in-law
29   Leaving the synagogue
       He went straight to the house
       Of Simon and Andrew
       With James and John

30   Now Simon's mother-in-law
       Was lying ill
       Stricken with fever
       And straight away
       They told him about her

31   He went to her
       And taking her hand
       He lifted her up
       The fever left her
       And she served them

Healing and teaching in Galilee

32   When evening came
       And the sun had set
       They brought to him
       All those who were sick
       Or possessed by demons

33   And the whole town
       Was gathered round the door

34   He healed many people
       Who suffered from various complaints
       And cast out many demons
       He did not allow
       The demons to speak
       Because they knew him

35   Very early in the morning
       While it was still night
       He rose up and went out
       He went away to a desert place
       And prayed there

36   Simon
       And those with him
       Pursued him

37   When they found him
       They said
           Everyone is searching for you

38   He said to them
           Let us go to other places
           And into the neighbouring towns
           So that I may also preach there
           It was for this
           That I came out

39   And he preached in their synagogue
Throughout Galilee
And cast out demons

The healing of a leper
40   A leper came to him
Entreating him
And falling on his knees
    He said to him
        If it is your will
        You have the power
        To make me clean

41   Filled with compassion
Jesus stretched out his hand
And touched him
    Saying
        I will
        You shall be clean

42   Instantly
The leprosy left him
And he was cleansed

43   Jesus sent him out at once
    With the stern warning
44   See that you
        Do not tell anyone anything
        But go and show yourself to the priest
        And offer for your cleansing
        What Moses commanded
        As a testimony to them

45   But he went out
And began to talk about it
Spreading the news
So that Jesus
Could no longer enter a town openly
But remained in the desert places
And they came to him
From all directions

2 *The healing of a paralytic*

1 Some days later
He again returned to Capernaum
And when the people heard
That he was at home
2 Such a crowd collected
That there was no more space
Not even round the door
And he preached the Word to them

3 A paralytic was brought to him
Carried by four bearers

4 As they could not reach him
Because of the crowd
They opened up the roof above him
When they had made an opening
They lowered the mat
On which the paralytic was lying

5 When Jesus saw their faith
   He said to the paralytic
      Child
      Your sins are forgiven

6 Some of the scribes
Were sitting there
Considering in their hearts
7 Why does he speak in this way?
He blasphemes
There is only one
Who has power to forgive sins
And that is God

8 Immediately
Jesus became aware in his spirit
What they were considering within themselves
   And he said to them
      Why are you considering this
      In your hearts?
9   Is it easier
      To say to the paralytic
      Your sins are forgiven
      Or to say

        Get up
        Take your mat
        And walk?
10   Only that you may know
        That the Son of Man
        Has authority on the earth
        To forgive sins

    Then he said to the paralytic
11   To you I say
        Get up
        Take your mat
        And go to your house

12 At once he got up
And taking his mat
Went out in front of them all
So that they were filled with awe
And praised God
    Saying
        We have never seen such a thing

The calling of Levi
13 Again
When he went out by the sea
Crowds came to him
And he taught them

14 As he was passing by
He saw Levi
The Son of Alphaeus
Sitting in the customs house
    And he said to him
        Follow me

He rose up
And followed him

Eating with outcasts
15 Now it happened
That he was having a meal
In his house
And many tax collectors

        And outcasts
        Were there with Jesus
        And with his disciples
        As many followed him

16   When the scribes of the Pharisees
        Saw that he was eating
        With outcasts
        And with tax collectors
            They said to his disciples
                Why does he eat
                With tax collectors
                And outcasts?

17   Hearing this
        Jesus said to them
            Those who have good health
            Do not need a doctor
            But those who are suffering
            I did not come
            To call the just
            But the outcasts

A question about fasting
18   Now John's disciples
        Were fasting
        As were those of the Pharisees
            So there were some people
            Who came to him and said
                Why do John's disciples
                And the Pharisees' disciples
            Fast?
            But your disciples
            Do not fast?

19   Jesus said to them
            The bridegroom's attendants
            Are not able to fast
            While the bridegroom is with them

            They cannot fast
            At the time
            When the bridegroom is there

20   But the day will come
          When the bridegroom
          Will be taken from them

          In that day
          They will fast

21   No one
          Sews a patch of untreated cloth
          On to an old cloak
          Or the quality of the new
          Will pull away from the old
          And the tear will be made worse

22   And no one
          Puts new wine
          Into old wineskins
          Or the wine
          Will burst the wineskins
          And the wine will be lost
          As also the skins
          But new wine
          Is put into fresh wineskins

In the cornfields on the sabbath

23   It happened
          That on the sabbath
          He was passing through the cornfields
          And his disciples
          Began picking the ears of corn
          Along the way

24   The Pharisees said to him
          See
          It is the sabbath
          So why are they doing something
          Which the Law forbids?

25   He said to them
          Have you never read
          What David did
          When he was in need
          And was hungry
          As were those who were with him?

26   How he entered the house of God
　　　　　　　　When Abiathar was high priest
　　　　　　　　And ate the loaves of offering
　　　　　　　　Which it was unlawful
　　　　　　　　For anyone to eat
　　　　　　　　Except the priests
　　　　　　　　And also gave some
　　　　　　　　To his companions?

27   And he said to them
　　　　　　　　The sabbath came into existence
　　　　　　　　For the sake of man
　　　　　　　　And not man
　　　　　　　　For the sake of the sabbath
28   So the Son of Man
　　　　　　　　Is also Lord of the sabbath

3

The healing of a man with a useless hand

1 Again
He went into a synagogue
And a man was there
Whose hand had wasted away

2 They watched him narrowly
To see if he would heal
On the sabbath
So that they could accuse him

3   He said to the man
　　　　　　　　With the shrunken hand
　　　　　　　　　　Come up into the centre

4   And he said to them
　　　　　　　　Is it lawful on the sabbath
　　　　　　　　To do good
　　　　　　　　Or to do evil?
　　　　　　　　To save soul-bearing life
　　　　　　　　Or to kill?

But they were silent

5   He looked round on them
　　With anger
　　Being saddened
　　By their closed hearts and minds
　　　　And said to the man
　　　　　　Stretch out your hand

　　He stretched it out
　　And his hand
　　Was made good

6   When they went away
　　The Pharisees
　　Immediately conferred with the Herodians
　　As to what could be done against Jesus
　　To destroy him

Crowds come to Jesus for help

7   He departed to the sea
　　With his disciples
　　And large numbers of people
　　Followed him
　　They came from Galilee
　　And from Judea
8   And Jerusalem
　　And Idumea
　　And beyond the Jordan
　　And from the country
　　Round Tyre and Sidon

　　Such a great many came to him
　　When they heard
　　About all that he was doing
9   That he told his disciples
　　That a little boat
　　Should remain close at hand
　　Because of the crowds
　　Who might press upon him

10   He healed many
　　And those who were afflicted
　　Struggled to touch him

11 The unclean spirits
    When they perceived him
    Fell down in front of him
        And cried out
            You are the Son of God

12 And he ordered them
    Not to make him known

    The calling of the twelve
13 He went up on to the mountain
    And called to him
    Those whom he wished
    And they came to him

14 And he appointed twelve
    Whom he could sent out
    To preach
15 And with authority
    To cast out the demons

16 The twelve
    Whom he appointed were
    Simon
    Whom he also named Peter
17 James the son of Zebedee
    And his brother John
    Whom he named Boanerges
    Which means
    Sons of Thunder
18 And Andrew
    Philip
    Bartholomew
    Matthew
    Thomas
    James the son of Alphaeus
    Thaddaeus
    Simon the Cananaean
19 And Judas Iscariot
    The one who betrayed him

20 Then Jesus entered a house
    And such a crowd

    Collected again
    That they could not even eat their meal

21   Hearing of this
    His own people set out
    To take charge of him
        Because they said
            He is out of his mind

The scribes accuse him

22   The scribes
    Who had come down from Jerusalem
    Said
        He is possessed by Beelzebub
        Through the ruler of the demons
        He casts out the demons

23   He called them to him
    And speaking to them in parables
        He said
            How can Satan
            Have power to cast out Satan?

24   If a kingdom
        Is divided against itself
        That kingdom
        Has no power to stand

25   If a house
        Is divided against itself
        That house
        Has no power to stand

26   If Satan
        Stood up against himself
        And was divided
        He would have no power to stand
        But would come to an end

27   For no one
        Has the power to enter
        A strong man's house
        To plunder his goods

Unless he first ties up
The strong man
And then he will plunder
His house

28 Certainly I say to you
That the sons of men
Will be freed from all sins
And from blasphemies
However they may blaspheme
29 But whoever blasphemes
Against the Holy Spirit
Will not be forgiven
Throughout the ages
But is guilty of sin
Unto the ending of time

30 This was because they had said
He has an unclean spirit

The family of Jesus
31 His mother
And his brothers
Came and stood outside
And sent to call him

32 But a crowd
Was sitting round him
So when they said to him
See how your mother
And your brothers
And your sisters
Are outside
Looking for you

33 He answered them
Who is my mother
And who are my brothers?

34 Looking round
At those sitting in the circle
He said

      See here my mother
      And my brothers

35   Whoever does the will of God
      Is my brother
      And my sister
      And my mother

4 *The parable of the sower*

1 Again
When he began to teach
Beside the sea
Such a great crowd surrounded him
That he embarked in a boat
And sat in it
Out on the water
While all the crowd remained on land
By the sea shore

2 He taught them many things
In parables
And when he was teaching
   He said
3   Now listen
      See how a sower
      Went out to sow

4   And it happened
      That as he sowed
      Some seed
      Fell beside the path
      Then came the birds
      And ate it up

5   Other seed
      Fell in rocky places
      Where it did not have much earth
      And sprouted immediately
      Because it had no depth of earth
6   When the sun rose
      It was scorched
      And as it had no root
      It withered

7   Other seed
Fell among the thorn bushes
As the thorns came up
They choked it
And it yielded no fruit

8   Other seed
Fell into cultivated ground
It sprouted and grew
And yielded fruit
Increased thirty times
Sixty times
And a hundred times

9   Then he said
Whoever has ears to hear
Should hear

10 When he was on his own
Others who were round him
With the twelve
Asked about the parables

11 He said to them
The mystery
Of the kingdom of God
Has been given to you
But for those outside
Everything is in parables

12 *That seeing*
They may see and not perceive
That hearing
They may hear and not understand
Lest they might turn again
And be forgiven

13 And he said to them
If you do not see the meaning
Of this parable
Then how will you understand
All other parables?

MARK 4

14   The sower sows the word

15   Those are the ones
      Where the word is sown
      Beside the path
      When they hear it
      Satan comes immediately
      And takes away the word
      Which was sown in them

16   Those are also the ones
      Where it is sown
      In the rocky places
      When they hear the word
      They immediately receive it with joy
17   But having no root in themselves
      It is short-lived
      When difficulties come about
      Or there is persecution
      Because of the word
      They give up at once

18   Others are the ones
      Where it is sown
      Among the thorn bushes
      The ones who hear the word
19   Then the problems of the times
      The enticement of riches
      And all other passionate desires
      Strangle the word
      And it yields no fruit

20   Those are the ones
      Where it is sown
      On the cultivated ground
      Who on hearing the word
      Welcome it
      And yield fruit
      Increased thirty times
      Sixty times
      And a hundred times

Jesus teaches in parables

21   And he said to them
        The lamp
        Is not brought in
        To be put under the corn measure
        Or under the bed
        But on the lampstand

22   For nothing is secret
        Except to be revealed
        Nor was concealed
        Except to be made visible

23   Whoever has ears to hear
        Should hear

24   And he said to them
        See that you listen

        With the measure you measure
        It will be measured to you
        And more will be added to you

25   Whoever has
        More will be a gift to him
        And whoever has not
        Even what he has
        Will be taken from him

26   And he said
        The kingdom of God
        Is like this

        As if a man
        Should throw the seed
        On to the earth
27   And should sleep
        And after each night
        Rise for the day

        Meanwhile the seed
        Sprouts and grows
        He does not know how

28   Of its own accord
The earth bears fruit
First the blade
Then an ear
Then full corn in the ear

29   But when the grain is ready
Immediately he sends out the sickle
Because the harvest has come

30   And he said
    To what should we compare
    The kingdom of God?
    Or what parable should we use?

31   It is like a mustard seed
When it is sown
On to the earth
It is smaller
Than all the seeds
On the earth

32   But when it is sown
And comes up
It grows taller
Than all other herbs

           And puts out
Such large branches
That the birds of heaven
Are able to nest in their shade

33   In many such parables
He spoke the word to them
As far as they had the ability
To hear it

34   And he only spoke to them
In parables
But when they were by themselves
He explained everything
To his own disciples

The calming of the storm

35   On that day
       When the evening had come
          Jesus said to them
             Let us cross over
             To the other side

36   They left the crowd
       And just as he was
       They took him in the boat
       And other boats
       Went with them

37   There came a great gale of wind
       And the waves
       Crashed into the boat
       So that it was now filled

38   But Jesus
       Was in the stern
       Asleep on a pillow

       They woke him
          And said to him
             Teacher
                Does it not matter to you
                That we are lost?

39   On waking
          He spoke sternly to the wind
          And said to the sea
             Be still
             Be silent

       The wind dropped
       And there was a great calm

40   And he said to them
            Why are you such cowards?
            Have you no faith?

41   They were terribly afraid
          And said to one another
             Who is this

      That both the wind
      And the sea
      Obey him?

5 *The healing of the man with legion*

1   On the other side of the sea
    They came to the district of the Gadarenes

2   As Jesus disembarked from the boat
    There met him a man
    Who came out from among the tombs
    And who had an unclean spirit.

3   He housed among the tombs
    And no longer did anyone
    Have the power
    To bind him with a chain

4   As he had often been bound
    With fetters and chains
    And he had burst the chains
    And broken the fetters
    And no one was strong enough
    To subdue him

5   He was always among the tombs
    And in the mountains
    Crying out night and day
    And cutting himself with stones

6   When he saw Jesus
    From a long way off
    He ran and worshipped him

7   And crying out in a loud voice
      He said
          What is there between me and you
          Jesus
          Son of the most high God?
          Swear by God
          Not to torment me

8   Because he had said
    To the unclean spirit
    That he should come out of the man

9   And Jesus asked him the question
        What is your name?

    He said to him
        My name is Legion
        Because we are many

10   And he implored him earnestly
    Not to send them
    Out of the district

11   A large herd of pigs
    Was feeding there
    On the mountain side

12   The unclean spirits implored him
        Saying
            Send us into the pigs
            So that we may go into them

13   And he allowed them to go

    They came out
    And went into the pigs
    And the whole herd
    Rushed headlong down the steep incline
    Into the sea
    There were about two thousand
    And they were drowned in the sea

14   The herdsmen fled
    And reported it in the town
    And in the countryside

    Then the people came out
    To see what had happened

15   When they came to Jesus
    And observed the demoniac
    The one who had the Legion
    Sitting clothed
    And come to his senses
    They were afraid

16   Those who had seen it
Told the story of what had happened
To the demoniac
And about the pigs

17   Then they began to beg Jesus
To leave their territory

18   As he embarked in the boat
The one
Who had been possessed by demons
Begged to go with him

19   He did not permit this
    But said to him
        Go to your house
        And to your people
        And tell them
        How the Lord pitied you
        And what he has done for you

20   He went away
And began to proclaim
Throughout the Decapolis
What Jesus had done for him
And every one was astonished

The cure of a woman and raising Jairus' daughter

21   When Jesus
Had crossed over again in the boat
And come to the other side
Crowds had gathered to meet him

He was beside the sea
22   When one of the leaders of the synagogue
Came to him
His name was Jairus
And when he saw Jesus
He fell at his feet

23   And imploring him insistently
    He said
        My little daughter

Is at the end
Come and lay your hands on her
So that she may be saved
And live

24 Jesus went with him
And a large crowd followed
Hemming him in

25 There was a woman
Who had suffered from severe bleeding
For twelve years

26 She had been treated
By a great many doctors
And spent all that she possessed
But nothing had helped
It had rather become worse

27 Because she had heard about Jesus
She came behind him in the crowd
And touched his cloak

28   As she said
      If I even touch his cloak
      I shall be saved

29 Instantly
The flow of her blood dried up
And she was aware in her body
That she was cured of her affliction

30 As Jesus
Knew at once within himself
That power
Had gone forth from him
He turned round in the crowd
   And said
      Who touched my cloak?

31   His disciples said to him
      You see the crowd jostling you
      And yet you say
      Who touched me?

32   Then he looked round
To see who had done this

33   The woman
Came in fear and trembling
As she was aware
Of what had happened to her
She fell down in front of him
And told him all the truth

34   And he said to her
        Daughter
        Your faith has saved you
        Go in peace
        And be cured of your affliction

35   While he was still speaking
Some people
Came from the leader's house
      Saying
        Your daughter has died
        Why do you trouble the Teacher?

36   But Jesus overheard
What they were saying
      And he said
      To the leader of the synagogue
        Do not be afraid
        Only have faith

37   And he allowed no one
To go with him
Except Peter and James
And John the brother of James

38   They came into Jairus' house
And Jesus observed a great commotion
With weeping
And crying out loud

39   As he went in
       He said to them
         Why do you make so much noise
         And weep?

       The child has not died
       She is sleeping

40   They laughed at him
      But he put them all outside

      Then he took the child's father
      And her mother
      Also those who were with him
      And went in where the child was

41   He took hold of the child's hand
         And said to her
           Talitha koum
           (Which is translated
           Young girl
           I say to you
           Get up)

42   At once
      The young girl rose up
      And walked

      She was twelve years old

      At that moment
      They were quite overcome with bewilderment

43   But Jesus
      Gave strict orders that no one
      Should be made aware of it
      And told them
      To give her something to eat

6
Jesus is not accepted in his native place

1   On going away from there
     He went to his native place
     And his disciples followed him

2   When the sabbath came
     He began to teach in the synagogue
     Many of those who heard him
     Were astonished

And said
>   Where does he get all this?
>   And what is the wisdom
>   Which is given to him?
>   How are such powerful deeds
>   Performed through his hands?

3   Is he not the carpenter
>   The son of Mary
>   The brother of James and Joses
>   And of Judas and Simon?
>   Are not his sisters
>   Here with us?

And they would not accept him

4   Jesus said to them
>   A prophet
>   Is not without honour
>   Except in his native place
>   Among his kinsmen
>   And in his own house

5   There
He was unable
To perform any powerful deeds
Only laying his hands
On a few sick people
He healed them
6   And he wondered at their lack of faith

Then he went about
Teaching in turn among the villages

The mission of the twelve
7   He called the twelve
To come to him
And began to send them out
Two by two
And gave them authority
Over the unclean spirits

8 He instructed them
To take nothing for the road
Except for a staff
Neither bread nor bag
Nor small coins in their belt
9 They should wear sandals with straps
But not put on two tunics

10   And he said to them
        Wherever
        You go into a house
        Stay until you leave that place
11   And wherever
        They do not receive you
        Or hear you
        When you go out
        Shake off the dust under your feet
        As a witness to them

12 They went out
Preaching a change of heart and mind
13 They cast out many demons
And anointing with oil
Many who were sick
They healed them

The death of John the Baptist
14 King Herod heard this
Because Jesus' name
Had become well known

    There were some who said
        John
        The one baptizing
        Has been raised from the dead
        Therefore these powerful deeds
        Are active in him

15   Others said
        He is Elijah

    While others said
        He is a prophet
        Like one of the prophets

16   But when he heard this
     Herod said
        John
        Whom I
        I beheaded
        Has been raised

17   For Herod
     Had himself sent to take John
     And held him bound in prison
     Because of Herodias
     The wife of his brother Philip
     Whom he had married
18   As John
     Had told Herod
     That it was not lawful
     For him to have his brother's wife

19   Now Herodias
     Was angry with him
     And wished to kill him
     But she had not the power

20   Because Herod
     Was afraid of John
     As he knew
     That he was a just and holy man
     And kept a watch on him

     When he heard him
     He was greatly disturbed
     Yet he was pleased to hear him

21   A suitable day came
     When Herod
     To celebrate his birthday
     Gave a supper for his courtiers
     The commanding officers
     And the chief men of Galilee

22   When the daughter of Herodias
     Came in herself and danced
     She pleased Herod
     And those at the table with him

Then the king
Said to the young girl
    Ask whatever you wish
    And I will give it to you

23   And he vowed to her
    I will give you
    Whatever you ask
    Even half of my kingdom

24   She went out
  And said to her mother
    What am I to ask?

She answered
    The head of John
    The one who baptizes

25   At once
She came swiftly
Into the king's presence
    And asked
        I wish you to give me immediately
        A dish with the head
        Of John the Baptist

26   The king became deeply distressed
But because of his oaths
And those at the table with him
He did not wish
To break faith with her

27   Straight away
The king sent an executioner
With orders to bring his head

He went and beheaded him
In the prison
28   And brought his head on a dish
And gave it to the young girl
And the girl
Gave it to her mother

29 When his disciples heard it
They came and took his dead body
And put it in a tomb

The feeding of the five thousand
30 The Apostles
Gathered again to Jesus
And gave him news
Of all that they had done
And had taught

31 He said to them
    Come away by yourselves
    To a desert place
    And rest a short while

For so many
Were coming and going
They did not even
Have the opportunity to eat

32 They embarked in the boat
And went away by themselves
To a desert place

33 Many people saw them going
And recognized them
So they came from all the towns
And running together on foot
Reached the place before them

34 When Jesus landed
He saw a large crowd
And had compassion on them
Because they were like sheep
Without a shepherd
And he began to teach them
About many things

35   As the hour grew late
      His disciples came to him
      And said
         This is a desert place
         And now the hour is late
36   Send them away
      So that they may disperse
         To the farms and villages round about
         And buy themselves
         What they need to eat

37   But he answered them
      You give them
      Something to eat

   So they said to him
      Shall we go away
      And spend two hundred denarii
      On bread
      And give it to them to eat?

38   And he said to them
      How many loaves have you?
      Go and see

   When they had discovered
   They said
      Five
      And two fishes

39   He ordered them
   To sit down for a meal
   In companies together
   On the green grass

40   So they sat down in squares
   Of a hundred
   And of fifty

41   He took the five loaves
   And the two fishes
   And looking up to heaven
   He said a blessing

He broke the loaves
And gave them to the disciples
To serve out to the people
And the two fishes
He divided among them all

42 They all ate
And were satisfied

43 And they took up
Twelve wicker baskets full of pieces
Including fragments from the fish

44 Those who had eaten the loaves
Were five thousand men

45 Then he demanded that his disciples
Should embark at once in the boat
And go ahead of him to Bethsaida
On the other side
While he sent the crowd away

46 After he had taken leave of them
He went on to the mountain
To pray

Jesus comes to the disciples on the sea
47 When evening came
The boat
Was in the midst of the sea
And he was alone
On the land

48 When he saw
That they were having difficulty in rowing
Because the wind was against them
He came to them
At about the fourth watch of the night
Walking on the sea
And would have passed by them

49 But as they saw him
Walking on the sea

They thought that it was a phantom
And cried out
50 Because they all saw him
And were troubled

    But he spoke to them at once
    And said
        Be brave
        I
        I AM
        Do not be afraid

51 Then he came into the boat
With them
And the wind dropped

Inwardly
They were filled with the greatest awe
52 Because they did not understand
About the loaves
As their hearts and minds
Were not open

Healings at Gennesaret

53 They crossed over
And reached the land at Gennesaret
Where they cast anchor

54 As they disembarked out of the boat
The people recognized him
55 And at once
They began to run around
All that countryside
Carrying round the sick on their mats
When they heard where he was

56 And wherever he went
Whether into the villages
Or into the towns
Or in the countryside
They brought the invalids
Into the open spaces
And begged him to allow them

To touch even the border of his cloak
And all who touched him
Were saved

7 *A discussion about tradition*
1 When the Pharisees
And some of the scribes
Who had come from Jerusalem
Were gathered round him
2 They saw some of his disciples
Eating with unclean hands
That is
Eating bread without having washed

3 Because the Pharisees
And indeed all the Jews
Do not eat
Unless they have first washed their hands
As they keep the tradition of the elders
4 When they come from the market
They do not eat
Without having first cleansed themselves

And there are many other things prescribed
Such as
How cups and utensils and copper pans
Should be washed

5 The Pharisees and the scribes
Asked him
    Why do your disciples
    Not follow the tradition of the elders
    But eat bread
    With unclean hands?

6 And Jesus said to them
    It was right
    What Isaiah prophesied
    About you hypocrites
    The people
    Honour me with their lips
    But their heart
    Is far from me

7   *They worship me in vain*
Teaching as doctrine
The commandments of men

8   You leave
The commandments of God
And hold fast
The tradition of men

9   And he said to them
    You succeed in setting aside
    The commandments of God
    So that you may keep
    Your own tradition

10   For Moses said
Honour your father and your mother
Whoever speaks evil
Of father or mother
Let him end in death

11   But you
You say that if a man
Declares to his father or mother
The help
Which I would have given to you
Is korban
Which means a gift to God

12   You no longer
Allow him to do anything
For his father or mother

13   Thus you annul the word of God
By your tradition
Which you received
As indeed you do many such things

Clean and unclean

14   Calling the crowds to him again
He said to them
    Listen all of you
    And understand

15 There is nothing
    Which enters into a man
    From outside
    Which has the power
    To make him unclean
    But it is those things
    Which come out of a man
    Which make him unclean

[16]

17 When he left the crowds
    And went into a house
    His disciples questioned him
    About the parable

18 And he said to them
    Are you
    You also without understanding?
    Do you not grasp
    That anything
    Which enters into a man
    From outside
    Has no power
    To make him unclean?

19 Because it does not enter his heart
    But his stomach
    And passes out into the drain
    Making all foods clean

20 And he said
    Those things
    Which come out of a man
    Make a man unclean

21 For from within
    Out of the hearts of men
    Come forth the evil thoughts
    Fornications and thefts and murders
22 Adulteries and greed and wickedness
    Deceit and indecency and envy
    Blasphemy and arrogance and folly
23 All these evil things
    Coming forth from within
    Make a man unclean

The healing of the Syrophoenician woman's daughter

24 Going up from there
Jesus went away
Into the district of Tyre

He went into a house
And wished no one
To be aware of it
But he could not be kept hidden

25 Straight away
A woman heard about him
Whose daughter had an unclean spirit
So she came
And fell at his feet

26 She was a Greek
By birth a Syrophoenician

And she asked him
To cast the demon
Out of her daughter

27   And he said to her
        First allow the children
        To be satisfied
        As it is not right
        To take the children's bread
        And to throw it to the house-dogs

28   She answered him
        Yes Lord
        But the house-dogs under the table
        Eat the children's crumbs

29   And he said to her
        Because of what you have said
        Go
        The demon has left your daughter

30 When she went away
To her house
She found the child

Laid on the bed
And the demon gone

The healing of the deaf man

31 Again leaving the district of Tyre
He came through Sidon
To the Sea of Galilee
Passing through the district
Of the Decapolis

32 They brought someone to him
Who was deaf
And had difficulty in speaking
And they begged him
To put his hand on him

33 Taking him on his own
Away from the crowds
He put his fingers into his ears
And spat and touched his tongue
34   Looking up to heaven
    He groaned
    And said to him
        Ephphatha
        (Which means Be opened)

35 His ears were opened
And at once
The bond of his tongue
Was loosened
And he spoke clearly

36 Jesus ordered them
To tell no one
But the more insistent he was
The more widely
They made it known

37 They were extremely astonished
    And said
        He has done everything well
        He makes both the deaf hear
        And the dumb speak

8   *The feeding of the four thousand*

1   During those days
Large crowds collected again
And they did not have anything to eat

2   Jesus called his disciples to him
       And said to them
           I have compassion on the people
           Because they have been with me
           For three days
           And do not have anything to eat
3   If I send them away to their homes
           Without food
           They will faint on the road
           For some of them
           Have come from far away

4   His disciples answered him
           Where could anyone
           Get enough bread
           To satisfy them
           Here in a desert place

5   He asked them
           How many loaves
           Have you?

       And they said
           Seven

6   He ordered the people
To sit down on the ground
And taking the seven loaves
He gave thanks
And broke them

   He gave them to his disciples
To serve out
And they served the people

7   They had a few little fish
And he blessed them
And told his disciples
To serve them also

8   They are and were satisfied
And they collected the fragments left over
In seven reed baskets

9   Now there were about four thousand
And he sent them away

The Pharisees seek for a sign

10   At once
He embarked in the boat
With his disciples
And went to the district of Dalmanutha

11   The Pharisees came out
And began to debate with him
Seeking from him
A sign from heaven
In order to test him

12   Groaning deeply in his spirit
      He said
          Why does this generation
          Seek a sign?
          Certainly I say to you
          No sign
          Will be given to this generation

The disciples fail to understand the signs

13   Leaving them again
He embarked
And went to the other side

14   His disciples
Had forgotten to take bread
And had only one loaf
With them in the boat

15   And he spoke to them severely
      Saying
          See that you take no notice

Of the yeast of the Pharisees
Or the yeast of the Herodians

16 They decided among themselves
That it was because
They had no bread

17 As he was aware of this
He said
>   Why have you decided
>   That it is because
>   You have no bread?
>   Do you still not grasp
>   Or understand?
>   Are your hearts and minds closed?

18 *Although you have eyes*
Do you not see?
Although you have ears
Do you not hear?
And do you not remember?

19 When I broke the five loaves
For the five thousand
How many wicker baskets
Full of fragments
Did you take up?

They said to him
Twelve

20 When the seven
For the four thousand
How many reed baskets
With the quantity of fragments
Did you take up?

And they said
Seven

21 And he said to them
Do you still not understand?

The healing of a blind man

22 They came to Bethsaida
And some of the people
Brought to him a blind man
And they begged him to touch him

23 Taking the blind man
By the hand
He led him away
Out of the village

Then he spat on his eyes
And putting his hands on him
   He asked him
      Do you see anything?

24 Looking up
He said
   I see men
   They are like trees
   That I observe walking

25 Again
He put his hands
On his eyes
And as he looked steadily
His sight was restored
And he saw everything distinctly

26   Jesus sent him to his house
   And said
      You should not go into the village

Peter declares Jesus to be the Christ

27 Jesus went out with his disciples
To the villages of Caesarea Philippi
And on the road
   He questioned his disciples
   Saying to them
      Whom do men believe me to be?

28   And they answered him
        John the Baptist
        And others Elijah
        But others say
        One of the prophets

29   He asked them
        But you
        Whom do you believe me to be?

    Peter answered him
        You are the Christ

30   And he warned them
    To tell no one about him

31   He began to teach them
    That it is necessary
    For the Son of Man
    To have great suffering
    And be rejected by the elders
    The chief priests
    And the scribes
    To be killed
    And after three days
    To rise again

32   He said this openly
    And Peter took him aside
    And began to speak sternly to him

33   But he turned
    And seeing his disciples
    He spoke sternly to Peter
        And said
            Get behind me
            Satan
            Because you are not thinking
            Of the concerns of God
            But of the concerns of men

Following Christ

34 He called the crowd to him
With his disciples
    And said to them
        If anyone
        Has the will to come after me
        He should not consider himself
        But take his cross
        And follow me

35   For whoever wishes to save
        His soul-bearing life
        Will lose it
        But whoever will lose
        His soul-bearing life
        For my sake
        And the Gospel
        Will save it

36   What use is it to a man
        To gain the whole world
        And suffer the loss
        Of his living soul

37   What could a man give
        As the price
        Of his living soul?

38   For whoever
        Is ashamed of me
        And of my words
        In this false and sinful generation
        The Son of Man
        Will be ashamed of him
        When he comes
        Revealing the glory of his Father
        With the holy angels

9 And he said to them
    Certainly I say to you
    That there are some standing here
    Who will surely not taste death
    Until they see the kingdom of God
    Come with power

The Transfiguration

2   After six days
    Jesus
    Took Peter and James and John
    And brought them up
    On to a high mountain
    Alone by themselves

    He was transformed
    In their presence
3   And his clothing
    Became shimmering white
    Very white like snow
    Such as no fuller on the earth
    Would be able to whiten

4   And there appeared to them
    Elijah with Moses
    Conversing with Jesus

5   Peter said to Jesus
            Rabbi
                It is right for us to be here
                Let us put up three tents
                One for you
                One for Moses
                And one for Elijah

6   He did not know
    How he answered
    As they were desperately afraid

7   And there came a cloud
    Which overshadowed them
        And a voice
            Came out of the cloud
                This is my Son
                The beloved
                Hear him

8   Suddenly
    As they looked round
    They no longer saw anyone
    Except only Jesus with them

9   Coming down from the mountain
    He ordered them
    Not to tell anyone
    The story of what they had seen
    Until the Son of Man
    Should have risen from the dead

10 So they kept close among themselves
    What he had said
    Discussing what that is
    To rise from the dead

11   They asked him
            Why do the scribes
            Say that Elijah must come first?

12   And he said to them
            Indeed Elijah comes first
            And will restore everything
            For what has been written
            About the Son of Man
            Except that he should suffer
            And be despised?

13   But I say to you
        That Elijah has come
        And they treated him
        Just as they wished
        As it has been written about him

The healing of a boy with a dumb spirit
14 When they came to the disciples
    They saw a large crowd round them
    And scribes discussing with them

15 Immediately
    When the people saw Jesus
    They were greatly astonished
    And came running to greet him

16   He asked them
            What are you discussing with them?

17   And one of the crowd
Answered him
> Teacher
> I have brought my son to you
> As he has a dumb spirit
18   > And wherever it seizes him
> It tears him
> And he foams at the mouth
> And grinds his teeth
> He is wasting away
> And when I asked your disciples
> To cast it out
> They had not the strength

19   Jesus answered them
> O generation without faith
> How long
> Shall I be with you?
> How long
> Shall I endure you?
> Bring him to me

20   They brought him to Jesus

When the spirit saw him
At once it threw the boy down
Who fell on the earth
And rolled there
Foaming at the mouth

21   Jesus asked his father
>> For how long a time
>> Has this been happening to him?

And he said
> From childhood
22   > And often
> It threw him into the fire
> And into the water
> To destroy him
> But if you have the power
> To do anything to help us
> Have compassion on us

23   Jesus said to him
           You say
           If you have the power
           Whoever has faith
           Has the power to do anything

24   The child's father
      Cried out at once
      In tears
           I do believe
           May you help my lack of faith

25   When Jesus
Saw that a crowd
Came running together
      He spoke sternly to the unclean spirit
      And said to it
           Dumb and deaf spirit
           I
           I command you
           To come forth out of him
           And you may never
           Enter him again

26   Shouting
And throwing him down violently
It came out
Leaving him as if dead
So that many people said
That he had died

27   But Jesus
Took hold of his hand
And lifted him
And he rose up

28   Then Jesus went into a house
And when his disciples
Were alone with him
      They asked him
           Why did we not have power
           To cast it out?

29   And he told them
        Nothing gives power
        To cast out this sort
        Except prayer

Teaching the disciples in Galilee and Capernaum
30 They went away from there
And passed through Galilee

He did not wish
That anyone should be aware of it
31 As he was teaching his disciples
    Saying to them
        The Son of Man
        Will be betrayed
        Into the hands of men
        And they will kill him
        Three days after being killed
        He will rise up

32 They did not understand
What he said
And were afraid to question him

33 They came to Capernaum
When they were in the house
    He asked them
        What were you discussing
        On the road?

34 They were silent
As on the road
They had been discussing
Who was the greatest

35 He sat down
    And calling the twelve
    He said to them
        If anyone wishes to be first
        He shall be last of all
        And be the server of all

36   Then he took a child
        And placed him in among them

        Taking him in his arms
            He said to them
37   Whoever receives
                One of such children
                In my name
                Receives me
                And whoever receives me
                Does not receive me
                But the one who sent me

38   John said to him
            Teacher
            We saw someone
            Casting out demons in your name
            Who does not follow us
            And because he does not follow us
            We forbade him

39   But Jesus said
            Do not forbid him
            For there is no one
            Who does powerful work
            In my name
            And who will soon be able
            To speak evil of me

40   He who is not against us
            Is for us

41   Whoever gives you
            A cup of water to drink
            In the name of Christ
            To whom you belong
            Certainly I say to you
            By no means
            Will he lose his reward

42   Whoever causes the downfall
            Of one of these little ones
            Who believe in me
            It would be right

MARK 9

        For him to have a great millstone
        Hung round his neck
        And to be thrown into the sea

43   If your hand
        Causes your downfall
        Cut it off
        It is right for you to enter maimed
        Into Life
        Rather than having two hands
        To go into the burning rubbish
        Into the fire
        Which cannot be put out

[44]
45   If your foot
        Causes your downfall
        Cut it off
        It is right for you to enter lame
        Into Life
        Rather than having two feet
        To be thrown into the burning rubbish

[46]
47   If your eye
        Causes your downfall
        Pluck it out
        It is right for you to enter one-eyed
        Into the kingdom of God
        Rather than having two eyes
        To be thrown into the burning rubbish
48   *Where their worm does not die*
        And the fire is never put out

49   For everyone
        Will be salted with fire
        And every sacrifice
        Will be salted with salt

50   Salt is useful
        But if the salt becomes saltless
        How will you season it?
        Have salt in yourselves
        And be at peace with one another

10 *A discussion about divorce*

1 He left there
And went up into Judea
Into the territory beyond the Jordan

Again
Crowds went with him
And again
He taught them
As was his custom

2 Some Pharisees came up to him
Asking him
In order to test him
Whether it is lawful
For a man to release a wife

3   He answered them
        What did Moses command you?

4   They said
        Moses
        Allowed a written document of divorce
        For her release

5   But Jesus said to them
        It was for your unyielding hearts
        That he wrote you this commandment

6   From the beginning of creation
        They were made male and female

7   Because of this
        A man shall leave
        His father and mother
        And be united with his wife
8   *And the two shall be one flesh*
        So that they are no longer two
        But one flesh

9   What God
        Joined together
        Man
        Should not separate

10 When they were in the house
The disciples
Questioned him again about this

11   He said to them
        Whoever releases his wife
        And marries another
        Commits adultery with her
12   And if she releases her husband
        And marries another
        She commits adultery

Children are brought to Jesus
13 They brought children to him
So that he might touch them
But the disciples reproved them

14 When Jesus saw this
He was indignant
    And said to them
        Allow the children
        To come to me
        Do not hinder them
        For as they are
        So is the kingdom of God

15   Certainly I say to you
        Whoever does not receive
        The kingdom of God
        As does a child
        There is no doubt
        That he shall not enter into it

16 And taking them in his arms
He blessed them
Putting his hands on them

The rich man

17 As he set out on the road
Someone came running up to him
And kneeling in front of him
    Asked him
        Good Teacher
        What shall I do
        To inherit life
        Throughout the ages

18   Jesus said to him
        Why do you call me good?
        No one is good
        Except God only

19   You know the commandments
        Do not kill
        Do not commit adultery
        Do not steal
        Do not witness falsely
        Do not cheat
        Honour your father and your mother

20   He answered him
        Teacher
        I have kept all this
        From my youth

21 But Jesus gazing into him
Loved him
    And said
        There is still something wanting
        Go and sell what you have
        And give it to the poor
        Then you will have treasure in heaven
        And come
        Follow me

22 He was downcast
At what was said
And went sadly away
As he had extensive possessions

23 Looking round
Jesus said to his disciples
How difficult it will be
For those who have riches
To enter the kingdom of God

24 The disciples
Were astounded at his words

Jesus said to them again
Children
How difficult it is
To enter the kingdom of God

25 It is easier for a camel
To go through the eye of a needle
Than for one who is rich
To enter the kingdom of God

26 They were absolutely astonished
And said to one another
Then who
Is able to be saved?

27 Gazing into them
Jesus said
With men it is impossible
But not with God
For with God
All things are possible

28 Peter began to say to him
You see
How we have left everything
And followed you

29 Jesus said
Certainly I say to you
There is no one
Who has left house
Or brothers or sisters
Or mother or father
Or children or lands
For my sake

     And for the Gospel
30   But will receive a hundred times more
     Houses
     And brothers and sisters
     And mothers and children
     And lands
     With persecutions
     Now at this season
     And in the time to come
     Life throughout the ages

31   But many that are first
     Will be last
     And the last first

The last prophecy of the Passion
32   They were on the road
     Going up to Jerusalem
     And Jesus
     Was leading them on

     They were astounded
     And those following
     Were afraid
     As taking the twelve again
      He began to tell them
      What was about to happen to him
33   Now see
      How we are going up to Jerusalem
      And the Son of Man
      Will be betrayed
      To the chief priests
      And to the scribes

     They will condemn him
     To death
     And will deliver him
     To the Gentiles
34   They will mock him
     And spit on him
     They will scourge him
     And kill him
     And after three days
     He will rise

The request of James and John

35 James and John
The sons of Zebedee
Came to him and said
    Teacher
    We wish you to do for us
    Whatever we ask

36 He said to them
    What do you wish me
    To do for you?

37 They said to him
    Grant us
    That we may sit
    One on your right
    And one on your left
    In your glory

38 But Jesus said to them
    You do not know
    What you ask
    Are you able to drink the cup
    Which I myself drink
    Or to be baptized with the baptism
    With which I
    I am baptized?

39 They said to him
    We are able

Jesus said to them
    You shall drink the cup
    Which I myself drink
    And be baptized with the baptism
    With which I
    I am baptized
40   But to sit on my right
    Or on my left side
    Is not mine to give
    But is for those
    For whom it has been prepared

41   When the ten heard this
      They began to be indignant
      About James and John

42   Jesus called them to him
          And said
              You know
              That those who think to rule the Gentiles
              Dominate them
              And their great ones
              Have authority over them

43   But it is not so
          Among you
          For whoever wishes to become great
          Among you
          Shall be your server

44   And whoever wishes to be first
          Among you
          Shall be the servant of all
45   For even the Son of Man
          Did not come to be served
          But to serve
          And to give his soul-bearing life
          As a ransom for many

The healing of blind Bartimaeus
46   They came to Jericho
      And as he left Jericho
      With his disciples
      And a considerable crowd
      A blind beggar
      Bartimaeus
      The son of Timaeus
      Was sitting at the side of the road

47   When he heard
      That it was Jesus of Nazareth
          He began to shout
              Jesus
              Son of David
              Pity me

48   Many ordered him to be quiet
        But he shouted all the more
            Son of David
            Pity me

49   Jesus stood still
      And said
            Call him

        And they called the blind man
        Saying to him
            Courage
            Get up
            He is calling you

50   So he threw off his cloak
      And leaping up
      He came to Jesus

51   Jesus asked him
            What do you wish me
            To do for you?

        The blind man said to him
            Rabboni
            That I may see again

52   Jesus said to him
            Go
            Your faith has saved you

      Immediately
      He could see again
      And followed him
      On the road

11 *The entry into Jerusalem*
1   When they came near Jerusalem
      To Bethphage and Bethany
      On the Mount of Olives
      He sent out two of his disciples
2   Saying to them
              Go into the village in front of you

And immediately you come into it
You will find a colt tied up
On which no man has yet sat
Untie it and bring it

3   If anyone says to you
Why are you doing this?
Say
The Lord needs it
And will send it here again
At once

4   They went and found a colt
Tied at a door
Outside in the street
And they untied it

5   Some of the people standing there
Said to them
    What are you doing
    Untying the colt?

6   They answered
As Jesus had told them
And they let them go

7   They brought the colt to Jesus
And threw their cloaks on it
And he sat on it

8   Many
Spread out their cloaks on the road
And others
A covering of greenery
Which they cut from the fields

9   Those who went in front
And those who followed
    Cried out
    Hosanna
    Blest be the one who comes
    In the name of the Lord

10   Blest be the coming kingdom
Of our father David

MARK 11

>   Hosanna
>   In the highest places

11 He entered Jerusalem
    And went into the Temple
    Where he looked round at everything
    And as the hour was now late
    He went out to Bethany
    With the twelve

The fig tree and the clearing of the Temple

12 On the next day
    As they went out of Bethany
    He was hungry
13 And seeing in the distance
    A fig tree in leaf
    He went to it
    As perhaps he might find
    Something on it

    When he came he found
    Nothing but leaves
    As it was not the season for figs

14   He spoke to it
        Saying
>   No more
>   May anyone eat of your fruit
>   Throughout the ages

    And the disciples heard him

15 They came to Jerusalem
    And entering the Temple
    He began to turn out
    Those who were selling
    And those who were buying
    In the Temple

    He overturned
    The tables of the money-changers
    And the seats
    Of those selling doves

16   And he did not allow anyone
To carry goods through the Temple

17   And he taught them
        Has it not been written
        My house
        Shall be called a house of prayer
        For all the nations
        But you yourselves
        Have made of it
        A robber's cave

18   The chief priests and the scribes
Heard it
And tried to find a way
To destroy him
As they were afraid of him
Because the crowds
Were all astonished at his teaching

19   When evening came
They left the city

20   As they passed by
Early in the morning
They saw the fig tree
Withered from the roots

21   Peter remembered
And said to him
        Rabbi
        See how the fig tree
        Which you cursed
        Has been withered

Teaching about prayer

22   Jesus said to them
        Have faith in God
23   Certainly I say to you
        Whoever says to this mountain
        Be taken up
        And thrown into the sea
        And does not waver in his heart

        But believes
        That it will happen as he says
        Then so it will be for him

24   Therefore I tell you
        If you believe that you received
        Everything for which you pray
        And for which you ask
        Then so it will be for you

25   When you stand and pray
        If you have anything against anyone
        Forgive them
        And your Father in the heavens
        Will forgive your shortcomings
26   But if you do not forgive
        Neither will your Father in the heavens
        Forgive your shortcomings

27 Again
    They came to Jerusalem

    As he walked in the Temple
        The chief priests
        The scribes
        And the elders
28   Came to him and said
            By what authority
            Are you doing these things?
            Or who gave you the authority
            Which allows you to do them?

29   Jesus said to them
        I will ask you one question
        Which you must answer me
        Then I will tell you
        By what authority
        I do these things

30   Was the baptism of John
        From heaven
        Or from men?
        You must answer me

31	They discussed it among themselves
	And said
	If we reply
	From heaven
	He will say
	Why then did you not believe him?
32	But what if we reply
	From men?

They were afraid of the crowd
For everyone held that John
Was really a prophet

33   So they answered Jesus
        We do not know

    And Jesus said to them
        Neither will I
        I say to you
        By what authority
        I do these things

12

The parable of the cruel farmers

1   And he began to speak to them
    In parables
        A man planted a vineyard
        He set a hedge round it
        And dug a pit for the wine press
        And built a watch-tower
        Then he let it to farmers
        And went out of the country

2   When the season came
    He sent a servant to the farmers
    To receive from them
    Some of the fruits of the vineyard

3   They took him
    And beat him
    Then sent him away with nothing

4   Again
    He sent another servant to them

MARK 12

That one
They wounded in the head
And insulted

5   He sent another
And that one
They killed

Then many more
Some were beaten
Others were killed

6   He still had one
A beloved son

He sent him to them
As the last
And said
They will respect my son

7   But those farmers
Said to one another
This is the heir
Come
Let us kill him
And the inheritance
Will be ours

8   They took him
And killed him
And threw him out
Outside of the vineyard

9   What
Will the Lord of the vineyard do?
He will come and destroy the farmers
And will give the vineyard to others

10 Do you not read in the Scripture
The stone
Which the builders rejected
Has become the head of the corner
11 *This comes from the Lord*
And is wonderful in our eyes?

12 Then they tried to take him
But because they were aware
That this parable had been for them
They were afraid of the crowd
So they left him
And went away

The Pharisees ask a question about taxes
13 They sent to him
Some of the Pharisees
And some of the Herodians
So that they could catch him
In what he said

14   They came and said to him
        Teacher
        We know that you tell the truth
        And that no one's position
        Matters to you
        For you do not look
        At the status of men
        But truthfully
        Teach the way of God

        Is it lawful or not
        To pay the tax to Caesar?
        Should we pay it
        Or should we not pay it?

15   But knowing their hypocrisy
    He said to them
        Why do you tempt me?
        Bring me a denarius
        So that I may see it

16   Then they brought it

    He said to them
        Of whom is this portrait
        And whose is the inscription?

And they told him
It is Caesar's

17 So Jesus said to them
What belongs to Caesar
Give back to Caesar
And to God
What belongs to God
And they were amazed at him

The Sadducees ask a question about resurrection
18 Sadducees
Who say that there is no resurrection
Came to him
To ask a question
And said
19 Teacher
Moses wrote for us
That if any man's brother should die
Leaving behind a wife
But not leaving a child
He may take the wife
And raise up children
For his brother

20 There were seven brothers
And the first took a wife
When he died
He left no children

21 And the second
Took her and died
Not leaving behind any children

And in the same way
The third

22 All the seven left no children

Last of all
The wife died

23   In the resurrection
        When they rise again
        To which of them
        Will she be wife?
        For all the seven
        Had her as wife

24   Jesus said to them
            Is not this where you are wrong
            That you do not know the Scriptures
            Or the power of God?
25   For when they rise from the dead
            They neither marry
            Nor are given in marriage
            But are like angels
            In the heavens

26   But concerning the dead
        That they are raised

        Have you not read
        In the book of Moses
        How God spoke to him
        At the thorn-bush
        Saying
        I
        The God of Abraham
        And God of Isaac
        And God of Jacob?

27   He is not God of the dead
        But of the living

        You are quite wrong

A scribe asks about the commandments
28 One of the scribes approached
    And heard the debate
    So when he knew that Jesus
    Was well able to answer them
        He asked him
            Which commandment
            Is first of all?

29 Jesus answered
This is the first
Hear O Israel
The Lord our God
Is one Lord
30 *And you shall love*
The Lord your God
With all your heart
And with all your soul
And with all your mind
And with all your strength

31 This is the second
You shall love
Your neighbour as yourself

There is no other commandment
Greater than these

32 The scribe said to him
It is right
Teacher
And the truth
When you say
That there is one
And there is no other
Beside him
33 And to love him
With all the heart
And with all the understanding
And with all the strength
And to love
One's neighbour as oneself
Is more
Than all the burnt offerings
And sacrifices

34 When Jesus
Saw that he answered sensibly
He said to him
You are not far
From the kingdom of God

And no one dared
To question him further

A warning about the scribes
35   When he was teaching
In the Temple
    Jesus said
        How is it
        That the scribes say
        The Christ is the son of David?

36   For David himself said
        When in the Holy Spirit
        The Lord
        Said to my Lord
        Sit on my right hand
        Until I put your enemies
        Under your feet

37   As David himself calls him Lord
        How can he be his son?

The vast crowds
Listened to him gladly

38   And in his teaching
He said
        Pay no attention to the scribes
        Who wish to walk about
        In long robes
        And be greeted
        In the public places
39   Also to have the first seats
        In the synagogues
        And the best places at meals
40   Who eat up
        The inheritance of widows
        And make pretence
        Of long prayers

        They will be judged
        With greater severity

The widow's gift

41 As he sat down opposite the treasury
He observed how the crowds
Threw their money into the treasury
And how many rich men
Threw in a great deal

42 One poor widow came
And threw in
Two of the smallest coins
Which together make up a quadrans

43   He called his disciples to him
   And said to them
      Certainly I say to you
      This poor widow
      Has put in more
      Than all those others
      Who have given to the treasury

44   They have all given
   From what they had over
   But she
   Out of her need
   Threw in all that she possessed
   Indeed all her living

13

Jesus prophesies war and persecution

1 As he went out of the Temple
   One of his disciples
   Said to him
      Teacher
      Look at the kind of stones
      And the kind of buildings
      That are here

2   Jesus said to him
      Do you see these great buildings
      By no means will stone
      Be left upon stone
      That will not be thrown down

MARK 13

3   He sat on the Mount of Olives
Opposite the Temple
> Then Peter
> James
> John
> And Andrew
> Questioned him on their own

4   >> Tell us
>> When will this be
>> And what will be the sign
>> When all this
>> Is about to come to an end?

5   So Jesus began to say to them
> Watch out that no one misleads you
6   > Many will come in my name
> Saying
> I
> I am
> And will mislead many people

7   > When you hear battles
> And hear tell of battles
> Do not be disturbed
> This must happen
> But it is not yet the end

8   > Nation will rise against nation
> And kingdom against kingdom
> In places there will be earthquakes
> There will be famines
> These are the beginning
> Of the pangs of birth

9   > Watch out for yourselves
> They will hand you over to councils
> You will be beaten in synagogues
> And will stand
> Before governors and kings
> For my sake
> As a witness to them

10 But first
The Gospel must be preached
To all the nations

11 When they lead you away
To arrest you
Do not be anxious beforehand
About what you will say
But say
Whatever is given to you
In that hour
Because it is not you
Who speaks
But the Holy Spirit

12 And a brother
Will betray a brother to death
And a father
A child
And children
Will rise against parents
And put them to death

13 Everyone will hate you
Because of my name
But the one
Who remains steadfast to the end
Will be saved

14 But when you see
The abomination of desolation
Stand where it should not
Whoever reads
Let him understand
Then those in Judea
Should flee to the mountains

15 Whoever is on the roof
Should not come down
Or go into his house
To take anything out

16 Whoever is in the fields
Should not turn back
To take the cloak
Which he left behind

17 Alas for the woman
In those days
Who carries a child in her womb
Or has one at her breast

18 But pray
That it may not be in winter
19 Because those will be days
Of such persecution
As there has not been
From the beginning of creation
Which God created
Until now
And indeed may not be again

20 And unless the Lord
Cut short those days
No flesh would be saved
But for the sake of the elect
Whom he chose
He cut short those days

21 Then if any one tells you
Look
Here is the Christ
Or there
Do not believe it

22 False Christs
And false prophets
Will rise up
And will perform signs and portents
And if it is possible
Will even mislead the elect

23 But you yourselves
Should watch out
For I have told you
Everything beforehand

The coming of the Son of Man

24   In those days
After the persecution
Then the sun
Will be darkened
And the moon
Will not shed her beams
25   And the stars
Will fall out of heaven
And the powers in the heavens
Will be shaken

26   Then they will perceive
The Son of Man
Coming in clouds
With great power and glory

27   He will send out the angels
And will gather the elect
From the four winds
From the bounds of earth
To the bounds of heaven

28   And learn this parable
From the fig tree

When the branch becomes tender
And puts out leaves
You are aware
That the summer is near

29   So you also
When you see
That these things are happening
Are aware that he is near
At the doors

30   Certainly I say to you
That this generation will not pass
Before all this will happen
31   Heaven and earth
Will pass away
But my words
Will not pass away

32   About that day
Or that hour
No one knows
Neither the angels in heaven
Nor the Son
Only the Father

33   Watch out
Be wakeful
For you do not know
When the moment will be

34   It is as if a man
Going out of the country
On leaving his house
Gives his servants authority
And to each his work
And commands the doorkeeper
To watch

35   Therefore you should watch
As you do not know
When the Lord of the house
Will come
Whether in the evening
Or at cockcrow
Or in the morning
36   As he might come suddenly
And find you sleeping

37   What I say to you
I say to all
Watch

14   *The anointing at Bethany*

1   Now it was two days
Before the Passover
And the feast of Unleavened Bread
When the chief priests and the scribes
Aimed to take him by stealth
In order to kill him

MARK 14

2. Because they said
>> Not at the festival
>> As it might lead to disorder
>> Among the people

3. As he was in Bethany
In the house of Simon the leper
And was sitting at the table
A woman came
With an alabaster jar
Of valuable ointment of pure nard
She broke the jar
And poured it over his head

4. Now there were some
Who were indignant
> Saying to themselves
>> Why has there been this loss
>> Of the ointment?
5. >> For could not this ointment
>> Have been sold
>> For more than three hundred denarii
>> To be given to the poor?

And they were displeased with her

6. But Jesus said
> Leave her
> Why do you make trouble for her?
> It is an honourable deed
> Which she has performed on me

7. > The poor
> You always have with you
> And whenever you wish
> You have the means
> To treat them well
> But you do not always have me

8. > She has done what she could
> She has anointed my body beforehand
> For burial

9   Certainly I say to you
     Wherever this Gospel is preached
     In the whole world
     What she did
     Will also be related
     As a memorial to her

The betrayal

10 Then Judas Iscariot
   One of the twelve
   Went to the chief priests
   To betray him to them

11 When they heard it
   They were glad
   And promised to give him money
   So he looked for the right moment
   To betray him

Preparations for the Passover

12 On the first day of Unleavened Bread
   When they sacrificed the passover
    His disciples said to Jesus
     Where do you wish us to go
     So that we may prepare for you
     To eat the passover?

13 He sent out two of his disciples
    Saying to them
     Go into the city
     And a man
     Will meet you
     Who is carrying a jar of water
     Follow him
14   And wherever he goes in
     Tell the master of the house
     The Teacher says
     Where is my guest room
     Where I may eat the passover
     With my disciples?

15   He will show you
A large upper room
Which has been set out ready
There prepare for us

16 The disciples went out
And came into the city
There they found everything
As he had told them
And they prepared the Passover

The Last Supper
17 In the evening
He came with the twelve

18 As they were eating at the table
    Jesus said
        Certainly I say to you
        One of you
        Will betray me
        One who is eating with me

19 They began to feel sad
    And to say to him
    One by one
        Surely not I?

20 And he said to them
    It is one of the twelve
    The one who is dipping with me
    Into the same bowl
21   For indeed the Son of Man
    Is going
    As it has been written about him
    But alas for that man
    Through whom the Son of Man
    Is betrayed
    It would be better for that man
    If he had not been born

22   As they were eating
He took bread
And blessing it
He broke it
And gave it to them
    And said
        Take this
        It is my body

23   Then he took a cup
And giving thanks
He gave it to them
They all drank from it
24   And he said to them
        This is my blood
        Of the Covenant
        Which is poured out for many

25   Certainly I say to you
        No more will I drink
        Of the fruit of the vine
        Until that day
        When I drink it new
        In the kingdom of God

26   When they had sung a hymn
They went out
To the Mount of Olives

Jesus foretells Peter's denial
27   Jesus said to them
        All of you will give up
        Because it is written
        I will strike the shepherd
        And the sheep will be scattered
28   But after I am raised
        I will go before you to Galilee

29   Peter said to him
        Even if all give up
        Yet not I

30 Jesus said to him
>> Certainly I say to you
>> Today
>> In this night
>> Before a cock crows twice
>> You will disown me three times

31 But he protested all the more
>> If I must die with you
>> It is certain
>> That I will not disown you

And they all said the same

Jesus prays at Gethsemane
32 When they came to a place
The name of which was Gethsemane
> He said to his disciples
>> Sit here while I pray

33 He took with him
Peter
James
And John
And beginning to be overwhelmed with distress
34 > He said to them
>> My living soul is sorrowful unto death
>> Stay here and watch

35 Going forward a little way
He fell on the ground
And prayed
That if it were possible
The hour might pass away from him
36 > Saying
>> *Abba*
>> Father
>> With thee everything is possible
>> Remove this cup from me
>> But not what I
>> I will
>> But thou

37   When he came
    He found them sleeping
        And said to Peter
            Simon
            Are you asleep?
            Had you no strength
            To watch one hour?
38   Watch and pray
            That you do not come into temptation
            Indeed the spirit is eager
            But the flesh is weak

39   Again
    He went away and prayed
    Saying the same words

40   Then again
    When he came
    He found them sleeping
    As their eyes had become heavy
    And they did not know
    How to answer him

41   The third time
        He came and said to them
            Sleep now and rest
            It is enough
            The hour has come
            You see that the Son of Man
            Is betrayed into the hands of sinners
42   Get up
            Let us go
            Look how near is my betrayer

The arrest

43   Immediately
    While he was still speaking
    Judas
    One of the twelve
    Arrived with a crowd
    With swords and clubs
    From the chief priests
    The scribes
    And the elders

44   The betrayer
      Had agreed to give them a signal
          Saying
              Whoever I kiss
              He it is
              Take him
              And lead him away securely

45   When he came
      He went up to him at once
          And said
              Rabbi

    And kissed him warmly

46   Then they laid their hands on him
      To take him

47   But one of those
      Who were standing there
      Drew his sword
      And struck the high priest's servant
      Taking off his ear

48   Jesus said to them
            Have you come out
            As if against a robber
            To capture me
            With swords and clubs?
49   I was with you every day
            Teaching in the Temple
            And you did not take me
            But the Scripture
            Should be fulfilled

50   Then they all left him
      And fled

51   And accompanying him
      Was a young man
      Who was wrapped round
52   With a linen cloth
      Over his nakedness

They took hold of him
And he left the linen cloth
And fled naked

Jesus before the council
53   They led Jesus away
     To the high priest
     Where all the chief priests
     The elders
     And the scribes
     Had come together

54   Peter followed him at a distance
     Until he was inside the courtyard
     Of the high priest
     Where he sat with the attendants
     And warmed himself in the firelight

55   The chief priests
     And all the council
     Looked for witnesses against Jesus
     To put him to death
     But they did not find any

56   There were many false witnesses
     Against him
     But their witness did not agree

57   Some false witnesses stood up
         And said
58   We heard him saying
             I myself
             Will overthrow this shrine
             Made with hands
             And after three days
             I will build another
             Not made with hands

59   But even then
     Their witness did not agree

60   The high priest
Rose up among them to question Jesus
    And asked him
        Do you not answer
        These witnesses against you?

61   But he was silent
And did not answer

    The high priest
    Questioned him again
        Are you the Christ
        The Son of the Blessed?

62   Jesus said
    I
    I AM
    And you will see
    The Son of Man
    Sitting on the right of the Power
    And coming with the clouds of heaven

63   The high priest
Tore his tunic and said
    Why do we need more witnesses
64   You heard the blasphemy
    How does it appear to you?

And they all condemned him to death

65   Some be to spit at him
And to cover his face
And strike him with their fists
    Saying to him
        Prophesy

Then the attendants
Took him and slapped him

Peter's denial
66   Peter was below in the courtyard
When one of the high priest's maidservants
67   Came and saw Peter warming himself
She looked closely at him

And said
> You were with Jesus
> The Nazarene

68 But he denied it
And said
> I neither know
> Nor can understand
> What you are saying

Then he went outside
Into the forecourt
And a cock crowed

69 The maidservant saw him
> And again
> > Began saying to those standing there
> > > He is one of them

70 But again
He denied it

After a little while
> Those standing there
> Said to Peter
> > It is true
> > > That you are one of them
> > > For you are a Galilean

71 He began to curse
> And to swear
> > I do not know the man
> > Of whom you are speaking

72 Immediately
A cock crowed a second time

Then Peter remembered the words
Which Jesus had said to him
Before the cock crows twice
You will disown me three times

And upon this
He wept

15 *Jesus before Pilate*

1   As soon as it was dawn
    The chief priests
    The elders
    And the scribes
    Together with the whole council
    Made their preparations

    Then having tied up Jesus
    They led him away
    And handed him over to Pilate

2   Pilate asked him
            Are you
                The King of the Jews?

    Jesus answered
        You say so

3   Then the chief priests
    Accused him of many things

4   Again
        Pilate asked him
            Do you not give any answer?
            See how they accuse you
            Of so much

5   But Pilate was astonished
    That Jesus answered nothing more

6   At a festival
    Pilate
    Released to them one prisoner
    For whom they entreated

7   There was a prisoner
    Called Barabbas
    Who had joined those rebels
    Who had committed murder in the rebellion

8   The crowds gathered
And began to ask Pilate
To do for them
As he had usually done

9   Pilate answered them
            Do you wish me
            To release to you
            The King of the Jews?

10   As he was aware
That it was because of their jealousy
The chief priests
Had handed him over

11   But the chief priests
Roused up the crowd
To have him release to them
Barabbas

12   Again
Pilate said to them
        What shall I do
        To him
        Whom you call
        The King of the Jews?

13   Again
They cried out
        Crucify him

14   But Pilate said to them
        Why
        What evil has he done?

They cried out all the more
        Crucify him

15   Pilate
Intent on satisfying the crowd
Released for them
Barabbas

Then having had Jesus scourged
He handed him over
To be crucified

Jesus mocked by the soldiers
16 The soldiers led him away
Into the courtyard
That is
Into the praetorium
And called the whole company together

17 They dressed him in purple
And plaiting a thorny crown
They placed it on him

18   Then they began to salute him
        Hail
        King of the Jews!

19 They struck his head
With a reed
And spat at him
And bending their knees
They worshipped him

20 When they had mocked him
They took the purple off him
And put on him his own clothes

Then they led him out
To crucify him

The Crucifixion
21 They pressed a passer-by into service
To carry his cross
He was Simon
A Cyrenian coming from the country
The father of Alexander and Rufus

22 They brought Jesus
To the place called Golgotha
Which means
The place of a skull

23   Where they gave him wine
       Mixed with myrrh
       But he did not receive it

24   Then they crucified him
       And divided his clothing
       Throwing dice
       As to what each should take

25   It was the third hour
       When they crucified him

26   And over him was written
       An inscription
       It was the accusation against him
       THE KING OF THE JEWS

27   With him they crucified two bandits
       One on his right
       And one on his left

28   So the Scripture was fulfilled
       Which said
       He was numbered
       With those who broke the Law

29   The people passing by blasphemed him
         Shaking their heads
         And saying
            Aha
            You who would overthrow the shrine
            And build it in three days
30   Save yourself
            Come down from the cross

31   The chief priests and scribes
       Also mocked him
         Saying to one another
            He saved others
            He cannot save himself
32   Let the Christ
            The King of Israel
            Come down from the cross
            So that we may see and believe

And those crucified with him
Reproached him

33 When the sixth hour had come
Darkness came over all the earth
Until the ninth hour

34 At the ninth hour
    Jesus called out in a loud voice
        Eloi
        Eloi
        Lama sabachthani?
        (Which is translated
        My God
        My God
        Why hast thou forsaken me?)

35 Some of those who stood there
When they heard it
Said
    See
    He calls Elijah

36 Then someone ran
And filling a sponge with vinegar
Put it on a reed
And gave it to him to drink
    Saying
        Leave him
        Let us see if Elijah
        Will come to take him down

37 But Jesus
Let out a loud cry
And drew his last breath

38 The curtain of the shrine
Was torn in two
From top to bottom

39 When the centurion
Who was standing there facing him
Saw that he thus
Drew his last breath

He said
> It is true that this man
> Was a Son of God

40 Some women
Were watching from a distance
Among them Mary Magdalene
Mary
Mother of the younger James and of Joses
And Salome
41 Who had followed him and served him
When he was in Galilee
And also many others
Who had come up with him
To Jerusalem

The burial

42 As it was the day of Preparation
Which is the day before the sabbath
When evening came
43 Joseph of Arimathea
A respected counsellor
Who himself was awaiting
The kingdom of God
Gathered his courage
And going into Pilate
He asked for the body of Jesus

44 Pilate
Wondered if he could already be dead
And calling the centurion
Enquired of him
Whether he had been dead for some time

45 On hearing from the centurion
He granted the dead body
To Joseph

46 He had purchased a length of linen
So taking him down
He wrapped him in the linen
And deposited him in a tomb
Which had been hewn out of the rock

Then he rolled a stone
Against the door of the tomb

47   Mary Magdalene
And Mary
The mother of Joses
Watched where he had been laid

16 *The women at the tomb*

1   When the sabbath was over
Mary Magdalene
Mary the mother of James
And Salome
Went to buy spices
So that when they came
They could anoint him

2   Very early
On the first day after the sabbath
They came to the tomb
As the sun was rising
3   And said to one another
Who will roll away the stone for us
From the door of the tomb?

4   On looking up they observed
That the great stone
Had been rolled back

5   Going into the tomb
They saw a young man
Clothed in a white robe
Sitting on the right side
And they were exceedingly astonished

6   But he said to them
Do not be so astonished
You are looking for Jesus
The Nazarene

MARK 16

    Having been crucified
    He was raised
    He is not here
    See the place where they laid him

7   Go and tell his disciples
    And Peter
    That he is going before you
    To Galilee
    There you will see him
    As he told you

8   And they went out
    And fled from the tomb
    For trembling and bewilderment
    Had taken hold of them
    And they said nothing to any one
    Because they were afraid

The shorter ending
They reported briefly
To Peter and those with him
All that had been commanded them

And after this
Jesus himself sent out through them
From the East as far as the West
Through all the ages
The sacred and imperishable
Message of salvation

The longer ending
9   Having risen early
    On the day following the sabbath
    He appeared first to Mary Magdalene
    From whom
    He had cast out seven demons

10   She brought the news
    To those who had been with him
    Who were mourning and weeping

11 When they heard
    That he is alive
    And she has had sight of him
    They did not believe her

12 After this
    As two of them
    Walked into the country
    He appeared to them
    In a different form

13 They brought back the news
    To the rest
    But they did not believe them either

14 Later
    He appeared to the eleven
    As they sat at table
    And he reproached them
    For their unbelief
    And closed hearts and minds
    Because they did not believe
    Those who had sight of him
    After he had been raised

15   And he said to them
            Go into all the world
            And preach the Gospel
            To all creation

16   Whoever believes
            And is baptized
            Will be saved
            But whoever does not believe
            Will be condemned

17   Those who believe
            Will have signs
            Which accompany them

18   In my name
            They will cast out demons
            And they will speak in new tongues
            They will pick up serpents

> And if they drink any poison
> It will certainly not hurt them
> They will place their hands
> On sick people
> And they will be well

19 Therefore after speaking to them
The Lord Jesus
Was taken up into heaven
And sat on the right of God

20 But they went out
And preached everywhere
The Lord working with them
And confirming the word
With the signs
Which accompanied them

The Gospel of Luke

1 *Prologue*

1 Since many have taken in hand
To set down an account
Of all those events
Which certainly took place among us
2 As they were committed to us
By those who from the beginning
Were themselves able to see
And to become ministers of the word
3 It seemed good to me also
Having been able to follow all things
From their outset
To write an orderly account for you
Most excellent Theophilus
4 So that you could be aware
Of the accuracy of the teaching
In which you have been instructed

The Angel comes to Zechariah

5 It so happened
That during the reign of Herod
King of Judea
That there was a certain priest
Belonging to the group of Abijah
Whose name was Zechariah

His wife was descended from Aaron
And she was called Elizabeth

6 They were both upright people
In the sight of God
Not failing to keep all the commandments
And regulations of the Lord
7 But they had no children
Because Elizabeth was barren
And they were both advanced in age

8   Then it happened
That he was acting as priest before God
In his order of service
9   And according to the custom of priesthood
It fell to him by lot
To enter the shrine of the Lord
And burn incense
10   While all the many people
Were praying outside
At the hour of the censing

11   An angel of the Lord
Appeared to him
Standing on the right side
Of the altar of incense

12   When he saw this
Zechariah was disturbed
And fear fell upon him

13   But the angel said to him
        Do not be afraid
        Zechariah
     Because your request has been heard
     Your wife Elizabeth
     Will bear you a son
     And you shall give him the name
     John

14   You will have joy
     And great happiness
     And many will rejoice
     At his birth
15   As he will be great
     In the sight of the Lord

     He shall not drink any wine
     Or strong drink
     He will be filled
     With the Holy Spirit
     Even from his mother's womb
16   And will turn many
     Of the sons of Israel
     To the Lord their God

17   He will go forth in his sight
            In the spirit and power of Elijah
            To turn the father's hearts
            To the children
            And the rebellious
            To an understanding of what is right
            Preparing for the Lord
            A people who are ready for him

18   Zechariah said to the angel
            How shall I become aware of this
            As I myself am an old man
            And my wife is advanced in age

19   The angel answered him
            I
            I am Gabriel
            Who stand in the presence of God
            I was sent out to speak to you
            And to bring you this good news

20   But see
            Now you will be silenced
            And not have the power to speak
            Until this happens
            Because you did not believe
            My words
            Which will be fulfilled
            In their season

21   The people were expecting Zechariah
        And they were astonished
        That he delayed in the shrine

22   When he came out
        He had not the power to speak
        And they became aware
        That he had seen a vision
        In the shrine
        As he signed to them
        And remained dumb

23 And when his term of service
    Came to an end
    He went back to his home

24 After this
    His wife Elizabeth conceived
    And hid herself for five months
        Saying
25   This is what the Lord
                Has done for me
                When he looked upon me
                To take away my disgrace
                Among the people

The Angel Gabriel comes to Mary
26 Now in the sixth month
    The angel Gabriel
    Was sent out from God
    To a town in Galilee
    Which was called Nazareth

27 To a virgin
    Promised in marriage
    To a man whose name was Joseph
    Belonging to the house of David
    And the virgin's name
    Was Mary

28 When he came to her
        He said
            Rejoice
            You have been shown favour
            The Lord is with you

29 She was much troubled
    By what he said
    And considered
    What sort of greeting
    This could be

30   And the angel said to her
            Do not be afraid
            Mary

31 Because you have found favour
    With God
    And see
    You will conceive
    And bear a son
    To whom you should give the name
    Jesus

32 He will be great
    And will be called
    The Son of the Most High
    And the Lord God
    Will give him the throne
    Of his father David

33 And he will reign
    Over the house of Jacob
    Throughout the ages
    And his kingdom
    Will have no end

34 Mary said to the angel
        How will this come about
        As I have no knowledge of man?

35 The angel answered her
        The Holy Spirit will come upon you
        And the power of the Highest
        Will overshadow you
        Therefore
        The child who will be born
        Will be called holy
        Son of God

36   And see
        Your cousin Elizabeth
        Has also conceived a son
        In her old age
        And this is her sixth month
        Although she was considered barren

37   Because nothing which he says
        Will be impossible for God

38   Mary replied
           See here
           The servant of the Lord
           Let it happen to me
           As you have said

And the angel
Went away from her

Mary visits her cousin Elizabeth

39 In those days
Mary set out
And hurried into the hill country
To a town in Judea
40 Where she entered Zechariah's house
And greeted Elizabeth
41 And so it happened
That when Elizabeth
Heard Mary's greeting
The unborn babe leaped in her womb

Elizabeth was filled with the Holy Spirit
42   And she called out
    With a loud cry
        Blessing on you among women
        And blessing
        On the fruit of your womb
43   What does this mean for me
    That the mother of my Lord
    Has come to me?
44   As indeed
    When the sound of your greeting
    Came to my ears
    The babe in my womb
    Leaped for joy

45   She is blessed
    Who has believed
    That what the Lord
    Has said to her
    Will be fulfilled

46 And Mary said
    My living soul
    Gives high praise to the Lord
47   And my spirit
    Rejoiced in God my saviour
48   Because he has looked upon
    His servant's humility

    See how from this time
    All generations will call me blessed
49   Because the Mighty One
    Has done great things for me
    And holy is his name

50   He is merciful
    To those who fear him
    From generation to generation

51   He acted
    With the strength of his arm
    He scattered the proud people
    Their hearts' desires came to nothing

52   He brought down the powerful
    From their thrones
    And raised up the humble

53   Those who were hungry
    He filled with good things
    Those who were rich
    He sent away empty

54   He gave help to his servant Israel
    Remembering mercy
    As he had said to our fathers
    To Abraham
    And to his descendants
    Until the ending of the age

56 Mary remained with her
For about three months
Then returned to her home

The birth of John the Baptist

57 When Elizabeth's time was fulfilled
She bore a son

58 Then her neighbours
And her family
On hearing that the Lord
Had shown her great mercy
Rejoiced with her

59 On the eighth day
They came to circumcise the child
And would have given him the name
Zechariah
After his father

60   But his mother said
        No
    He must be called John

61   And they said to her
        No one in your family
        Has been given this name

62 They made signs to the father
As to what name
He wished him to have

63   He asked for a writing tablet
        And wrote
            His name is John

And they were all astonished

64 Instantly
His mouth was opened
And when his tongue was set free
He spoke in praise of God

65 Fear came upon all the neighbourhood
And these things were discussed
In the hill country of Judea

66 All those who heard of them
Kept them in their hearts
   And said
      What will become of this child?

67 As indeed
The hand of the Lord
Was with him

68 His father Zechariah
Was filled with the Holy Spirit
   And he prophesied
   Saying
      Blessing on the Lord God of Israel
      Because he has come to his people
      And he has obtained their release
69   Raising for us
      A powerful saviour
      From the house of his servant David
70   As he told us
      Through the mouth
      Of his holy prophets of old
71   That we should be saved
      From our enemies
      And out of the hands
      Of all who hate us

72   This mercy
      He granted to our forefathers
      In remembrance of his holy covenant
73   And the oath
      Which he swore to our father Abraham
      That he would give us

74   As we have been delivered
      Out of the hands of our enemies
      We may serve him without fear
75   With piety and justice in his sight
      All our days

76   And you child
      Will also be called
      A prophet of the Most High
      As you will go before the Lord

	To make ready his road
77	Bringing knowledge of salvation
	To his people
	In forgiving their sins

78	Because of the compassionate mercy
	Of our God
	Whereby the sun
	Which rises in high heaven
	Will visit us
79	Appearing
	To those who sit in darkness
	And in the shadow of death
	To guide our feet
	On to a road of peace

80	The child grew
	And became strong in spirit

He was in the desert
Until those days
When he appeared openly
Among the people of Israel

2 *The birth of Jesus in Bethlehem*

1	Now it happened in those days
	That a decree
	Went out from Caesar Augustus
	That all those living in the land
	Should be registered

2	This first registration
	Was made when Quirinius
	Governed Syria
3	And all the people
	Went to be registered
	Every one to his own city

4	Therefore Joseph
	Also went up out of Galilee
	From the town of Nazareth
	To Judea
	To the city of David
	Which is called Bethlehem

Because he belonged
   To the house and family of David

5 To be registered with Mary
   His promised bride
   Who was with child

6 Now it so happened
   That while they were there
   The number of her days was completed
7 And she gave birth
   To her first born son

   She wrapped him in linen bands
   And laid him in a manger
   Because there was no room for them
   In the inn

8 In that region there were shepherds
   Who remained out in the fields
   Guarding their flock during the night

9 And an angel of the Lord
   Came upon them
   And the glory of the Lord
   Shone around them
   And they were shaken with fear

10   The angel said to them
           Do not be afraid
           See how I bring you
           News of great joy
           Which will come to all the people

11   Today
       In the city of David
       A saviour has been born to you
       Who is Christ the Lord

12   And this will be a sign
       For you
       You will find a new born babe
       Wrapped in linen bands
       And lying in a manger

13 All of a sudden
A great heavenly host
Was there with the angel
    Giving praise to God and saying
14   Glory to God in the heights
        And peace on the earth
        Among men of good will

15 When the angels
Had gone away from them
Into heaven
    The shepherds said to one another
        Let us go to Bethlehem
        And see what has taken place there
        Which the Lord
        Has revealed to us

16 They came with all speed
And found Mary and Joseph
With the new-born babe
Who was lying in the manger

17 When they had seen it
They spread the news
Of what had been said to them
Concerning this child

18 And all who heard it
Were astonished
At what the shepherds told them

19 But Mary
Stored up all these things
Dwelling on them in her heart

20 And the shepherds returned
Giving glory and praise to God
As all
That they had heard and seen
Was just as they had been told

Jesus is circumcised
21 After eight days
    He was circumcised
    And he was given the name
    Jesus
    Which he was called by the angel
    Before he was conceived in the womb

Jesus is presented in the Temple
22 When the days of their purification
    Were completed
    According to the Law of Moses
    They took him up to Jerusalem
    To present him to the Lord

23 As it is written in his Law
    Every male who is the first born
    Shall be called holy to the Lord
24 And to make an offering
    As it is laid down
    By the Law of the Lord
    A pair of turtle doves
    Or two little pigeons

25 Now there was a man in Jerusalem
    Whose name was Simeon
    This man was upright and devout
    Expecting comfort for Israel
    And the Holy Spirit was upon him

26 He had been warned
    By the Holy Spirit
    That he should not see death
    Before he had seen
    The Lord's Christ

27 Lead by the Spirit
    He came into the Temple
    When the child Jesus' parents
    Brought him in
    To do for him
    What was required of them
    By the custom of the Law

28 He took him into his arms
And praised God
   And said
29   Now Master
      Release your servant
      To go in peace
      According to what you have said
30   Because my eyes have seen
      Your salvation
31   Which you have made ready
      In the sight of all the peoples
32   A light of revelation
      To the Gentiles
      And the glory of your people Israel

33 His father and mother
Were astonished
At what was said about him

34 Simeon blessed them
   And said to his mother Mary
      See
      This is the one who is destined
      To cause the fall and resurrection
      Of many in Israel
      And for a sign which is disputed
35   And a sword
      Will also pierce your own soul
      That the thoughts of many hearts
      May be revealed

36 There was Anna
A prophetess
Who was a daughter of Phanuel
Of the tribe of Asher

She was advanced in age
Having lived with her husband
Seven years from her virginity
37 And then as a widow
Until she was eighty-four years old

Now she did not leave the Temple
Serving night and day
With fasting and earnest prayer

38 Coming upon them
Just at that hour
She gave thanks to God
And she spoke about him
To all those in Jerusalem
Who were expecting their deliverance

39 When everything had been done
According to the divine Law
They went back to Nazareth in Galilee
Which was their home town

40 The child grew
Becoming strong and filled with wisdom
And the grace of God
Was upon him

The twelve year old Jesus in the temple
41 His parents
Went up to Jerusalem every year
For the Passover festival
42 And when he reached twelve years old
They went up to the festival
According to their custom

43 When the days
Were at an end
And they set out to return
The boy Jesus remained in Jerusalem
Although his parents
Did not become aware of it

44 But thinking he was in the company
They went a day's journey
Before they looked for him
Among their relations
And the people whom they knew

45 When they did not find him
   They went back to Jerusalem
   To search for him

46 And it so happened
   That after three days
   They found him in the Temple
   Sitting surrounded by the teachers
   Listening to them
   And asking them questions

47 Everyone who heard him
   Was astonished
   At his understanding
   And his answers

48 When they saw him
   They were amazed
      And his mother said to him
         Child
         Why have you done this to us?
         See how your father
         And I myself
         Have been searching for you
         In great distress

49 And he said to them
      Why were you searching for me
      Did you not know
      That I must be in my Father's house?

50 But they did not understand
   What he said to them

51 Going down with them
   He came to Nazareth
   And obeyed them
   But his mother
   Guarded all these things carefully
   In her heart

52 And Jesus progressed in wisdom
   And in stature

And in the favour of God
And of his fellow men

3　　*The preaching of John the Baptist*
1　　Now in the fifteenth year
　　Of the government of Tiberius Caesar
　　When Pontius Pilate
　　Was governing Judea
　　And Herod
　　Was ruling as Tetrarch of Galilee
　　And his brother Philip
　　Ruling as Tetrarch
　　Of the country of Ituraea and Trachonites
　　And Lysanias as Tetrarch of Abilene
2　　When Annas and Caiaphas
　　Were the high priests

　　Word came from God
　　To John
　　Son of Zechariah
　　Who was in the desert

3　　And he came into all the region
　　Of the Jordan
　　Preaching a baptism
　　To change heart and mind
　　For the forgiveness of sins

4　　As it is written in the scroll
　　Of the words of Isaiah the prophet
　　A voice calling in the desert
　　Prepare the road of the Lord
　　Make his paths straight

5　　*Every hollow will be filled up*
　　And every mountain and hill
　　Will be brought low
　　The crooked ways
　　Will be made straight
　　And the rough roads
　　Made into smooth

6 *And all flesh*
Will see the salvation of God

7 So he said to the crowds
Who came out
To be baptized by him
> Offspring of vipers
> Who warned you
> To escape from the anger
> Which is to come?

8 > Therefore bear fruits
> Worthy of your change of heart
> And do not begin
> To say among yourselves
> We have Abraham as our father
> As I say to you
> God has the power
> To raise up children to Abraham
> Even from these stones

9 > The axe is already laid
> At the root of the trees
> So that every tree
> Which does not bear sound fruit
> Is cut down
> And thrown into the fire

10 And the people asked him
> What should we do?

11 He answered them
> Anyone who has two tunics
> Should share with whoever has none
> And anyone who has food
> Should do the same

12 Tax collectors
Also came to be baptized
And they said to him
> Teacher
> What should we do?

13   He said to them
           Only carry out your instructions

14   Serving soldiers asked him
           We also
           What should we do?

       And he told them
           Do not intimidate anyone
           Or accuse them falsely
           And be satisfied with your pay

15 The people expected something
But they were all
Questioning in their hearts
About John
If perhaps he could be the Christ

16   But he answered them all
           I
           I indeed baptize you
           With water
           But there is one who is coming
           Who is stronger than I
           The thong of whose sandals
           I am not worthy to untie
           He will baptize you
           With Holy Spirit
           And with fire

17   The winnowing fan is in his hand
      He will sweep clean
      His threshing floor
      And gather the wheat
      Into his barn
      But the chaff
      He will burn with a fire
      That cannot be put out

18 Giving advice to the people
In many different ways
He brought the good news

Herod puts John in prison

19 But Herod the tetrarch
When he was rebuked by him
Because of Herodias
His brother's wife
And because of all the wicked things
Which Herod had done
20 Added this above all
That he shut up John in prison.

The Baptism of Jesus Christ

21 Now it happened
When all the people had been baptized
And Jesus had been baptized
And was praying
That the heaven was opened
22 And the Holy Spirit
Descended on him
In visible form
As a dove

> And a voice came out of heaven
>> You are my son
>> The beloved
>> Today I have brought you to birth

The ancestry of Jesus

23 And Jesus himself
Began his work
When he was about thirty years old
Being
As he was supposed
The son of Joseph
Who was the son of Heli

24 The son of Matthat
The son of Levi
The son of Melchi
The son of Jannai
The son of Joseph

25 Who was the son of Mattathias
The son of Amos
The son of Nahum
The son of Esli
The son of Naggai

26 Who was the son of Maath
The son of Mattathias
The son of Semein
The son of Josech
The son of Joda

27 Who was the son of Joanan
The son of Rhesa
The son of Zerubbabel
The son of Shealtiel
The son of Neri

28 Who was the son of Melchi
The son of Addi
The son of Cosam
The son of Elmadam
The son of Er

29 Who was the son of Joshua
The son of Eliezer
The son of Jorim
The son of Matthat
The son of Levi

30 Who was the son of Simeon
The son of Judah
The son of Joseph
The son of Jonam
The son of Eliakim

31 Who was the son of Melea
The son of Menna
The son of Mattatha
The son of Nathan
The son of David

32 Who was the son of Jesse
The son of Obed

The son of Boaz
The son of Sala
The son of Nahshon

33 Who was the son of Amminadab
The son of Admin
The son of Arni
The son of Hezron
The son of Perez
The son of Judah

34 Who was the son of Jacob
The son of Isaac
The son of Abraham
The son of Terah
The son of Nahor

35 Who was the son of Serug
The son of Reu
The son of Peleg
The son of Eber
The son of Shelah

36 Who was the son of Cainan
The son of Arphaxad
The son of Shem
The son of Noah
The son of Lamech

37 Who was the son of Methuselah
The son of Enoch
The son of Jared
The son of Mahalaleel
The son of Cainan
38 The son of Enos
The son of Seth
The son of Adam
Who was the son of God

4 *The Temptation*
1 Jesus returned from the Jordan
Full of the Holy Spirit

LUKE 4

2   For forty days
He was led in the spirit
Through the desert
Tempted by the devil

And during those days
He did not eat anything
So that when they came to an end
He was hungry

3   And the devil said to him
If you are God's son
Tell this stone
To become a loaf of bread

4   Jesus answered him
It has been written
Mankind
Shall not only live on bread

5   He led him high up
And showed him
All the kingdoms of the civilized world
In a moment of time

6   And the devil said to him
I will give you
All this authority
And their glory
Because it has been delivered to me
And I may give it
To whom ever I wish

7   If therefore
You will bow down before me
All will be yours

8   Jesus answered him
It has been written
You shall worship
The Lord your God
And you shall only serve him

9   He led him to Jerusalem
      And set him
      On the parapet of the Temple
          And said to him
              If you are God's son
              Throw yourself down from here
10   As it has been written
              He will command his angels
              To watch over you
11   *And on their hands*
              They will carry you
              Lest you strike your foot
              Against a stone

12   Jesus answered him
          It has been said
          You shall not
          Put the Lord your God
          To the test

13   When the devil
      Had come to the end
      Of all the temptations
      He went away from him
      Until there should be an opportunity

Jesus preaches in Nazareth
14   Jesus returned to Galilee
      In the power of the spirit
      And there was talk of him
      Throughout the countryside

15   He taught in the synagogues
      And all the people praised him

16   He came to Nazareth
      Where he had been brought up
      And on the sabbath day
      As was usual with him
      He went into the synagogue
      And stood up to read

17   A scroll of the prophet Isaiah
Was given to him
He unwound the scroll
And found the place
Where there was written

18   *The spirit of the Lord*
Is upon me
Because he has anointed me
To preach good news to the poor

He has sent me
To announce the release
Of those taken prisoner
To give sight to the blind
And liberty
To those who are oppressed
19   *To proclaim a year*
Which is acceptable to the Lord

20   When he had wound up the scroll
And returned it to the attendant
He sat down
And the eyes
Of all those in the synagogue
Were fastened on him

21   Then he began to speak to them
    And said
        Today has this Scripture
        Been fulfilled in your ears

22   Everyone paid attention to him
And they were astonished
At the gracious words
Which came from his mouth

    And they said
        Is he not Joseph's son?

23   He said to them
        You will certainly quote to me
        This proverb
        Physician

                Heal yourself
                We have heard
                What has happened in Capernaum
                Now do these things
                Here in your native place

24   And he said
                Certainly I say to you
                No prophet is accepted
                In his native place

25   But I am telling you the truth
                There were many widows
                In Israel
                In the days of Elijah
                When the heavens were closed
                For three years and six months
                And there was great famine
                Over all the land

26   And Elijah
                Was not sent
                To any one of them
                But to a woman
                Living in Zarephath in Sidon

27   And there were many lepers
                In Israel
                When Elisha was a prophet
                But not one of them
                Was cleansed
                Except Naaman the Syrian

28   All those in the synagogue
        Were filled with anger
        When they heard this

29   And they rose up
        And cast him out of the town

        They led him
        To a ridge of the hill
        On which their town was built

So that they could throw him down
Over the precipice

30　But he passed between them
And went away

A demoniac is healed in Capernaum
31　He went down to Capernaum
Which is a town in Galilee
And he taught them on the sabbath
32　They were amazed at his teaching
Because his words had authority

33　There was a man in the synagogue
Who had the spirit of an unclean demon
　　And he shouted out aloud
34　　　Ah
　　　What is between us and you
　　　Jesus Nazarene?
　　　Have you come to destroy us?
　　　I know who you are
　　　The Holy One of God

35　Jesus spoke sternly to him
And said
　　Be silenced
　　And come out of him

And throwing him down
Among them all
The demon came out of him
Without doing any harm

36　They were all astonished
　　And said to one another
　　　What word is this?
　　　Because with authority and power
　　　He commands the unclean spirits
　　　And they come out

37　The echo
Of what he was doing
Went out into all the surrounding country

LUKE 4

The healing of Simon's mother-in-law

38 He rose up
And left the synagogue

Then he went into Simon's house
Where Simon's mother-in-law
Was suffering from a high fever
And they asked him about her

39 He stood over her
And spoke sternly to the fever
And it left her

At once she rose up
And served them

Jesus heals at sunset

40 When the sun was setting
All those
Who had anyone suffering
From any kind of disease
Brought them to him
And putting his hands
On each one of them
He healed them
41 And as the demons
Also came out of many people
    They cried out and said
        You are the Son of God

He silenced them
And would not allow them
To speak
Because they knew him
To be the Christ

Jesus preaches throughout the land

42 At day break
He went out to a desert place

> The people searched for him
> And when they came to him
> They tried to prevent him from leaving them

43   But he said to them
>> I must also preach the good news
>> Of the kingdom of God
>> In other towns
>> Because it was for this
>> That I have been sent out

44 And he preached
In the synagogues of Judea

5

Simon's great catch of fish

1 It happened
When the people crowded round him
To hear the word of God
That he was standing
By the lake of Gennesaret

2 And he saw two small boats
Beside the lake
But the fishermen had left them
And were washing the nets

3 He embarked
In one of the boats
Which belonged to Simon
And asked him to put out
A little way from the land

Then sitting in the boat
He taught the crowds

4 When he had finished speaking
> He said to Simon
>> Put out into deep water
>> And let down your nets
>> for a catch

5   Simon answered
> Master
> We have worked hard all night

                    And have taken nothing
                    But as you ask
                    I will let down the nets

6   They did this
    And enclosed a great many fish
    Tearing their nets

7   They beckoned to their partners
    In the other boat
    To come and help them
    And they came
    And filled both the boats
    So that they were sinking

8   When Simon Peter saw this
    He fell at the feet of Jesus
        And said
            Leave me
            Lord
            Because I am a sinful man

9   He was overcome with amazement
    At the catch of fish
    Which they had taken
10 As were all those with him
    Both James and John
    The sons of Zebedee
    Who shared with Simon

        Jesus said to Simon
            Do not be afraid
            From now on
            You will capture men

11 They brought the boat to land
    And left everything
    To follow him

    The healing of a leper
12 He was in one of the towns
    And there was a man
    Full of leprosy

When he saw Jesus
He fell on his face
   And entreated him
      Lord
      If you will
      You are able to make me clean

13 Jesus stretched out his hand
And touched him
   Saying
      I will
      You shall be clean

At once
The leprosy left him

14 But Jesus impressed on him
That he should not tell anyone
   And said
      Go and show yourself
      To the priest
      And offer for your cleansing
      What Moses commanded
      As evidence to them

15 The news about him
Spread all the more
And large crowds went with him
To listen
And to be healed of their disabilities

16 But he withdrew into the desert
And prayed

The healing of a paralytic
17 It so happened on one of these days
When he was teaching
That Pharisees
And teachers of the Law
Were sitting there
They had come from every village
In Galilee and Judea
And from Jerusalem

And the power of the Lord
Was in him to heal

18   Then there came some men
Carrying on a mattress
A man who was paralysed
And they made efforts
To bring him in
And to lay him down
In the presence of Jesus

19   Because of the crowd
They could not find a way
To bring him in
So they went up on to the roof
And let him down through the tiles
So that he lay on his mattress
Among them all
In front of Jesus

20   When he saw their faith
   He said
      Man
      Your sins have been forgiven you

21   The scribes and the Pharisees
Began a discussion
   And said
      Who is this?
      He speaks blasphemies
      Who has the power to forgive sins
      Except God alone?

22   But Jesus
Knew what they discussed
   And answered them
      Why are you considering this
      In your hearts

23   Is it easier to say
   Your sins are forgiven
   Or to say
   Get up and walk?

24   Only that you may know

That the Son of Man
Has authority on the earth
To forgive sins

He said to the man
Who was paralysed
   I say to you
   Get up
   And taking you mattress
   Go to your home

25 He rose up at once
In front of them
And taking the mattress
On which he had been lying
He went away to his house
Praising God

26 Astonishment
Took hold of them all
And they praised God

Filled with fear
   They said
      We saw strange things today

The calling of Levi
27 After this he went out
And beheld a tax-gatherer
Whose name was Levi
Sitting in the custom house
   And he said to him
      Follow me

28 He rose up
And leaving everything
Followed him

Jesus teaches in Levi's house
29 Then Levi
Made him a great feast
In his own house

Where a large number of tax-collectors
And of others
Were with them at the table

30   The Pharisees and the scribes
Grumbled at his disciples
   Saying
      Why do you eat and drink
      With tax-collectors
      And with outcasts?

31   But Jesus answered them
   It is not
   Those who have good health
   Who need a doctor
   But those who are suffering
32   I have not come
   To call the just
   But the outcasts
   To change their ways

33   They said to him
   John's disciples often fast
   And make requests in prayer
   As do those of the Pharisees
   But yours eat and drink

34   Jesus said to them
   Can you
   Make the bridegroom's attendants fast
   While the bridegroom is with them?
35   But the days will come
   When the bridegroom
   Is taken from them
   In those days they will fast

36   He also told them a parable
   No one
   Tears a piece from a new cloak
   To put it on an old cloak
   Otherwise he will tear the new
   And the patch from the new
   Will not match the old

37 No one
Puts new wine
Into old wineskins
Otherwise the new wine
Will burst the old wineskins
It will pour out
And the wineskins will be destroyed
38 But new wine
Must be put into fresh wineskins

39 No one
Who has drunk the old
Wishes for the new
As he says
The old is better

6

In the cornfields on the sabbath

1 It so happened
That on a sabbath
He went through the cornfields
And his disciples
Picked the ears of corn
And ate them
Rubbing them in their hands

2   Some of the Pharisees said
        Why are you doing this
        Which is unlawful
        On sabbath days?

3   Jesus answered them
        Have you not read
        What David did
        When he was hungry
        As were those who were with him

4   How he went
        Into the house of God
        And taking the loaves of offering
        Which it is not lawful
        For anyone to eat
        Except the priest
        He ate them

>   And also gave them
>   To his companions?
>
> 5   And he said to them
>   The Son of Man
>   Is Lord of the sabbath

The healing of a man with a useless hand

> 6   On another sabbath
> He entered the synagogue
> And taught
> And there was a man
> Whose right hand
> Had wasted away
>
> 7   The scribes and the Pharisees
> Watched him narrowly
> To see if he will heal
> On the sabbath
> So that they could find something
> With which to accuse him
>
> 8   But he knew
> What they were considering
>   And he said to the man
>   Who had the wasted hand
>   Get up
>   And stand in the centre
>
> So he rose up
> And stood there
>
> 9   And Jesus said to them
>   I am asking you
>   If it is lawful
>   To do good or to do evil
>   On the sabbath
>   To save soul-bearing life
>   Or to destroy it?
>
> 10   Then looking round at them all
>   He said to him
>   Stretch out your hand

He did that
And his hand was made good

11 They became utterly unreasonable
And discussed with one another
What they could do to Jesus

Jesus chooses the twelve apostles
12 It happened in those days
That he went out
On to the mountain
To pray
And spent the whole night
In prayer to God

13 When the day came
He called his disciples to him
And chose twelve from among them
Whom he named apostles

14 Simon
Whom he also named Peter
His brother Andrew
James and John
Philip
Bartholomew
15 Matthew
Thomas
James son of Alphaeus
Simon called the Zealot
16 Judas son of James
And Judas Iscariot
Who became a traitor

The sermon on the plain
17 He came down with them
And stood on the level ground
With a large crowd of his disciples
And very many people
From all parts of Judea

           And from Jerusalem
           And the sea coast of Tyre and Sidon
18   Who came to hear him
           And be cured of their diseases
           Also those who were tormented
           By unclean spirits
           Were healed

19   Everyone in the crowd
           Was trying to touch him
           Because power came from him
           Which healed them all

20   He lifted up his eyes
           On his disciples
               And said
                   Blessed are you
                   Who are beggars
                   Because yours
                   Is the kingdom of God

21   Blessed are you
                   Who are hungry now
                   Because you will be satisfied

                   Blessed are you
                   Who weep now
                   Because you will laugh

22   Blessed are you
                   When your fellow men hate you
                   And when they separate you from them
                   And reproach you
                   And cast out your name as evil
                   For the sake of the Son of Man

23   In that day
                   Leap and rejoice
                   As indeed in heaven
                   You have a great reward
                   Because their forefathers
                   Did the same to the prophets

24 But woe to you
Who are rich
Because you have received
Your consolation

Woe to you
Who are satisfied now
Because you will be hungry

25 Woe to you
Who laugh now
Because you will mourn and weep

26 Woe to you
When all your fellow men
Speak well of you
Because their forefathers
Did the same to the false prophets

27 But I say
To you who listen
Love your enemies
Give help to those who hate you
28 Bless those who curse you
Pray for those who ill treat you

29 If anyone
Hits you on the cheek
Turn to him the other as well

And if anyone
Takes your cloak
Do not prevent him
From taking your tunic

30 Give to everyone
Who asks you
And if anyone
takes your possessions
Do not ask for them back

31 What ever you wish
That your fellow men

Should do to you
Do the same for them

32 If you love those who love you
What thanks should you have?
Because even outcasts
Love those who love them

33 If you do good
To those who do good to you
What thanks should you have?
Because even the outcasts
Do the same

34 If you lend
To those from whom
You hope to receive
What thanks should you have?
Because even the outcasts
Lend to outcasts
So that they may receive
The same again

35 But love your enemies
And do good and lend
Never giving up
Then your reward will be great
And you
Will be sons of the Most High
Because he is kind
To the unthankful
And the wicked

36 You should be merciful
As your Father is merciful

37 Do not judge others
So that you
May not be judged
Do not condemn others
So that you
May not be condemned
Release others
And you will be released

38   Give
And it will be given to you
A sufficient measure
Pressed down
Shaken together
And running over
Will it be given into your lap
As it is the measure
With which you measure
That will be measured to you
In return

39 And he told them
This parable
    A blind man is not able to guide
Another who is blind
Or both
Will fall into a ditch

40   A disciple
Is not above his teacher
But when he has learnt
Every one
Will be like his teacher

41   And why do you see
The splinter in your brother's eye
And do not pay attention to the beam
In your own eye

42   How can you say to your brother
Brother
Allow me to take the splinter
Out of your eye
When you yourself
Do not see the beam
In your own eye?

Hypocrite
First take the beam
Out of your own eye
Then you will see clearly
To take out the splinter
Which is in your brother's eye

43 Because there is no sound tree
　　Which produces rotten fruit
　　Nor is there a rotten tree
　　Which produces sound fruit

44 As every tree
　　Is recognized by its own fruit
　　They do not gather figs
　　From thorns
　　Nor from a thorn bush
　　Do they gather grapes

45 The good man
　　Brings forth the good
　　Out of the good treasure
　　Of his heart
　　And the evil man
　　Brings forth the evil
　　Because his mouth speaks
　　Out of his overflowing heart

46 Why do you call me
　　Lord
　　Lord
　　And not do what I say?

47 Everyone
　　Who comes to me
　　And who hears my words
　　And does them
　　I will show you
　　To whom he is like

48 He is like a man
　　Building a house
　　And when he dug
　　He went deep
　　And laid a foundation
　　On the rock
　　When there was a flood
　　The waters dashed against that house
　　And were not able to shake it
　　Because it was properly built

49 But whoever hears my words
And does not do them
Is like a man
Who built a house
On the earth
Without a foundation
When the waters dashed against it
It collapsed at once
And the ruin of that house
Was complete

7

The healing of the centurion's servant

1 When he had finished speaking
And the people had heard
All that he had to say
He entered Capernaum

2 Now there was a centurion
Who had a servant
Having fallen ill
He was about to die

The centurion valued him greatly
3 And hearing of Jesus
He sent elders of the Jews
To request him to come
And save his servant

4 When they came to Jesus
They begged him earnestly
  Saying
    You should grant this
    Because he deserves it
5   He loves our nation
    And built us a synagogue

6 So Jesus went with them

While he was still some distance
From the house
The centurion sent friends
  Who said to him

       Do not take the trouble
       As I am not worthy
       That you should enter under my roof

7   Therefore I did not presume
       To come to you myself
       But speak the word
       Which says that my attendant
       Should be healed

8   For I myself
       Am also a man under authority
       And I say to one
       Go
       And he goes

       And to another
       Come
       And he comes
       And to my servant
       Do this
       And he does it

9   When he heard this
    Jesus was astonished at him
    And turning to the crowd
    Who were following
       He said
           I say to you
           In Israel
           I have not found such faith

10 Returning to the house
    Those who had been sent out
    Found that the servant had recovered

The widow's son is restored to life
11 On the next day
    He went to a town called Nain
    With him
    Were his disciples
    And a large crowd

12 When he had almost reached the town gate
One who had died
Was being carried out
He was his mother's only son
And she was a widow
With her
There came many people from the town

13 When he saw her
The Lord had compassion on her
    And said to her
        Do not weep

14 He went to the bier
And touched it
The bearers stood still
    And he said
        Young man
        I say to you
        Rise

15 The dead man sat up
And began to speak
And he gave him to his mother

16 Fear took hold of them all
And they praised God
    Saying
        A great prophet
            Has risen among us
    And
        God has visited his people

17 This was said about him
Throughout Judea
And in all the surrounding country

John sends his disciples to Jesus
18 John's disciples
Brought to him the news
Of all that had happened

       Then John
       Called two of his disciples
19   And sent them to the Lord
          To ask him
              Are you the one who is coming
              Or may we expect someone else?

20   When they came to him
          The men said
              John the Baptist
              Has sent us to you
              To ask
              Are you the one who is coming
              Or may we expect someone else?

21   In that hour
       He healed many people
       Who had diseases
       Or suffered torments
       Or had evil spirits
       And he granted sight
       To many who were blind

22   And he answered them
            Go and give the news to John
            Of what you have heard and seen
            The blind have sight again
            And the lame walk
            Lepers are cleansed
            The deaf hear
            The dead are raised up
            The poor receive the Gospel
23   And all who do not reject me
            Are blessed

Jesus talks to the people about John
24   When John's messengers
       Had gone away
          He began to talk to the people
          About John
              What did you
              Go out into the desert
              To behold?
              A reed shaken by the wind?

25   But what did you
Go out to see?
A man wearing fine clothes?
Those who wear splendid clothes
And live in luxury
Are in kings' courts

26   But what did you
Go out to see?
A prophet?

I say to you
Yes
And more than a prophet

27   This is he
Of whom it has been written
Behold I sent out my messenger
Before thy face
Who will make ready the road
In front of thee

28   I say unto you
Among those born of women
No one is greater than John
But the least
In the kingdom of God
Is greater than he is

29 All the people
And the tax-collectors
Who heard this
Recognized the justice of God
As they had been baptized by John

30 But the Pharisees and the lawyers
Rejected God's purpose for themselves
Not having been baptized by him

31   Then to whom shall I compare
The men of this generation
And what are they like?

32   They are like children
     Sitting in the market
     And calling to one another
     We piped to you
     And you did not dance
     We mourned
     And you did not weep

33   John the Baptist
     Has come
     Neither eating bread
     Nor drinking wine
     And you say
     He has a demon

34   The Son of Man
     Has come
     Eating and drinking
     And you say
     Look
     This is a man who is greedy
     And a wine drinker
     A friend of tax-collectors
     And of outcasts

35   But wisdom
     Has been proved to be right
     By all her children

The woman who anointed Jesus

36   There was one of the Pharisees
     Who asked Jesus to eat with him
     So he went into the Pharisee's house
     And took his place
     On a couch at the table

37   And now
     A woman living in the town
     An outcast
     When she learned
     That he was dining in the Pharisee's house
     Brought an alabaster jar of ointment

38   And stood behind him
　　　　Weeping

　　　　She began to wet his feet
　　　　With her tears
　　　　And to wipe them
　　　　With the hair of her head

　　　　Then she kissed his feet
　　　　And anointed them with the ointment

39   When he saw this
　　　　The Pharisee who had invited him
　　　　　　Said to himself
　　　　　　　　If he was a prophet
　　　　　　　　He would have been aware
　　　　　　　　What sort of woman it is
　　　　　　　　Who is touching him
　　　　　　　　As she is an outcast

40   But Jesus answered him
　　　　　　Simon
　　　　　　I have something to say to you

　　　　And he said
　　　　　　Teacher
　　　　　　Say it

41   A certain creditor had two debtors
　　　　　　　　One owed five hundred denarii
　　　　　　　　And the other owed fifty

42   As they were not able to pay
　　　　　　　　He pardoned both of them fully
　　　　　　　　So which of them
　　　　　　　　Will love him most?

43   Simon answered
　　　　　　I suppose
　　　　　　The one
　　　　　　To whom the most was pardoned

　　　　And Jesus said to him
　　　　　　You have judged rightly

44   Then turning to the woman
        He said to Simon
            Do you see this woman?
            I came into your house
            And you did not give me
            Any water for my feet
            But she wet my feet
            With her tears
            And she wiped them with her hair

45   You did not give me a kiss
            But since I came in
            She has not ceased
            To kiss my feet

46   You did not anoint
            My head with oil
            But she has anointed
            My feet with ointment

47   This is my reason
            Why I say to you
            Her many sins have been forgiven
            Because she loved very much
            But the one
            To whom little is forgiven
            Will only love a little

48   And he said to her
        Your sins have been forgiven

49   Then those
Who were at the table with him
Began to say among themselves
        Who is this
        Who even forgives sins?

50   But he said to the woman
        Your faith has saved you
        Go in peace

8 *The parable of the sower*
1. And it happened soon afterwards
That he travelled
Through towns and villages
Preaching the good news
Of the kingdom of God
And the twelve were with him

2. As were also some women
Who had been healed from evil spirits
And disabilities
Mary called Magdalene
From whom seven demons had gone out
3. And Joanna
The wife of Herod's steward Chuza
And Susanna
And many others
Who cared for them
Using their own resources

4. A great many people from the towns
Had gathered together
And when they came to him
   He said in a parable
5.   A sower
    Went out to sow his seed
    And as he sowed
    Some fell beside the path
    And were trodden down
    And the birds of heaven
    Ate it up

6.   And other seed
    Fell on the rock
    And when it grew up
    It withered
    Because it had no moisture

7.   Other seed
    Fell among the thorn bushes
    And the thorns grew up with it
    And choked it

8   Other seed
     Fell on to the good earth
     And when it grew
     It produced fruit
     Increased a hundred times

When he had said this
   He called out
      Whoever has ears to hear
      Should hear

9   His disciples asked him
    What this parable could mean

10   And he said
          To you
          It has been given
          To become aware of the mysteries
          Of the kingdom of God
          But for the rest
          They are in parables
          So that seeing
          They may not see
          And hearing
          They may not understand

11   Now this is the parable

       The seed is the word of God
12   Those beside the path
       Are the ones who hear
       Then the devil comes
       And takes the word
       From their hearts
       So that they may not believe
       And be saved

13   Those on the rock
       Are the ones
       Who when they hear the word
       Receive it with joy
       But because they have no root
       Although they believe for a while

In a period of trial
They fall away

14 Those who fell among the thorn bushes
Are the ones who hear
But on their way
Are choked
By the anxieties
And riches
And pleasures of life
So that nothing comes to perfection

15 Those on the cultivated ground
Are the ones
Who when they hear the word
Hold it fast
In a worthy and good heart
And bear fruit with endurance

16 No one
Who has lit a lamp
Covers it with a bowl
Or puts it underneath a bed
But on a lampstand
So that those who come in
See the light

17 As nothing is secret
Which will not be revealed
Nor concealed
Which will not certainly be known
And come out into the open

18 Therefore
See how you listen

Because whoever has
Will receive
And whoever has not
Even what he thinks that he has
Will be taken from him

The mother and the brothers of Jesus

19 His mother and his brothers
Came to him
But were not able to reach him
Because of the crowd

20   And he was told
        Your mother and your brothers
        Are standing outside
        As they want to see you

21   But he answered them
        My mother and my brothers
        Are those
        Who hear the word of God
        And do it

Jesus calms the storm

22 One day it happened
That he embarked in a boat
With his disciples
    And he said to them
        Let us cross over
        To the other side of the lake
        So they set out

23 As they sailed he fell asleep
And a gale of wind
Came down on the lake
The boat was filling up
And they were in danger

24 They went to him
And woke him
    Saying
        Master
        Master
        We are perishing

But when he had been woken up
He spoke sternly to the wind
And to the rough water
It all ceased
And there was a calm

25 Then he said to them
        Where is your faith?

They were afraid and astonished
    And said to one another
        Who then is this
        Who can even command
        The winds and the water
        And they obey him?

The healing of the Gadarene demoniac
26 They sailed over
    To the country of the Gadarenes
    Which is opposite Galilee

27 As he disembarked on to the land
    A man met him
    Who belonged to the town
    He had demons
    And it was a long time
    Since he had put on clothes
    Nor would he remain in a house
    But among the tombs

28 When he saw Jesus
    He cried out
    And fell down in front of him
        Shouting in a loud voice
            What is there between me and you
            Jesus
            Son of the Most High God?
            I pray to you not to torment me
29 As Jesus had commanded
    The unclean spirit
    To come out of the man

    Because it had often
    Taken hold of him
    And although he was guarded
    And bound with chains and fetters
    He had broken the bonds
    And been driven by the demons
    Into the deserts

30 Jesus asked him the question
        What is your name?

    And he said
        Legion

    As many demons
    Had entered him

31 And they begged him
    Not to order them
    To depart into the abyss

32 Now there was a large herd of pigs
    Feeding on the hillside
    And they begged him to allow them
    To enter those pigs
    And he allowed them to do so

33 So the demons
    Came out of the man
    And went into the pigs
    Then the herd
    Rushed headlong down a steep incline
    Into the lake
    And were drowned

34 When the herdsmen
    Saw what had happened
    They fled
    And brought the news
    To the town and the countryside

35 The people went out
    To see what had happened
    And when they came to Jesus
    They found the man
    From whom the demons had gone out
    Now clothed
    And come to his senses
    Sitting at Jesus' feet
    And they were afraid

36   Those who had seen it
       Told them
       How the one possessed by demons
       Had been healed

37   And all the people
       From the surrounding country of the Gadarenes
       Asked Jesus to go away from them
       Because intense fear
       Had taken hold of them

       So he embarked in a boat
       And returned

38   The man
       From whom the demons had gone out
       Prayed to go with him
       But he sent him away
          Saying
39   Go back to your home
              And tell them
              What God has done for you

       And he went through the whole town
       Proclaiming
       What Jesus had done for him

Cure of a woman and Jairus' daughter is raised
40   Now when Jesus returned
       The crowd welcomed him
       Because they were all expecting him

41   And now there came a man
       Whose name was Jairus
       A leader of the synagogue
       He fell at Jesus' feet
       Praying him earnestly
       To come to his house
42   Because his only daughter
       Who was about twelve years old
       Was dying

As Jesus was on his way
The crowds hemmed him in
43 And there was a woman
Who had suffered from severe bleeding
For twelve years
And whom no one
Was able to heal

44 She came behind him
And touched the fringe of his cloak
At once
The flow of her blood stopped

45   And Jesus said
        Who is touching me?

When everyone denied it
    Peter said
        Master
        The crowds are hemming you in
        And jostling you

46 But Jesus said
    Somebody touched me
    As I
    I am aware
    That power
    Has gone forth from me

47 When the woman
Saw that she was not hidden
She came trembling
And falling down in front of him
She explained
In the presence of all the people
The reason why she had touched him
And how she was cured at once

48   And he said to her
        Daughter
        Your faith has saved you
        Go in peace

49   While he was still speaking
       Someone came from the house
       Of the leader of the synagogue
          And said
              Your daughter has died
              Do not trouble the teacher
              Any further

50   But Jesus heard this
       And answered him
          Do not be afraid
          Only believe
          And she will be saved

51   When he entered the house
       He would not allow anyone
       To come in with him
       Except Peter and John and James
       And the father and mother
       Of the child

52   Everyone was weeping
       And mourning for her
          But he said
              Do not weep
              She has not died
              She is sleeping

53   They laughed at him
       Because they knew
       That she had died

54   But he took her hand
          And called
              Child
              Get up

55   Her spirit returned
       And at once she rose up
       And he instructed them
       To give her something to eat

56 Her parents were astonished
But he ordered them
Not to tell anyone
What had happened

9

The mission of the twelve

1 When he had called the twelve together
He gave them power and authority
Over all the demons
And to cure diseases
2 And sent them
To preach the kingdom of God
And to heal

3   And he said to them
        Take nothing for the road
        Neither a staff
        Nor a bag
        Nor bread
        Nor silver
        And do not each have two tunics

4   Remain in what ever house you enter
        Until you leave the place
5   And if anyone does not receive you
        When you leave that town
        Shake the dust off your feet
        As a witness against them

6 So they went out
And travelled through the villages
Bringing the good news
And healing everywhere

Herod wishes to see Jesus

7 Herod the Tetrarch
Heard all that was happening
And was bewildered
Because it was said by some
That John
Had been raised from the dead
8 And by some

That Elijah had appeared
And by others
That one of the prophets from the past
Had risen again

9   But Herod said
        I myself beheaded John
        But who is this
        About whom I hear such things?

And he was anxious to see him

The feeding of the five thousand
10   When they returned
The apostles told Jesus
What they had done

Then he took them away
On their own
To a town which is called Bethsaida

11   But when the crowds
Became aware of this
They followed him

He welcomed them
And spoke to them
About the kingdom of God
And cured those in need of healing

12   The day
Began to draw to an end
And the twelve came to him
    And said
        Send the people away
        So that they may go to the villages
        And to the farms round about
        Where they may find lodging
        And provisions
        Because we are here
        In a lonely place

13   He said to them
            You
                Give them something to eat

        But they said
            We have only five loaves
            And two fishes
            Unless we go away
            And buy food for all these people

14   There were about five thousand men

        He said to his disciples
            Make them sit down for a meal
            In groups of about fifty each

15   They did so
        Making them all sit down

16   He took the five loaves
        And the two fishes
        Then looking up to heaven
        He blessed and broke them
        And gave them to his disciples
        To set before the people

17   They all ate
        And were satisfied
        Then they took up twelve wicker baskets
        Of the pieces that were left over

        Peter's confession of faith
18   Now it happened
        That when he had been praying alone
        His disciples were with him
            And he asked them the question
                Whom do the people
                Believe me to be?

19   They answered
    John the Baptist
    But others say Elijah
    And others
    That one of the prophets from the past
    Has risen again

20   And he said to them
    But you
    Whom do you
    Believe me to be

  Peter answered
    The Christ of God

21 But he gave them strict orders
  Not to tell this to anyone

First prophecy of the Passion
22   And he said
    It is necessary
    For the Son of Man
    To have great suffering
    To be rejected by the elders
    The chief priests
    And the scribes
    To be killed
    And to be raised
    On the third day

23   Then he said to all
    If anyone
    Has the will to come after me
    He should not consider himself
    But take his cross every day
    And he should follow me

24   As whoever wishes to save
    His soul-bearing life
    Will lose it
    But whoever loses
    His soul-bearing life

        For my sake
        Will save it

25   Because what use is it to a man
        If he gains the whole world
        At the cost of losing or damaging
        Himself

26   As whoever
        Is ashamed of me
        And of my words
        The Son of Man
        Will be ashamed of him
        When he comes
        In the revelation of his glory
        And in the glory of the Father
        And the holy angels

27   But I am telling you the truth
        There are some standing here
        Who will certainly not taste death
        Until they see
        The kingdom of God

The Transfiguration

28   Then about eight days
        After these words
        He took Peter and John and James
        And went up into the mountain
        To pray

29   It happened that as he prayed
        The appearance of his face changed
        His clothing
        Became as a lightning flash
30   And two men were seen
        Conversing with him

        They were Moses and Elijah
31   Who appeared in glory
        And spoke of his exodus
        Which he was about to achieve
        In Jerusalem

32 But Peter
And those with him
Were heavy with sleep

As they woke
They saw the revelation of his glory
And also the two men
Who were standing with him

33 It was when they had parted from him
That Peter said to Jesus
It is right for us to be here
Let us put up three tents
One for you
One for Moses
And one for Elijah

He did not know
What he was saying

34 But as he said this
There came a cloud
Which overshadowed them
And they were afraid
As they passed into the cloud

35 Then a voice
Came out of the cloud
Which said
This is my Son
Who has been chosen
Hear him

36 After the voice had come
Jesus was found to be alone

They kept silent
And in those days
They did not report to anyone
Anything that they had seen

The healing of the demoniac boy

37 It so happened that on the next day
When they came down from the mountain
A large crowd met him

38 Then a man called out
From out of the crowd
Teacher
I beg you
To look at my son
Because he is my only child

39 As indeed
A spirit takes hold of him
And crying out
Suddenly throws him down
Foaming at the mouth
And after hurting him
It departs from him reluctantly

40 I begged your disciples
To cast it out
But they had not the power

41 Jesus answered
O perverted generation
Without faith
How long shall I be with you
And endure you?

Bring your son here

42 As he came close to Jesus
The demon tore him
And hurled him to the ground

Jesus spoke sternly
To the unclean spirit
He healed the boy
And gave him back to his father

43 And they were all astonished
At the majesty of God

Second prophecy of the Passion

44   As everyone was wondering
       At all that he did
          He said to his disciples
             Keep these words in your ears

          The Son of Man
          Is about to be betrayed
          Into the hands of men

45   But they did not understand
       What he said
       It was veiled from them
       Lest they should perceive it
       And they were afraid to ask him
       About this statement

Who is the greatest?

46   They entered into a discussion
       Among themselves
       As to which of them
       Might be the greatest?

47   But as Jesus knew
       What they were considering
       In their hearts
       He took a child
       And stood him by his side

48   Then he said to them
          Whoever receives this child
          In my name
          Receives me
          And whoever receives me
          Receives the one who sent me

          Whoever is the least
          Among you all
          Is the one who is great

49   John spoke up
       Saying

>   Master
>   We saw someone
>   Casting out demons
>   In your name
>   And we tried to prevent him
>   Because he does not follow us

50   But Jesus answered
>   Do not prevent him
>   As whoever is not against you
>   Is for you

On the road to Jerusalem

51   Then
As the days of his ascension
Drew near
He set out
To go to Jerusalem

52   And sent his messengers ahead
To prepare for him

On their way
They entered a Samaritan village

53   Which did not welcome him
Because he was making for Jerusalem

54   When they saw this
>   His disciples James and John
>   Said
>>   Lord is it your will
>>   That we tell fire
>>   To come down from heaven
>>   And destroy them?

55   But he turned
And spoke sternly to them

56   And they went to another village

57   As they were on the road
>   One of them said to him
>>   I will follow you
>>   Wherever you go

58 Jesus said to him
    The foxes have holes
    And the birds of heaven
    Have their dwellings
    But the Son of Man
    Has nowhere to lay his head

59 He said to another
    Follow me

But he answered
    First allow me to go away
    And bury my father

60 Jesus said to him
    Leave the dead
    To bury their own dead
    But you
    You go and announce
    The kingdom of God

61 There was another who said
    I will follow you
    Lord
    But first
    Let me say goodbye
    To those in my house

62 But Jesus said
    No one
    Who has put his hand to the plough
    And then looks back
    Is fit for the kingdom Of God

10 *The mission of the seventy*

1 After this
The Lord appointed seventy others
And sent them out two by two
To go ahead of him
Into every town and place
Where he himself was coming

2   And he said to them
              Indeed there is a great harvest
              But there are few labourers
              Therefore pray the lord of the harvest
              To speed labourers into his harvest

3   Go forth
              See how I send you out
              Like lambs among wolves

4   Do not carry a purse
              Nor a bag
              Nor sandals
              And greet no one
              On the road

5   When you go into a house
              First say
              Peace be to this house
6   And if a son of peace
              Is present there
              Your peace shall rest on him
              If otherwise
              It shall return to you

7   Stay on in the same house
              Eating and drinking with them
              Whatever they have
              Because the workman deserves his wage
              Do not remove from house to house

8   When you enter a town
              And you are welcomed
              Eat what is set before you
9   Heal the sick who are there
              And say to them
              The kingdom of God
              Has come close to you

10   But when you enter a town
              And you are not welcomed
11   Go out into the streets
              And say
              Even the dust of your town

> Which sticks to our feet
> We wipe off on to you
> However
> You should be aware of this
> That the kingdom of God
> Has come close

12
> I say to you
> That on that day
> It will be more bearable for Sodom
> Than for that town

13
> Woe to you
> Chorazin
> Woe to you
> Bethsaida
> Because if the powerful deeds
> Had been done in Tyre and Sidon
> Which have been done in you
> They would have altered long ago
> Sitting in sackcloth and ashes

14
> However
> At the judgment
> It will be more bearable
> For Tyre and Sidon
> Than for you

15
> And you Capernaum
> Were you lifted up
> As far as heaven?
> You shall go down
> As far as Hades

16
> Whoever listens to you
> Listens to me
> And whoever rejects you
> Rejects me
> And whoever rejects me
> Rejects the one who sent me

Return of the seventy

17 The seventy
Returned with joy
   Saying
      Lord
      Even the demons
      Surrender to us in your name

18   And he said to them
     I perceived Satan
     Fall as lightning
     Out of heaven

19   See how I have given to you
     The authority
     To tread on snakes and scorpions
     And on all the power
     Of the enemy
     And there is nothing
     That will hurt you in any way

20   However
     Do not be glad
     That the spirits submit to you
     But be glad
     That your names
     Have been written in the heavens

Jesus prays to the Father

21 In that very hour
He was filled
With the joy of the Holy Sprit
   And said
      I give praise to you
      Father
      Lord of Heaven
      And of Earth
      Because you have hidden these things
      From the wise and the able
      And have revealed them to babes
      Yes Father
      As thus it was pleasing in your sight

22   All things
     Were handed over to me
     By my Father
     And no one understands
     Who the Son is
     Except the Father
     And who the Father is
     Except the Son
     And those to whom
     It is the will of the Son
     To reveal him

23 He turned to his disciples
    Saying only to them
     Blessed are the eyes
     Which see the things which you see

24   As I say to you
     That many prophets and kings
     Wished to have sight
     Of the things which you see
     But did not have sight of them
     And to hear
     The things which you hear
     But did not hear them

The good Samaritan
25 Now there was a lawyer
  Who stood up to test him
    Saying
     Teacher
     What shall I do
     So that I may inherit life
     Throughout the ages

26 Jesus said to him
    What has been written in the Law
    How do you read it?

27 And he answered
    You shall love the Lord your God
    From all your heart
    And with all your soul

And with all your strength
And with all your mind
And your neighbour as yourself

28 He said to him
    You have given the right answer
    Do this and you will live

29 But as he wanted
    To do himself justice
        He said to Jesus
            And who is my neighbour?

30 Jesus took up what he had said
    And replied
        There was a man
        Who was going down from Jerusalem
        To Jericho
        When he fell in with robbers
        Who stripped him
        And after raining blows on him
        Went away
        Leaving him half dead

31   Just then
        There was a priest
        Who came down that road
        And when he saw him
        Went past on the other side

32   There was also a Levite
        Who came to the place
        And when he saw him
        Went past on the other side

33   But there was a Samaritan
        Travelling on the road
        Who came upon him
        And when he saw him
        Was filled with compassion

34   Going to him
        He bound up his wounds
        Pouring on oil and wine

           Then he put him on his own mount
           Brought him to an inn
           And took care of him

35   On the next day
           He took out two denarii
           And gave them to the innkeeper
           Saying
           Take care of him
           And if you spend more
           When I myself return
           I will repay you

36   Which of these three
           Do you think
           Became a neighbour to the man
           Who fell among the robbers?

37   He said
               The one who was merciful to him

       Jesus said to him
               Go
               And do the same yourself

       Martha and Mary
38   As they went on their way
       He came to a village
       Where a woman
       Whose name was Martha
       Welcomed him into her home

39   She had a sister
       Called Mary
       Who sat by the Lord
       At his feet
       And listened to his words

40   But as Martha
       Was distracted by so much serving
           She came to him
           And said

            Lord
            Does it not matter to you
            That my sister
            Has left me to serve alone?
            Therefore say to her
            That she should help me

41   The Lord answered her
            Martha
            Martha
            You are anxious and worried
            About all sorts of things
            But few are necessary
42   Indeed only one
            Mary
            Has chosen the good part
            Which shall not be taken away from her

11 *The Lord's Prayer*
1   And it happened
        As he was praying somewhere
        When he had come to an end
            One of his disciples said to him
                Lord
                Teach us to pray
                Just as John
                Taught his disciples

2   And he said to them
            When you pray
            Say

            FATHER
            MAY YOUR NAME BE KEPT HOLY
            YOUR KINGDOM COME
3   THE BREAD WE NEED EVERY DAY
            GIVE US EACH DAY
4   AND FORGIVE US OUR DEBTS
            AS WE OURSELVES FORGIVE EVERYONE
            WHO IS INDEBTED TO US
            AND DO NOT BRING US TO THE TEST

Teaching about prayer

5   Then he said to them
        Which of you
        Who has a friend
        Would go to him at midnight
        And say to him
        Friend
        Lend me three loaves

6   Because a friend of mine
        Has arrived on a visit to me
        And I have nothing
        With which to serve him

7   And the one inside would answer
        Do not trouble me
        Now that the door is shut
        And my children
        Are with me in bed
        I cannot get up
        To give them to you?

8   I say to you
        Even if he will not get up
        And give them to him
        Because he is his friend
        Because of his demands
        He will get up
        And give him as many as he needs

9   And I myself say to you
        Ask
        And it will be given to you
        Seek
        And you will find
        Knock
        And it will be opened for you

10   As everyone who asks
        Receives
        And the one who seeks
        Finds
        And for the one who knocks
        It will be opened

11 Which of you who is a father
When his son asks for a fish
Instead of a fish
Would give him a snake?
12 Or if he asks for an egg
Would give him a scorpion?

13 Therefore
If you who are evil
Know how to give good gifts
To your children
How much more
Will the heavenly Father
Give the Holy Spirit
To those who ask him

Casting out demons
14 He was casting out a demon
Which was dumb
And it happened
That as the demon left him
The dumb man spoke
And the crowds were astonished

15 But some of them said
He casts out demons
By Beelzebub
The ruler of demons

16 And others
In order to test him
Asked him for a sign
Out of heaven

17 But he knew their thoughts
And said to them
Every kingdom
Which is divided against itself
Is made a desert
And house on house
Falls into ruins
18 And if Satan
Was divided against himself

How would his kingdom stand?
For you say
That I cast out
Demons by Beelzebub

19 But if I
I cast our demons
By Beelzebub
By whom do your sons
Cast them out
Therefore
They shall be your judges

20 But if I
I cast out demons
By the finger of God
Then the kingdom of God
Has come upon you

21 When a strong man
Who is fully armed
Guards his own forecourt
His possessions are safe

22 But when one who is stronger
Comes upon him
And wins the victory over him
He takes away his armour
In which he put his trust
And distributes the spoil

23 The one who is not with me
Is against me
And whoever
Does not gather with me
Scatters

24 When the unclean spirit
Has gone out of a man
He goes through waterless places
Looking for rest
When he does not find it
He says

    I will go back to my house
    Which is where I came from

25   When he comes
    He finds it swept
    And put in order

26   Then he takes seven other spirits
    More evil than himself
    And goes in there to stay
    So the last state of that man
    Becomes worse than the first

27 It happened as he said this
That a woman in the crowd
  Called out to him
    Blessed is the womb
    That bore you
    And the breasts
    That you have sucked

28   But he said
    Indeed
    It is rather those
    Who hear the word of God
    And who keep to it
    Who are blessed

The sign of Jonah
29 As the crowds gathered round him
  He started saying
    This generation
    Is an evil generation
    It looks out for a sign
    But no sign
    Will be given to it
    Except the sign of Jonah

30   Just as Jonah
    Became a sign to the Ninevites
    So will the Son of Man
    Become to this generation

31
    At the judgment
    The Queen of the South
    Will rise up
    With the men of this generation
    And will condemn them
    As she came
    From the bounds of the earth
    To hear the wisdom of Solomon
    And now
    Here is one
    Who is greater than Solomon

32
    At the judgment
    The men of Nineveh
    Will rise up with this generation
    And will condemn it
    As they changed their ways
    At the preaching of Jonah
    And now
    Here is one
    Who is greater than Jonah

33
    No one
    Who has lit a lamp
    Keeps it hidden
    Or puts it under a corn measure
    But on the lamp stand
    So that those who come in
    See the light

34
    The lamp of your body
    Is the eye
    When the eye sees clearly
    The whole of your body
    Will also shine
    But if it sees falsely
    Your body will also be dark

35
    Therefore keep watch
    That the light which is in you
    Is not darkness

36
    If then all your body
    Is shining

And has no part that is dark
It will shine
As if a lamp with its flashing
Enlightens you

Woe to the Pharisees and the lawyers

37 After Jesus had spoken
A Pharisee
Invited him to eat with him

So he went in
And sat down at the table

38 But the Pharisee was astonished
When he saw
That he had not first washed
Before the meal

39 But the Lord said to him
Now you Pharisees
Clean the outside
of the cup and the dish
But within
You are full of grasping
And wickedness

40 That is senseless
Has not the one
Who made the outside
Also made the inside?

41 But give generously
From what you have
Then indeed
Everything will be clean for you

42 But woe to you Pharisees
Because you take a tenth
Of peppermint and rue
And every other herb
And pass by judgment
And the love of God

> These are the things you should do
> While not neglecting the others

43
> Woe to you Pharisees
> Because you love
> The first seats in the synagogues
> And greetings in the public places

44
> Woe to you
> Because you are like tombs
> Which are not noticed
> And men walking over them
> Do not know that they are there

45
> In response
> One of the lawyers said to him
>> Teacher
>> When you say such things
>> You also insult us

46
> And he said
>> Woe to you also
>> Lawyers
>> Because you burden men
>> With burdens
>> Which are hard to bear
>> But you
>> Do not touch the burden
>> With one of your fingers

47
> Woe to you
> Because you build the tombs
> of the prophets
> And your fathers killed them

48
> Therefore you are witnesses
> And support the deeds of your fathers
> Because they killed them
> And you build their tombs

49
> As it was said
> By the wisdom of God
> I will send to them
> Prophets and apostles

50   And some they will kill and persecute
So that the blood of all the prophets
Poured out
From the foundation of the world
May be demanded of this generation

51   From the blood of Abel
To the blood of Zechariah
Destroyed between the altar of sacrifice
And the House of the Lord
Yes I tell you
It will be demanded of this generation

52   Woe to you lawyers
Because you
Have taken the key of knowledge
And not having entered yourselves
You have prevented others
From entering

53 When he left there
The scribes and Pharisees
Began to be terribly angry
And tried to make him speak
About very many things
54 Lying in wait
To catch him out
In what he said

12 *Jesus warns his disciples*

1 In the meantime
When thousands of people
Had gathered together
So that they even trod on one another
    He first said to his disciples
        Guard yourselves
        Against the yeast of the Pharisees
        Which is hypocrisy

2   Nothing is covered up
Which will not be uncovered
Or secret
Which will not become known

3   So what you have said
    In the dark
    Will be heard
    In the light
    And what was spoken by you
    In the inner room
    Will be proclaimed
    On the rooftops

4   And I say to you
    My friends
    Do not be afraid
    Of those who kill the body
    And afterwards
    Have nothing more
    That they can do

5   But I will warn you
    Whom you should fear
    Fear the one who kills
    And afterwards
    Has the authority
    To cast into the valley of burning
    I say to you
    That is the one you should fear

6   Are not five sparrows
    Sold for two small copper coins
    And not one of them
    Has been forgotten
    In the sight of God

7   And on your head
    Even the hairs
    Have all been counted

    Do not be afraid
    You are worth more
    Than many sparrows

8   But I say to you
    That anyone
    Who acknowledges me
    In the presence of men

      The Son of Man
      Will acknowledge him
      In the presence
      Of the angels of God

9   And whoever disowns me
      In the presence of men
      Will be disowned
      In the presence
      Of the angels of God

10   And everyone
      Who says a word
      Against the Son of Man
      Will be forgiven
      But whoever blasphemes
      Against the Holy Spirit
      Will not be forgiven

11   When they bring you
      Before the synagogues
      And before rulers and authorities
      Do not be anxious
      About how to answer
      Or what you should say
12   As in that hour
      The Holy Spirit
      Will teach you what you should say

Parable of the rich landowner

13   Someone from among the crowd
      Said to him
          Teacher
          Order my brother
          To divide the inheritance with me

14   But he said to him
          Man
          Who has appointed me
          As judge or divider among you?

15   Then he said to them
        Watch out
        And guard against all greed
        Because no one's life
        Consists in the amount that he owns

16   And he told them a parable
        There was a certain rich man
        Whose land was fruitful
17   And he said to himself
        What shall I do
        Because I have nowhere
        To store my harvest?

18   So he said
        This is what I will do
        I will pull down my barns
        And build larger ones
        There I will store my wheat
        And all my goods

19   Then I will say to my living soul
        Soul
        You have many good things
        Stored up for the years to come
        Take your ease
        Eat and drink
        And be happy

20   But God said to him
        Senseless man
        In this night
        They will reclaim your living soul
        From you
        Then who will possess
        What you have prepared?

21   Such is the one
        Who has treasure for himself
        But is not rich in the realm of God

Trust in God

22   And he said to his disciples
Therefore I will tell you
Do not be anxious
About what you should eat
To support your life
Or about what you should wear
To clothe your body

23   The soul-bearing life
Is more than food
And the body more than clothes

24   Consider the ravens
How they do not sow or reap
And have neither a store house
Nor a barn
But God feeds them
How much more are you worth
Than the birds?

25   But which of you
By his concern
Can alter the way he is made?

26   If you have not the power
To do the smallest thing
Why are you anxious
About the rest?

27   Consider the lilies
How they neither spin nor weave
But I say to you
That Solomon in all his glory
Was not robed like one of them

28   And if in the fields
Where there is grass today
Which tomorrow
Will be thrown into an oven
It was clothed in this way
By God
How much more will he clothe you
You that have little faith

29   Do not look out
      For what you should eat
      Or what you should drink
      And do not have them
      On your mind

30   In all the nations of the world
      People run after these things
      But your Father
      Knows that you need them

31   Instead
      Look for his kingdom
      And all these things
      Will be yours also

32   Do not be afraid
      Little flock
      Because it has pleased your Father
      To give you the kingdom

33   Sell what you have
      And give to those
      Who are in need
      Make purses for yourselves
      Which will not wear out
      And have treasure in the heavens
      Which will not fail
      Where no thief comes near
      And no moth destroys
34   Because where your treasure is
      There your heart
      Will be also

Be watchful

35   Tuck up your tunics
          And have your lamps burning

36   Be like men
          Who are expecting their Lord
          So that when he returns
          From the marriage
          And comes knocking
          They open to him at once

LUKE 12

37 Blessed are those servants
    Whom the Lord will find watching
    When he comes
    Certainly I tell you
    That he will tuck up his tunic
    And making them sit at table
    He will come and serve them

38 If it is in the second
    Or in the third part of the night
    That he comes
    And finds them watching
    Blessed are those servants

39 Be aware of this
    If the householder had known
    At what hour the thief would come
    He would not have allowed
    His house
    To have been broken into

40 So be prepared
    Because it is at the hour
    When you do not expect him
    That the Son of Man
    Will come

41 Peter said
        Lord
        Is this parable meant for us
        Or for everyone?

42 And the Lord said
        Who is that faithful and trustworthy steward
        Whom the lord
        Will appoint over his household
        To give them their measure of corn
        When it is due

43   Blessed is that servant
        Whom the lord
        Will find doing so
        When he comes

44   Certainly I say to you
       That he will give him charge
       Over all his possessions

45   But if that servant
       Says in his heart
       My lord delays his coming
       And begins to hit the menservants
       And the maidservants
       Also eating and drinking
       Until he is drunken

46   Then the lord of that servant
       Will come
       On a day which he did not expect
       And in any hour
       Of which he was not aware
       And will cut him off
       And his place
       Will be among the unbelievers

47   But that servant
       Who was aware
       Of the will of his lord
       But has not made preparation
       Or acted according to that will
       Shall be severely beaten
48   While the one who was unaware
       Although what he has done
       Deserved a beating
       Shall be beaten less severely

       Because from everyone
       To whom much has been given
       Much will be required
       And from those
       To whom much has been entrusted
       Even more will be asked

49   I came to cast fire
       On the earth
       And how I wish
       That it was already lighted

50   I have a baptism
With which to be baptized
And how I am oppressed
Until it is completed

51   Do you think
That I came to give peace
To the earth?
Not so
But rather to bring separation

52   Because from now on
There will be five in one house
Who will be divided
Three against two
And two against three

53   There will be divisions
Father against son
And son against father
Mother against daughter
And daughter against mother
Mother-in-law against her daughter-in-law
And daughter-in-law against her mother-in-law

Right judgment

54   Then speaking to the crowds
He said
    When you see a cloud
    Rising in the west
    Immediately you say
    That a rain storm is coming
    And it will happen

55   And when the wind
Blows from the south
You say
That there will be heat
And it will happen

56   Hypocrites
You know how to interpret
The face of the earth

And of the heavens
But this present season
You cannot interpret

57 And why do you yourselves
Not make the right judgment?

58 As you go with your opponent
To a magistrate
Take the trouble
To be freed from him
While you are on the road
Or else he
May drag you to the judge
And the judge
Will throw you into prison

59 I say to you
That is certain
You will not come out of there
Until you have paid
The last copper

13 *The death of the Galileans*
1 At that same season
There were people present
Who gave him the news of Galileans
Whose blood
Pilate had mixed with their sacrifices

2 He answered them
Do you think that those Galileans
Were more sinful
Than all other Galileans
Because they suffered in this way?

3 No
I say to you
That unless you
Change heart and mind
All of you
Will also perish

LUKE 13

4   Or those eighteen
Who were killed
When the tower of Siloam
Fell upon them
Do you think that they were debtors
More than all the men
Living in Jerusalem?

5   No
I say to you
That unless you
Change heart and mind
You will perish
In the same way

Parable of the fig tree

6   And he told this parable
There was a man
Who had planted a fig tree
In his vineyard
And when he came
To look for the fruit
He did not find any

7   And he said to the vine dresser
For three years
I have come
To look for fruit
On this fig tree
And have not found any
Cut it down
Why should it use up the ground?

8   But he answered him
Sir
Leave it this year as well
Until I have dug round it
And spread manure

9   If it bears fruit in the future
Well and good
If not
Cut it down

Healing of a woman who was disabled

10 He was teaching
In one of the synagogues
On the sabbath

11 And now
There was a woman
Who had suffered from a disabling spirit
For eighteen years
She was bent double
And had not the power
To stand up straight

12 When Jesus saw her
He called her to him
    And said to her
        Woman
        You have been set free
        From your disability

13 He put his hands on her
And at once
She straightened up
And gave praise to God

14 Because he was indignant
That Jesus healed on the sabbath
    The ruler of the synagogue
    Said to the crowd
        There are six days
        On which work should be done
        So it is on them
        That you should come to be healed
        And not on the sabbath day

15 But the Lord answered him
    Hypocrites
    Does not each one of you
    On the sabbath
    Untie his ox or ass
    From the manger
    And lead them away to drink?

16   And should not this woman
    A daughter of Abraham

Whom Satan has bound
For as long as eighteen years
Be set free from her bondage
On the sabbath day?

17 When he said this
All those who opposed him
Were shamed
And the whole crowd rejoiced
At all the glorious things
Which were happening through him

18 Therefore he said
    To what can the kingdom of God
    Be compared?
    And to what shall I compare it?

19   It is like a mustard seed
    Which a man took
    And threw into his garden
    It grew into a tree
    So that the birds of heaven
    Nested in its branches

20 Again he said
    To what shall I compare
    The kingdom of God?

21   It is like yeast
    Which a woman took
    And hid in three measures
    Of fine flour
    Until it was all leavened

Teaching on the road to Jerusalem

22 As he travelled through towns and villages
Teaching
And making his way to Jerusalem
23   Someone said to him
        Lord
        Will only a few be saved?

LUKE 13

24   And he said to them
        Make every effort
        To go in through the narrow door
        Because I tell you
        That many will try to enter
        And will not succeed

25   When the master of the house
        Has got up and shut the door
        Then you will stand outside
        And begin to knock on the door
        Saying
        Lord open to us

        And he will answer
        I do not know
        Where you have come from

26   Then you will say at once
        We ate and drank in your presence
        And you taught in our streets

27   But he will speak out
        And say to you
        I do not know
        Where you have come from
        Withdraw from me
        All those who do what is unjust

28   There will be weeping
        And gnashing of teeth
        When you see Abraham
        And Isaac and Jacob
        With all the prophets
        In the kingdom of God
        While you are thrown out
        To the outside

29   The people will come
        From east and west
        And from north and south
        To sit at table
        In the kingdom of God

30   But look
            There are those who are last
            Who will be first
            And there are those who are first
            Who will be last

31   In that same hour
         There came some Pharisees
            Who said to him
               Leave here
               And go away
               Because Herod wishes to kill you

32   But he said to them
            Go and tell this fox
            See how I cast out demons
            And bring about cures
            Today and tomorrow
            And on the third day
            I shall be made perfect

33   However
            It is necessary for me
            To continue my journey
            Today and tomorrow
            And on the following day
            Because it is not possible
            That a prophet should perish
            Outside Jerusalem

34   Jerusalem
         Jerusalem
            Who killed the prophets
            And stoned those sent out to her
            How often
            I wished to gather your children
            As a bird gathers her nestlings
            Under her wings
            But you would not

35   Look how your house
         Is left to you

I say to you
That you shall certainly not see me
Until it will be
That you say
Blest is the one who comes
In the name of the Lord

14   *Healing of a man suffering from water retention*
1   It so happened that on a sabbath
He went to the house
Of one of the leading Pharisees
To have a meal
And they watched him narrowly

2   Now there in front of him
Was a man
Whose body was swollen

3   Jesus said to the lawyers
And the Pharisees
Is it lawful to heal on the sabbath
Or is it not?

4   But they kept quiet

Then he took the man
And having healed him
Sent him away

5   And he said to them
Which of you
Having an ass or an ox
Which has fallen into a well
On the sabbath day
Will not pull it up at once?

6   They were unable to retort to this

Humility and care for the poor
7   He told a parable
To those who had been invited
Because he noticed

That they chose the best seats
And he said to them
8 When you are invited by anyone
To a wedding feast
Do not sit down at the table
In the best seat
As someone may have been invited
Who is more valued than you are

9 Then your host
Who has invited you both
Will come and say to you
Make room for this man
So that you will be ashamed
And make your way
To the last place

10 But when you are invited
Go and sit down
In the lowest place
So that when your host comes
He will say to you
Friend
Go up higher
Then you will be honoured
In front of all those
Who are at the table with you

11 Because everyone who exalts himself
Will be humbled
And he who humbles himself
Will be exalted

12 He also said to his host
When you make a dinner or supper
Do not call your friends
Or your brothers
Or your relations
Or your neighbours
As they may invite you in return
And you will be repaid

13 But when you make a feast
Invite the poor
The crippled
The lame and the blind
14 And because they have nothing
With which to repay you
You will be blessed
And will be repaid
At the resurrection of the just

Parable of the great feast
15 On hearing this
One of those sitting at the table
Said to him
> Blessed is the one
> Who eats bread
> In the kingdom of God

16 But Jesus said to him
> There was once a man
> Who made a great feast
> And invited many guests

17 At the time of the feast
He sent out his servant
To say to those who had been invited

Come
Because it is now ready

18 Then one and all
Began to make excuses

The first one said to him
I have bought a farm
And need to go out to see it
So I ask you
To have me excused

LUKE 14

19 And another said
I have brought five yoke of oxen
And I am going to try them
So I ask you
To have me excused

20 Another said
I have married a wife
And therefore I am not able to come

21 The servant returned
And brought this news
To his lord
Then the master of the house
Became angry
And said to his servant
Go out quickly
Into the streets and lanes of the city
And bring in here
The poor
The crippled
The blind and the lame

22 And the servant said
Sir
What you ordered
Has been done
And there is still room

23 Then the lord
Said to the servant
Go out on to the highroads
And into the byways
And demand that they come in
So that my house
May be filled

24 As I tell you
That none of those men
Who were invited
Shall taste my feast

Following Christ

25 A large crowd gathered
And when they came to him
    He turned to them and said
26   If anyone comes to me
        Who does not <u>disregard</u>
        His father and mother
        His wife and children
        And his brothers and sisters
        As well as his own soul-bearing life
        He cannot be my disciple

27   Whoever does not carry his cross
        And come after me
        Cannot be my disciple

28   Which of you
        Who intends to build a watch tower
        Does not first sit down
        And count the cost
        To find out if he has enough
        To see it through?

29   Otherwise
        When he has laid the foundation
        And has not the means to finish
        Everyone who sees it
        Will begin to taunt him
30   Saying
        This man started to build
        But was not able to finish

31   Or what king
        Who is going to make war
        On another king
        Will not sit down and consider
        If with ten thousand
        He has the power
        To meet the one who comes upon him
        With twenty thousand

32   If he cannot
        He will send out an embassy
        To sue for peace

While that king
Is still a long way off

33 Therefore every one of you
Who does not take leave
Of all his possessions
Cannot be my disciple

34 Salt is useful
But if the salt becomes useless
With what will it be seasoned?
35 It is neither fit for earth
Nor for the manure heap
So it will be thrown outside

Whoever has ears to hear
Should hear

15 *The lost sheep*

1 Now all the tax-collectors and outcasts
Came to listen to him
2 But both the Pharisees and the scribes
Were complaining a great deal
    And saying
        This is the man
        Who welcomes outcasts
        And eats with them

3 Then he told them this parable
4   What man among you
    Who has a hundred sheep
    If he loses one of them
    Does not leave the ninety nine
    In the desert
    And go after the sheep
    Which has got lost
    Until he finds it?

5   And when he has found it
    He puts it on his shoulders
    And full of joy
6   He returns home

Then he collects his friends
And the neighbours
And says to them
Rejoice with me
Because I have found
The sheep which I had lost

7 I say to you
That in heaven
There will be more joy
Over one sinner
Who changes both heart and mind
Than over ninety nine upright people
Who do not need to change

The lost coin

8 Or what woman
Who has ten coins
If she loses one coin
Does not light a lamp
And sweeping the house
Search carefully
Until she finds it?

9 And when she has found it
She collects her friends
And the neighbours
And says to them
Rejoice with me
Because I have found
The coin which I had lost

10 Even so I say to you
That in the presence
Of the angels of God
There is joy
Over one sinner
Who changes both heart and mind

The lost son

11 And he said
There was a man
Who had two sons

12 And the younger of them
    Said to his father
    Father
    Give me the share of the property
    Which should come to me
    And he divided the living
    Between them

13 After a few days
    The younger son
    Collected everything together
    And went away
    To a distant country
    Where he lived wildly
    And wasted his property

14 But when he had spent everything
    There was a severe famine
    Throughout the land
    And he began to be in need
15 So he joined one of the inhabitants
    Of that country
    Who sent him into his fields
    To feed the pigs

16 And he longed to fill his stomach
    With the pods
    Which the pigs were eating
    But no one gave him anything

17 When he came to himself
    He said
    How many of my father's paid workers
    Have plenty of food
    But here I
    I am perishing with hunger

18 I will set out
    And go to my father
    And will say to him
    Father
    I have sinned against heaven
    And in your sight
19 I am no longer worthy

To be called your son
Make me
Like one of your paid workers

20 He set out
And went to his father

When he was still a long way off
His father saw him
And was filled with compassion
So he ran
And falling on his neck
He kissed him warmly

21 Then his son said to him
Father
I have sinned against heaven
And in your sight
I am no longer worthy
To be called your son
Make me
Like one of your paid workers

22 But his father said to the servants
Bring out the finest robe
And clothe him
Put a ring on his hand
And sandals on his feet
23 Bring the calf
Which is being fattened
And kill it
Let us eat and be glad
24 Because this son of mine
Was dead
And has returned to life
He was lost
And has been found

They began feasting

25 But his elder son
Was out in the fields
And as he came near the house
He heard music and dancing

26	So he called
	To one of the farm hands
	To ask what this meant

27	And he answered
	Your brother has come
	And your father
	Has killed the calf
	Which was being fattened
	Because he has received him back
	Safe and sound

28	He was angry
	And did not want to go in

	So his father came out
	And tried to persuade him

29	Then he answered his father
	Look how many years
	I have served you
	And I
	Never disobeyed your orders
	But you
	Never gave me a kid
	So that I could feast
	With my friends

30	But when this son of yours came
	Who has wasted your livelihood
	With prostitutes
	For him
	You have killed the calf
	Which was being fattened

31	And he said to him
	Child
	You are always with me
	And everything that I have
	Is yours

32	It was right
	That we should feast and rejoice
	Because this brother of yours

Who was dead
Has returned to life
He was lost
And has been found

16 *The untrustworthy agent*

1   He also said to his disciples
There was a rich man
Who had an agent
Of whom he heard complaints
That he was wasteful
With his property

2   So he called him
And said to him
What is this
That I hear about you?
Render an account of your management
As you cannot be agent any longer

3   The agent said to himself
What shall I do
Now that the lord
Takes the management away from me?
I have not the strength to dig
And I am ashamed to beg

4   I know what to do
So that when I have been dismissed
As agent
They will accept me into their homes

5   And he called his lord's debtors
One at a time
And said to the first
How much do you owe my lord?

6   And he answered
A hundred measures of oil

So he said to him
Sit down at once

Take your account
And write fifty

7   Then he said to another
And you
How much do you owe?

And he answered
A hundred measures of wheat

So he said to him
Take your account
And write eighty

8   And the Lord
Praised the untrustworthy agent
Because he acted with forethought
And said
The sons of this age
Show more forethought
In their own generation
Than the sons of light

9   But I
I say to you
Make yourselves friends
By means of the unjust wealth
So that when it fails
They may receive you into tents
Which remain throughout the ages

10   The one who is faithful
In very little
Is also faithful in much

And the one who is dishonest
In very little
Is also dishonest in much

11   If therefore
You were not faithful
With unjust wealth
Who will entrust to you
The true riches?

12   And if you were not faithful
With what belonged to another
Who will give you
What is your own?

13   No household servant
Can serve two overlords
As either he will hate the one
And love the other
Or he will hold to the one
And despise the other
You cannot serve God and riches

Christ answers the Pharisees

14   The Pharisees heard all this
And as they loved money
They scorned him

15   But he said to them
You are the ones
Who feel yourselves to be justified
In the opinion of your fellow men
But God
Knows your hearts
Because what is highly thought of
Among men
Is an abomination
In the sight of God

16   Until John
There were the Law and the prophets
Since then
The kingdom of God
Is being preached
And everyone
Is pressing to enter it

17   But it is easier
For heaven and earth to pass away
Than for one detail
To fall away from the Law

18 Everyone
Who releases his wife
And marries another
Commits adultery
And a woman
Who is released by her husband
And marries another
Commits adultery

The rich man and Lazarus

19 Now there was a man
Who was rich
And was accustomed to dress
In a purple robe
And in fine linen
And to eat splendidly every day

20 Lying beside his entrance
There was a beggar
Whose name was Lazarus

He was covered with sores
21 And he longed to be fed
With the pieces which were falling
From the rich man's table

Even the dogs
Came and licked his sores

22 It so happened
That the beggar died
And was carried away by the angels
Into the care of Abraham

The rich man also died
And was buried

23 In Hades
Where he was in torment
He lifted up his eyes
And saw Abraham
In the far distance
With Lazarus in his care

24   He called out
Father Abraham
Pity me
And send Lazarus
To dip the end of his finger
In water
To cool my tongue
Because I am in deep distress
In this flame

25   But Abraham said
Child
Remember
That during your lifetime
You received the good that was yours
Just as Lazarus
The evil
But now he is comforted here
And you are in deep distress

26   But as well as all this
A great chasm has been fixed
Between us and you
So that whoever has the desire
To pass over to you
Has not the power
Nor may anyone cross over
From where you are
To us

27   And he answered
Then I ask you
Father
To send him to my father's house
28   As I have five brothers

He should be a witness to them
And prevent them also
From coming to this place of torment

29   But Abraham said
They have Moses and the prophets
Let them hear them

30   And he replied
No
Father Abraham
But if someone from among the dead
Would go to them
They will change their hearts and minds

31   But he said to him
If they do not hear
Moses and the prophets
Neither will they be convinced
If someone should rise again
From among the dead

17 *Christ teaches the disciples*

1   And he said to his disciples
It is impossible
That temptations should not come
But woe to the one
Through whom they come

2   It would be better for him
If a millstone
Were hung around his neck
And he was cast into the sea
Than that he should cause the downfall
Of one of these little ones

3   You yourselves should take care

If your brother sins
Speak sternly to him
And if he changes heart and mind
Forgive him

4   And if he sins against you
Seven times in the day
And seven times he turns to you
Saying
I will change
You should forgive him

5   The apostles said to the Lord
            Add to our faith

6   Then the Lord said
            If your faith
            Was the size
            Of a grain of mustard seed
            You would have said
            To this mulberry tree
            Be uprooted
            And planted in the sea
            And it would have obeyed you

7   Which of you
            Having a servant
            Who has been ploughing
            Or tending sheep
            Would say to him
            When he comes in from the fields
            Sit down at the table at once?

8   But will say to him
            Prepare my supper
            Then tuck up your tunic
            And serve me
            While I eat and drink
            After this
            You may eat and drink yourself

9   Does he thank his servant
            Because he carried out his orders?

10   In the same way
            When you carry out your orders
            You too should say
            We are not useful servants
            We have only done
            What was asked of us

Ten lepers are healed

11   As he was going to Jerusalem
       He passed through the border
       Between Samaria and Galilee

12   When he entered a village
        Ten men met him
        They stood some distance away
        Because they were lepers

13   Raising their voices
          They called out
              Jesus
              Master
              Pity us

14   When he saw them
        He said to them
            Go
            Show yourselves to the priests

       Then it happened
       That as they went
       They were cleansed

15   But one of them
        When he saw that he was cured
        Turned back
        Praising God with a loud voice

16   Falling on his face
        At Jesus' feet
        He thanked him
        And he was a Samaritan

17   Jesus answered
            Have not ten been cleansed
            But where are the nine?
18   Was it only this outsider
            Who turned back
            To give praise to God?

19   And he said to him
        Rise up and go
        Your faith has saved you

20   When the Pharisees questioned him
        Asking when the kingdom of God
        Was coming

He answered them
    You cannot observe
    The coming of the kingdom of God
    And they will not say
    It is here or there
    As indeed
    The kingdom of God
    Is within you

The coming of the Son of Man

And he said to his disciples
    The days will come
    When you will long to see
    One of the days
    Of the Son of Man
    And will not see it

And they will say to you
    Look there
    Look here
    But do not go after them
    Or follow them

Just as the lightning flashes
    Shining from one part of heaven
    To the other
    So the Son of Man
    Will be in his day

But first
    He must suffer greatly
    And be rejected by this generation

As it was
    In the days of Noah
    So will it be also
    In the days of the Son of Man
They were eating and drinking
    Marrying
    And giving in marriage
    Until the day when Noah
    Entered the ark

When the flood came
And destroyed them all

28 Just as it was
In the days of Lot
They were eating and drinking
Buying and selling
Planting and building
29 Until the day when Lot
Went away from Sodom
When it rained
Fire and sulphur from heaven
And destroyed them all

30 It will be the same
In the day
When the Son of Man is revealed

31 In that day
Whoever is on the housetop
With his belongings in the house
Should not come down to take them
And whoever is in the fields
Should not turn back

32 Remember Lot's wife

33 Whoever seeks to save
His soul-bearing life
Will lose it
But whoever would lose it
Will save it alive
34 I say to you
In this night
There will be two men
In one bed
One will be taken
And the other will be left

35 Two women
Will be grinding together
One will be taken
But the other will be left

36   Two men
           Will be in the fields
           One will be taken
           And the other will be left

37   They asked him
           Where
           Lord?

      And he said to them
           Where the body is
           There the eagles
           Will gather together

18 *Parable of the determined widow*

1   He told them a parable
    To show that they should always pray
    And not give up
2   He said
        In a certain town
        There was a judge
        Who neither feared God
        Nor respected his fellow men

3   And in that town
        There was also a widow
        Who came to him
        Saying
        Defend my cause against my opponent

4   For a time
        He would not do it

        But after a while
        He said to himself
        Although I do not fear God
        Nor respect my fellow men
5   In the end
        Because this widow troubles me
        I will defend her cause
        So that she no longer comes
        To wear me out

6   The Lord said
            You should note
            What the unjust judge is thinking

7   Will not God
            Be patient with his elect
            And come to their defence
            When they cry out to him
            Day and night?

8   I tell you
            That at once
            He will come to their defence

            However
            When the Son of Man comes
            Will he find faith
            On the earth?

The parable of the Pharisee and the tax-collector
9   And he also told this parable
        To some who considered themselves
        To be in the right
        And looked down on the rest

10   Two men
            Went up to the Temple to pray
            One was a Pharisee
            The other a tax-collector

11   The Pharisee stood praying within himself
            And said
            God
            I thank you
            That I am not like other men
            Greedy
            Unjust
            An adulterer
            Or even like this tax-collector

12   I fast twice between sabbaths
        And give a tenth
        Of all that I receive

13   The tax-collector
        Standing far off
        Would not lift up his eyes
        To heaven
        But beat his breast
        And said
        God
        Be gracious to me
        A sinner

14   I say to you
        This man
        Went back to his home
        With his prayer heard
        Rather than the other
        Because everyone who exalts himself
        Will be humbled
        And whoever humbles himself
        Will be exalted

Children are brought to Jesus
15   They brought babies to him
        So that he could touch them
        When the disciples saw it
        They turned them away

16   But Jesus called them to him
            And said
                Allow the children to come to me
                And do not hinder them
                Because of such as they are
                So is the kingdom of God

17   Certainly I say to you
                Whoever
                Does not receive the kingdom of God
                Like a child
                In no way
                Will enter into it

The problem of riches

18 A leader among the Jews
Put a question to him
Saying
    Good teacher
    What should I do
    To inherit life
    Throughout the ages?

19 Jesus said to him
    Why do you call me good?
    No one is good
    Except God only

20   You know the commandments
    Do not commit adultery
    Do not kill
    Do not steal
    Do not witness falsely
    Honour your father and your mother

21 But he answered
    I have kept all this
    From my youth

22 On hearing this
Jesus said to him
    But there is still something wanting
    Sell everything that you have
    And distribute it to the poor
    Then you will have treasure
    In the heavens
    And come
    Follow me

23 When he heard this
He grew deeply distressed
Because he was enormously rich

24 Jesus looked at him
    And said
        How difficult it is
        For those who have possessions
        To enter the kingdom of God

25   It is easier for a camel
To enter through the eye of a needle
Than for a rich man
To enter the kingdom of God

26   Those hearing him said
Then who can be saved?

27   And he said
What is impossible with men
Is possible with God

28   Peter said
See how we have left
What belongs to us
And have followed you

29   And he said to them
Certainly I say to you
There is no one
Who has left house or wife
Or brothers or parents or children
For the sake of the kingdom of God
30   Who will not receive much more
In this present season
And in the age to come
Life throughout the ages

Third prophecy of the Passion
31   He took the twelve
And said to them
Now
We are going up to Jerusalem
And everything will be completed
Which has been written through the prophets
About the Son of Man

32   He will be delivered to the Gentiles
And will be mocked
Insulted
And spat upon

33   When they have scourged him
They will kill him
And on the third day
He will rise

34 But they did not understand
Any of this
As what was said
Had been hidden from them
And they did not comprehend
These words

Healing of a blind man
35 Then it happened
That as he came near Jericho
There was a blind man
Sitting by the wayside
Begging

36 As he heard a crowd passing
He enquired what this meant

37 And they gave him the news
That Jesus of Nazareth
Was going past

38   He cried out
        Jesus
        Son of David
        Pity me

39 Those who went in front
Told him sternly
That he should be quiet

    But he cried out all the more
        Son of David
        Pity me

40 Jesus stood still
And ordered him
To be brought to him

      As he came close
          He put the question to him
41   What do you want me
                To do for you?

      He said
          Lord
          That I may see again

42   And Jesus said to him
          See again
          Your faith has saved you

43   Immediately
      He could see again
      And followed him
      Praising the revelation of God

      And all the people who saw this
      Gave praise to God

19

Jesus and Zacchaeus

1   On coming to Jericho
      He passed through it

2   And there was a man
      Whose name was Zacchaeus
      He was a high-ranking tax collector
      And he was rich

3   He was anxious to see Jesus
      To know how he looked
      But he could not see him
      Because of the crowd
      And because he was small himself

4   When he had run on ahead
      He climbed up into a sycamore tree
      So that he could see Jesus
      As he would be passing that way

5   On coming to the place
Jesus looked up
    And said to him
        Zacchaeus
        Come down quickly
        Because today
        I must stay at your house

6   He came down quickly
And welcomed him with joy

7   When they saw this
They all complained
    And said
        He has gone to stay
        With a man who is an outcast

8   Zacchaeus stood
    And said to the Lord
        Half of my property
        O Lord
        I give to the poor
        And if I have cheated anyone
        I return it four times over

9   And Jesus said to him
        Today
        Salvation has come to this house
        Because he too
        Is a son of Abraham

10   For the Son of Man
        Came to look for what has been lost
        And to save it

Parable of the ten servants

11   When they had heard all this
He also told them a parable
Because he was near Jerusalem
And they thought
That the kingdom of God
Would appear immediately

12	Therefore he said to them
	There was a man of noble birth
	Who was going into a distant land
	To receive a kingdom for himself
	And then to return

13	When he had called ten of his servants
	He gave them money
	Distributing among them
	Ten silver minas
	And he said to them
	Trade with these until I come back

14	But his fellow citizens hated him
	And sent a deputation after him
	Saying
	We do not want this man
	To reign over us

15	It happened
	That when he returned
	After having received the kingdom
	He ordered those servants
	To whom he had given the money
	To be called before him
	So that he might find out
	From each one
	What they had gained by trading

16	When the first came
	He said
	Lord
	Your mina has gained ten minas

17	And he said to him
	Well done
	Good servant
	Because you have been faithful
	In very little
	You shall have authority
	Over ten towns

18	The second came And said Your mina O Lord Has made five minas
19	He also said to that one You shall be over five towns
20	Then the other came and said Lord See here is your mina Which I had stored away In a linen cloth
21	I was afraid of you Because you are a strict man You take up What you did not put down And you reap What you did not sow
22	He said to him I judge you By what you have said yourself You bad servant Did you know indeed That I I am a strict man Taking up What I had not put down And reaping What I had not sown?
23	So why did not you Give my money to the bankers So that when I came myself I could have claimed it back With interest?
24	To those who were standing there He said Take the mina away from him

And give it to the one
Who has ten minas

25 And they said to him
Lord
He has ten minas

26 He answered them
I tell you
That everyone who has
Will be given more
But if anyone has not
Even what he has
Will be taken away

27 But bring those enemies of mine
Who did not want me
To reign over them
And execute them in my presence

The entry into Jerusalem
28 After he had said this
He led the way
Going up towards Jerusalem

29 And it happened
When he came to Bethphage and Bethany
Near the hill called after the olive trees
That he sent two of his disciples
   Saying to them
30   Go to the village opposite
And when you come into it
You will find a colt tied up
On which no man has yet sat
Untie it and bring it here

31 And if anyone says to you
Why are you untying it?
This is what you should say
Because the Lord needs it

32   Those who had been sent out
     Came and found everything
     Just as he had told them

33   While they were untying the colt
         The people to whom it belonged
         Said to them
             Why are you untying the colt?

34   They answered
             Because the Lord needs it

35   They brought it to Jesus

     And when they had cast their cloaks
     Over the colt
     They placed Jesus on it

36   And the people
     Spread their cloaks on the road
     As he passed

37   When he had almost reached
     The descent of the Mount of Olives
     The whole crowd of his disciples
     Began to rejoice with great shouts
     And to praise God
     For all the powerful deeds
     Which they had seen
38   Saying
             Blest be the one who comes
             As the king
             In the name of the Lord
             Peace in heaven
             And revelation in the highest places

39   Some of the Pharisees
     Who were in the crowd
     Said to him
         Teacher
         Speak sternly to your disciples

40   And he answered
         I tell you

If these kept silent
The stones would cry out

Jesus weeps over Jerusalem
41 As he came nearer
And saw the city
He wept over it
42   And said
        If only
        Even you
        Could know today
        What it is that brings peace
        But now
        It has been hidden
        From your eyes

43   As the days will come to you
    When your enemies
    Will encircle you with a palisade
    And oppress you on all sides
44   They will level you with the ground
    Both you and your children
    Who are within your walls

    There is not one stone
    Which will be left standing upon another
    Because you did not recognize
    The right moment
    When it came upon you

Jesus clears the Temple
45 When he entered the Temple
He began to turn out the traders
46   Saying to them
        It has been written
        My house
        Shall be a house of prayer
        But you yourselves have made it
        A robber's cave

47	He was teaching every day
	In the temple
	And the leaders of the people
	Were looking for a way to destroy him
48	But they did not find anything
	That they could do
	Because the people
	All hung upon his words

20

Jesus questions the elders about John

1 It happened one day
That as he was in the Temple
Teaching the people
And preaching the Gospel
    The chief priests and scribes
    Together with the elders
    Came up and spoke to him
2   Saying
        Tell us
        By what authority
        Are you doing these things
        Or who gave you
        This authority?

3   He answered them
        I myself
        Will also ask for a word from you
        Tell me
4   Was John's baptism
        From heaven or from men?

5   They discussed it among themselves
    And said
        If we say
        From heaven
        He will say
        Why did you not believe him?

6   And if we say
    From men
    All the people will stone us
    Because they are convinced
    That John was a prophet

7   So they answered
           We do not know
           Where it came from

8   And Jesus said to them
           Neither will I
           I say to you
           By what authority
           I do these things

Parable of the wicked farmers

9   He began to tell the people
      This parable
           A man planted a vineyard
           And let it out to farmers
           Then he went out of the country
           For a long time

10   In due season
      He sent his servant
      To the farmers
      So that they should give him
      The fruit of the vineyard
      But the farmers beat him
      And sent him away with nothing

11   He sent another servant as well
      But him they also insulted
      And after beating him
      They sent him away with nothing

12   He also sent a third
      But they injured him
      And threw him out

13   Then the owner of the vineyard said
      What shall I do?

      I will send my beloved son
      Perhaps they will respect him

14 When they saw him
The farmers discussed it together
And said
This is the heir
Let us kill him
So that the inheritance
May be ours

15 Then throwing him out
Outside of the vineyard
They killed him

What therefore
Will the owner of the vineyard
Do to them?

16 He will come and destroy the farmers
And will give the vineyard to others

When they heard this
They said
May that never happen

17 Jesus looked at them
And said
What therefore
Is this that has been written
The stone which the builders rejected
Has become the headstone of the corner

18 Anyone who falls on that stone
Will be broken to pieces
But anyone on whom it falls
Will be crushed to powder

A question about taxes
19 At that same hour
The chief priest and the scribes
Made efforts to lay hands on him
But they were afraid of the people
Because they were conscious that this parable
Had been told about them

20 They watched him narrowly
And sent men
Who pretended to be honest
To take hold of his words
So that they might hand him over
To the jurisdiction and authority
Of the governor

21   And they asked him this question
        Teacher
        We know that when you teach
        You speak out plainly
        Without regard to anyone's position
        But truthfully teach the way of God
22   Is it lawful for us
    To give tax to Caesar
    Or is it not lawful?

23 As he considered their trickery
    He said to them
24   Show me a denarius
        Whose is this portrait
        And inscription?

    They said
        It is Caesar's

25   And he said to them
        So give back to Caesar
        What belongs to Caesar
        And to God
        What belongs to God

26 Their position was not strong enough
In the presence of the people
To take up what he said
And marvelling at his answer
They fell silent

    The Sadducees' question
27 Then came some of the Sadducees
Those who deny
That there is a resurrection

To ask him the question
28 Teacher
Moses wrote for us

If any man
Has a brother who dies
Leaving a wife but no children
Then that man
Should take his brother's wife
And raise up children
For his brother

29 Now there were seven brothers
And the first
Having taken a wife
Died childless

30 Then the second brother took her
31 And then the third

So that all the seven
Having died without children
Had done the same

32 Finally the woman
Also died

33 Therefore in the resurrection
Of which of them
Will she become the wife
Because all the seven
Had her as a wife?

34 But Jesus said to them
The sons of this age
Marry
And are given in marriage
35 But those considered worthy
To attain to the age to come
And to the resurrection of the dead
Neither marry
Nor are given in marriage

36	They are not able to die any more
	But are equal to the angels
	And are the sons of God
	As they are sons of the resurrection
37	That the dead are raised
	Was shown by Moses
	At the thorn-bush
	As he calls the Lord
	The God of Abraham
	And the God of Isaac
	And the God of Jacob
38	He is not the God of the dead
	But of the living
	As indeed
	All live to him
39	Some of the scribes
	Answered him
	Teacher
	What you say is right
40	Because they did not have the courage
	To ask him any more questions

Jesus questions the scribes

41	But he said to them
	How is it that they say
	The Christ is David's son?
42	Because David himself says
	In the scroll of the Psalms
	The Lord said to my Lord
	Sit at my right hand
43	*Until I make your enemies*
	A footstool for your feet
44	Therefore if David calls him Lord
	How is he his son?

45   All the people heard
         How he said to his disciples
46   Be on your guard against the scribes
            Who wish to walk about in long robes
            And who like greetings in the markets
            The first seats in the synagogues
            And the best places at meals
47   And who eat up the inheritance of widows
            And make pretence of long prayers

         They will be judged
         With greater severity

21   *The widow's offering*
1   He looked up
     And saw that the rich
     Were throwing their gifts into the treasury

2   Then he saw one poor widow
     Throwing in two of the smallest coins

3   And he said
            Certainly I say to you
            This poor widow
            Has put in more
            Than all of them
4   Because their gifts
            Came from what they have over
            But out of her need
            She has put in all the living
            Which she has

     Jesus prophesies disasters and persecution
5   When some people
     Were talking about the Temple
     Saying that it was made beautiful
     By fine stones and votive offerings
         He said
6   You observe all this
            The days will come
            When there will not be a stone
            Left standing upon a stone
            Which will not be thrown down

7   And they questioned him
Saying
    Teacher
    When will this be?
    And what will be the sign
    That this is going to happen?

8   And he said
    Watch out
    That you are not misled
    As there are many
    Who will come in my name
    Saying
    I
    I am

    And also
    The right moment is near

    But you should not go after them

9   When you hear about wars
    And revolutions
    Do not be dismayed
    As these things must first happen
    But the end
    Will not come at once

10   Then he said to them
    Nation
    Will rise against nation
    And kingdom
    Against kingdom

11   There will be mighty earthquakes
    And in places
    There will be plagues and famines
    And there will be terrors
    And mighty signs from heaven

12   But before all this
    They will lay hands on you
    And will persecute you
    Giving you up to the synagogues

LUKE 21

And to imprisonment
They will bring you before kings
And before governors
Because of my name

13 You will be landed with bearing witness
14 But hold in your hearts
That you need not practise your defence

15 Because I myself will give you
Such grace of speech and wisdom
That all those who oppose you
Will neither be able to withstand
Nor to contradict it

16 You will be betrayed
By parents and brothers
And by relations and friends
Some of you
Will be condemned to death

17 Because of my name
Everyone will hate you
18 But not even a hair of your head
Will perish

19 It is through your patience
That you will gain possession
Of your living souls

20 But when you see Jerusalem
Surrounded by encampments
Then you will be aware
That it will soon be desolate

21 Then those who are in Judea
Should escape to the mountains
And those within the city
Should leave it
While those should not go there
Who are out in the country

22   Because these are days of vengeance
      When all that has been written
      Will be fulfilled

23   Alas for the woman
      In those days
      Who carries a child in her womb
      Or has one at her breast
      Because there will be great want
      Throughout the land
      And wrath upon the people

24   They will fall
      By the edge of the sword
      And will be taken as captives
      Among all the nations

      And Jerusalem
      Will be trodden down by strangers
      Until the era of the heathen
      Comes to an end

The coming of the Son of Man

25   There will be signs
      In sun
      And moon
      And stars
      And on the earth
      Nations in distress
      Anxious at the sound of the sea
      And of the ocean surge

26   Men fainting from fear
      And the expectation of what is coming
      To the inhabited earth
      For the powers of the heavens
      Will be shaken

27   Then will they behold
      The Son of Man
      Coming in a cloud
      With power and great glory

LUKE 21

28   When these things begin to happen
             Stand erect
             And lift up your heads
             Because your deliverance
             Is coming close

29   And he told them a parable
             You observe the fig tree
             And all the trees
30   When they put out leaves
             You see for yourselves
             And are aware
             That the summer is now near

31   So also
             When you observe these things
             You are aware
             That the kingdom of God is near

32   Certainly I say to you
             That this generation
             Will not pass away
             Until it will all happen

33   Heaven and earth
             Will pass away
             But my words
             Will never pass away

34   But look to yourselves
             Lest your hearts
             Become burdened
             With overindulgence
             Drunkenness
             And the cares of living

             Because that day
             Will come upon you suddenly
35   And trap you
             As it will come on all those
             Who are dwelling
             On the face of the whole earth

36	Be watchful at all seasons
	Begging for strength
	To escape all those things
	Which are coming soon
	And to stand in the presence
	Of the Son of Man
37	Now during the daytime
	He was teaching in the Temple
	But at night he went out
	And stayed on that hill
	Which is called the Mount of Olives
38	Rising early in the morning
	All the people came to him
	To hear him

22 *The betrayal*

1	Now the festival of Unleavened Bread
	Which is called Passover
	Was coming close
2	And the chief priests and the scribes
	Looked for a way to destroy Jesus
	Because they were afraid of the people
3	Then Satan
	Entered into Judas called Iscariot
	Who was counted among the twelve
4	He went away
	And discussed with the chief priests
	And with the Temple officers
	How he could betray him to them
5	They were overjoyed
	And agreed to give him money
6	Which he accepted
	Then he looked for an opportunity
	To betray him
	Away from the crowds

Preparation for the Passover

7 When the day of Unleavened Bread came
On which the Passover lamb
Should be killed
8   He sent Peter and John
    Saying
        Prepare the Passover for us
        So that we may eat it

9   They said to him
        Where
        Do you wish us to prepare it?

10   And he told them
        Now when you enter the city
        A man will meet you
        Who is carrying a jar of water
        Follow him
        Into the house where he is going

11   Then speak
    To the master of the house
    Saying
    The teacher says to you
    Where is the guest room
    So that I may eat the Passover there
    With my disciples?

12   He will show you
    A large upper room
    Which has been set out ready
    Prepare for us there

13 They went
And found everything
As he had told them
And they prepared the Passover

The Last Supper

14 When the hour came
He sat at the table
And the apostles were with him

15   Then he said to them
           With great longing
           I have desired to eat this Passover
           With you
           Before I suffer

16   As I say to you
      It is certain
      That I shall not eat it again
      Until it is fulfilled
      In the kingdom of God

17 He took a cup
And when he had given thanks
    He said
        Take this
        And divide it among yourselves
18   As I tell you
      From now on
      It is certain
      That I shall not drink
      The fruit of the vine
      Until the kingdom of God comes

19 He took bread
And when he had given thanks
He broke it
And gave it to them
    Saying
        This is my body
        Which is being given for you
        Do this
        In memory of me

20 After the supper
He did the same with the cup
    And said
        This is the cup
        Of the new covenant
        In my blood
        Which is shed for you

21 But look how the hand
Of the one who is betraying me
Is with me on the table

22 It is certain
That the Son of Man
Will go
According to what has been determined
But woe to that man
By whom he is betrayed

23 And they began to debate
Among themselves
Which of them it might be
Who was about to undertake
Such a thing

Rivalry among the disciples
24 And it happened
That there was rivalry among them
As to which of them
Should be thought
To be the greatest

25 So he said to them
   The kings of the nations
   Are their overlords
   And those who have authority over them
   Are called benefactors

26 But not among you

   There the greatest
   Must become the youngest
   And the leader
   Like the one who serves

27 For who is the greatest
   The one sitting at the table
   Or the one who is serving?
   Surely the one sitting at the table
   But I
   I am among you
   As the one who serves

28 You are the ones
    Who have stayed with me
    Throughout my trials

29 And I
    I appoint you a kingdom
    As the Father has appointed me
30 So that you may eat and drink
    At my table in my kingdom
    And you will sit on thrones
    Judging the twelve tribes of Israel

Jesus foretells Peter's denial

31   Simon
        Simon
        See how Satan
        Demanded to have you all
        To sieve out like wheat
32   But I
        I have prayed for you
        That your faith
        Might not fail
        And when you have come to yourself
        Support your brothers

33 And he answered him
        Lord
        I am ready to go with you
        Both to prison
        And to death

34 But Jesus said
        I tell you
        Peter
        Today a cock will not crow
        Until you have denied three times
        That you know me

35 And to all of them
    He said
        When I sent you out

Without a purse
Or a bag
Or sandals
Were you in need of anything?

They said
Nothing

36 Then he said to them
But now
Whoever has a purse
Let him take it
And whoever has a bag
Should do the same
And he who has no sword
Should sell his cloak
And buy one

37 Because I tell you
In me
The Scripture is fulfilled
Which says
He was numbered with those
Who broke the Law
As indeed
All that was written of me
Has an end

38 They said
Lord
See here are two swords

And he said to them
It is enough

Jesus prays on the Mount of Olives
39 On leaving there
He went to the Mount of Olives
As was his habit
And his disciples followed him

40 When he came to the place
He said to them

Pray
That you may not give way to temptation

41 He withdrew from them
About a stone's throw
And he knelt down and prayed
42 Saying
Father
If it is your desire
Take this cup away from me
However
It is not my will
But yours
Which should be done

43 Then an angel from heaven
Appeared to him
Giving him strength

44 As he was in agony
He prayed ever more urgently
And his sweat
Became like clots of blood
Falling on to the ground

45 When he rose up from prayer
He came to the disciples
And found them asleep
Because of their sorrow

46 And he said to them
Why are you sleeping
Rise up
And pray
That you may not give way to temptation

The arrest
47 While he was still speaking
They saw a crowd
Led by one of the twelve
Called Judas

He came up to Jesus
To kiss him

48   But Jesus said to him
        Judas
        Do you betray the Son of Man
        With a kiss?

49   When those who were around him
Saw what was going to happen
        They said
        Lord
        Shall we strike with a sword?

50   And one of them
Struck the high priest's servant
And cut off his right ear

51   Jesus answered
        Let them have their way

And touching his ear
He healed him

52   Then Jesus
Said to the chief priests
To the captains of the Temple Guard
And to the elders
Who had come for him
        Have you come out with swords
        And with clubs
        As if against a bandit?

53   Every day
When I was with you
In the Temple
You did not stretch out your hands
Against me
But this is your hour
And the authority of the darkness

Peter's denial

54 When they had taken him
They led him away
And brought him into the high priest's house

Peter followed at a distance

55 In the centre of the courtyard
A fire had been lighted
And when the company sat down together
Peter sat down with them

56 One of the maidservants
Saw him sitting in the firelight
    And looking at him closely
    She said
        That one was with him

57   But he denied it
    And said
        Woman
        I do not know him

58 After a little while
Another man saw him
    And said
        And you are one of them

    But Peter said
        Man
        I am not

59 About an hour later
    Another insisted
    Saying
        It is true
        That this one also
        Was with him
        As he is certainly a Galilean

60   But Peter said to him
        Man
        I do not know
        What you are saying

At once
While he was still speaking
A cock crowed

61 The Lord turned
And looked at Peter

Then Peter remembered
What the Lord had said
When he told him
Before a cock crows today
You will disown me three times

62 He went outside
And wept bitterly

Jesus is mocked and beaten
63 Then the men who had taken Jesus
Mocked him and beat him

64 They blindfolded him
   And said to him
      Prophesy
      Which is the one
      Who is the one hitting you?

65 And blaspheming
They said many other things
Against him

Jesus before the Council
66 At daybreak
The assembly of the elders of the people
Consisting of both chief priests and scribes
Had Jesus brought before their Council
67   And said to him
      If you are the Christ
      Tell us

   And he said to them
      If I tell you
      It is certain that you will not believe

68	And if I question you
	You will certainly not answer

69	But from now on
	The Son of Man
	Will be sitting at the right hand
	Of the power of God

70	They all said
	Are you therefore
	The Son of God?

And he answered them
    You say that I
    I AM

71	Then they said
	Why do we still need witnesses
	As we heard it ourselves
	From his own mouth?

23 *Jesus is brought before Pilate*

1	Then the whole assembly rose up
	And brought him before Pilate

2	They began to accuse him
	And said
	We found this person
	Misleading our nation
	Preventing us from giving tribute to Caesar
	And saying of himself
	That he is Christ
	A king

3	Pilate put the question to him
	Are you the King of the Jews?

And he answered
    You say so

4	Then Pilate said to the chief priests
	And to the crowds

I do not find any crime
In this man

5 But they persisted
And said
>He rouses up the people
>Teaching throughout Judea
>He started in Galilee
>And then came here

Jesus is sent to Herod
6 When Pilate heard this
He asked
If the man was a Galilean

7 On discovering
That he came from Herod's district
He sent him over to Herod
Who was also in Jerusalem
During those days

8 When Herod saw Jesus
He was filled with joy

He had wanted to see him
For a long time
Because of what he had heard
About him
And he hoped to see some sign
Performed by him

9 He questioned him at length
But he did not answer

10 The chief priests and scribes
Stood by
Making great efforts to accuse him

11 Herod and his soldiers
Despised him
They threw a shining garment round him
And mocked him
Then sent him back to Pilate

12   On that same day
      Herod and Pilate became friends
      As before this
      There had been ill will between them

      Pilate fails to release Jesus
13   Then Pilate called together
      The chief priests
      The leaders
      And the people
14   And said to them
              You have brought this man to me
              Because He is turning the people away
              But now I myself
              Have examined him in your presence
              And I do not find this man
              Guilty of the crimes
              Of which you accuse him
15   And neither did Herod
              As he sent him back to us

              So now
              As he has done nothing
              Which deserves death

16   When he has been disciplined
              I will let him go

17   But at the festival
      He had to release one prisoner for them

18   So the whole crowd cried out
              Take this man away
              And release for us
              Barabbas

19   Barabbas had been thrown into prison
      Because of some disturbance
      And murder
      Which had happened in the city

20   Pilate
      Called out to them again
      As he wished to release Jesus

21   But they shouted
           Crucify him
           Crucify him

22   He said to them a third time
           But what has he done wrong?
           I found nothing in him
           Which deserves death
           Therefore
           I will discipline him
           And let him go

23   But they held to it
      And with loud voices
      Asked for him to be crucified
      And their voices prevailed

24   So Pilate decided
      That what they demanded
      Should be carried out

25   He released the one
      For whom they asked
      A man who had been thrown into prison
      For creating a disturbance
      And for murder

      But Jesus
      He handed over to their will

The Crucifixion

26   As they led him away
      They took hold of Simon
      A Cyrenian coming from the country
      And put the cross on him
      To carry it behind Jesus

27   A large crowd of people
      Followed
      Also many women
      Who wailed and mourned for him

28   Jesus turned to them
  And said
    Daughters of Jerusalem
    Do not weep for me
    But weep for yourselves
    And for your children

29   Look
    The days are coming
    When they will say
    Blessed are the barren
    The wombs that did not bear
    And the breasts that did not give milk

30   Then they will begin
    To say to the mountains
    Fall on us
    And to the hills
    Cover us

31   Because if they do these things
    When the wood is green
    What will happen
    When it is dry?

32   Two others
  Who were evil-doers
  Were led away
  To be put to death with him

33   When they came to the place
  Which is called the Skull
  There they crucified him
  And the evil-doers with him
  One on the right
  And one on the left

34   Then Jesus said
     Father
     Forgive them
     Because they do not know
     What they are doing

So that they could divide his clothing
They threw dice

35 The people
Stood looking on
The rulers
Also scorned him
    They said
        He saved others
        Let him save himself
        If he is Christ
        The one chosen by God

36 And the soldiers
Mocked him
Coming up to him
And offering him vinegar
37   Saying
        If you are the King of the Jews
        Save yourself

38 There was also a superscription
Over him
THIS IS THE KING OF THE JEWS

39 And one of the evil-doers
Who was being hanged
    Blasphemed him saying
        Are you not the Christ?
        Save yourself and us

40   But the other
    Spoke sternly to him
    And said
        Do you not fear God
        Because you too have been sentenced?
41   And we indeed justly
        Because the result of what we undertook
        Comes back to us
        But he has not undertaken
        Anything harmful

42   And he said
        Jesus

>   Remember me
>   When you come into your kingdom

43   He answered him
>   Certainly I say to you
>   Today
>   You will be with me
>   In Paradise

44   It was now about the sixth hour
And there was darkness
Over all the land
Until the ninth hour
45   As the sun failed

The veil of the shrine
Was torn down the centre

46   And Jesus cried out
With a loud voice
>   Father
>   Into your hands
>   I commit my spirit

As he said this
He drew his last breath

47   When the centurion
Saw what was happening
>   He praised God
>   And said
>   >   This was certainly a just man

48   And the crowds
Who had come together at this spectacle
When they beheld what was happening
Beat their breasts and returned

49   All those whom he had known
Stood at a distance
Watching all this

With them were the women
Who had accompanied him
From Galilee

The burial

50 And now there was a man
Whose name was Joseph
He came from the Jewish town of Arimathea
And was a member of the Council

He was a good and just man
51 Who awaited the kingdom of God
And he had not agreed
With their intention
Or with what they had carried out

52 This man went to Pilate
And asked for the body of Jesus

53 On taking it down
He wrapped it in linen
And placed it in a tomb
That was cut out of rock
And where no one
Had so far been laid

54 As it was the day of Preparation
And the sabbath was approaching
55 The women
Who had followed him from Galilee
Took note of the tomb
And saw how his body was placed

Then they went back
To prepare spices and ointment

56 They remained quiet on the sabbath
As ordered by the commandment

24 *The Resurrection*

1   At day break
On the first day after the sabbath
They came to the tomb
Carrying the spices
Which they had prepared

2   And they found that the stone
Had been rolled away from the tomb

3   When they went inside
They did not find the body
Of the Lord Jesus

4   They were at a loss about this
When see
Two men stood by them
Clothed in lightning

5   As they were filled with fear
And bowed their faces to the earth
    The men said to them
        Why are you
           Looking for the one who lives
           Among those who are dead?

6   He is not here
        But has been raised
        Remember what he told you
        While he was still in Galilee
7   When he said
        The Son of Man
        Must be given up
        Into the hands of sinful men
        And be crucified
        To rise again on the third day

8   And they remembered his words

9   Then they returned from the tomb
To give the news to the eleven
And to all the others

10   Now it was Mary Magdalene
Joanna
Mary the mother of James
And the other women with them
Who told all this to the apostles
11   And their words
Appeared to them to be nonsense
So that they did not believe them

12   But Peter got up
And hurried to the tomb
He stooped down
And saw only the linen cloths
So he went home
Filled with wonder at what had happened

The road to Emmaus
13   On the same day
Two of them were on their way
To a village called Emmaus
Which was about seven miles from Jerusalem

14   And they talked to each other
About everything that had taken place

15   Then it happened
That as they were deep in conversation
And were discussing together
Jesus himself approached them
And travelled with them

16   But their eyes
Were prevented from recognizing him

17   And he said to them
          What are the words
             Which fly back and forth between you
          As you walk along?

They stood still
Looking depressed

18   The one who was called Cleopas
Said to him

Are you the only stranger in Jerusalem
Who does not know
About the events which have happened there
In recent days

19 He said to them
What events?

And they answered him
Those connected with Jesus
The Nazarene
A man who was a prophet
Powerful in deed and in word
In the sight of God
And of all the people

20 How both our chief priests
And our rulers
Handed him over
To be condemned to death
And crucified him

21 We were hoping
That he was the one
Who was about to ransom Israel

As well as all this
It is now the third day
Since it happened
22 And we were astonished
By some of our women
Who had been early at the tomb
23 And not finding his body
Came and reported
Having seen a vision of angels
Who said that he lives

24 Some of those who were with us
Went to the tomb
And found that it was indeed
As the women had said
But they did not see him

25   Jesus said to them
        O you are senseless
        And your hearts are so slow
        That you did not believe
        All that the prophets said

26   Was it not necessary for the Christ
       To suffer in this way
       And to enter into his glory?

27 And beginning with Moses
He went through all the prophets
Interpreting for them
All those parts of the Scriptures
Which concerned himself

28 When they came near the village
To which they were travelling
He made as if to go further

29   But they persuaded him
    Saying
        Stay with us
        Because it will soon be evening
        And the day
        Draws to a close

And he went in
To stay with them

30 It happened
That when he sat at table with them
He took bread
And blessed it
And when he had broken it
He gave it to them

31 Their eyes were opened
And they recognized him

Then he was no longer
Visible to them

32 They said to one another
    Did not our hearts
    Burn within us
    As he talked to us on the road
    Explaining the Scriptures to us

33 In that same hour
They set out
And returned to Jerusalem
Where they found the eleven
And those who were with them
Gathered together

34   They were saying
    The Lord
      Has certainly been raised
      And has appeared to Simon

35 Then they told them
What had happened on the road
And how they recognized him
When he broke the bread

Jesus appears to the disciples
36 As they were talking about this
He stood among them
    And said to them
        Peace be with you

37 But they were dismayed
And filled with fear
Because they supposed
That they beheld a spirit

38   He said to them
    Why are you distressed
    And why do such thoughts
    Rise up in your hearts
39   Look at my hands and my feet
    Make sure that I
    I am indeed myself
    Handle me
    Because a spirit

> Does not have flesh and bones
> As you behold that I have

40 When he had said this
He showed them
His hands and his feet

41 Overcome with joy and astonishment
They still did not believe
> So he said to them
>> Have you anything to eat here?

42 And they gave him
Part of a cooked fish
And a piece of honeycomb
43 Which he took and ate
In their presence

44 > And he said to them
>> While I was still with you
>> I told you it was necessary
>> For everything to be fulfilled
>> That has been written about me
>> In the Law of Moses
>> And in the prophets and the psalms

45 Then he opened their minds
So that they understood the Scriptures
46 > Saying to them
>> This is what has been written
>> The Christ must suffer
>> And rise from the dead
>> On the third day

47 >> And in his name
>> There shall be proclaimed
>> To all the nations
>> Beginning from Jerusalem
>> The need to change heart and mind
>> For the forgiveness of sins

48 >> You are witnesses
>> To all of this

49   And see
          I
          I send out upon you
          The promise of my Father
          But you should stay in the city
          Until you are clothed with power
          From above

The Ascension

50   Then he led them out
      Almost as far as Bethany
      And lifting up his hands
      He blessed them

51   And it happened
      That as he blessed them
      He passed from them

52   They returned to Jerusalem
      With great joy
53   And were always in the Temple
      Praising God

The Gospel of John

1   *Prologue*
1. In the Beginning
   Was the Word
   And the Word
   Was with God
   And the Word
   Was God
2. He was in the Beginning
   With God

3. Through him
   Everything entered into existence
   And without him
   Nothing entered into existence

   What existed
4. Was life in him
   And the life was the light of mankind
5. And the light
   Shines in the darkness
   But the darkness
   Has not taken hold of it

6. There entered into existence
   A man sent out from God
   His name was John

7. He came as a witness
   To bear witness to the Light
   So that everyone
   Might believe through him

8. He was not the Light
   But should bear witness to the Light
9. The true Light
   Who enlightens every human being
   Coming into the world

10   He was in the world
Through him the world
Entered into existence
And the world
Was not aware of him

11   He came into his own
And those who were his own
Did not receive him

12   To all who accepted him
He gave the authority
For their existence as children of God

For those who believe in his name
13   It was not of blood-streams
Nor of the will of the flesh
Nor of the will of mortal man
But of God
That they were born

14   In the flesh
The Word entered into existence
And made his dwelling among us
And we beheld the glory of his revelation
Revealed as an only-born from his Father
Full of grace and truth

15   John bears witness to him
And has cried out
This was the one
Of whom I spoke
The one
Who coming after me
Has existed before me
Because he preceded me

16   Out of his fullness
We have all received grace
In the place of grace
17   Because the Law
Was given through Moses
But grace and truth
Entered into existence through Jesus Christ

18   No one has ever had sight of God
      The only-born Son
      Who is within the being of the Father
      He is the interpreter

      The witness of John the Baptist
19   And this is the witness of John
      When the Jews
      Sent out priests and Levites from Jerusalem
      So that they could ask him
      You
      Who are you?

20   He confessed
          And did not deny it
          But confessed
              I
              I am not the Christ

21   They asked him
              Then are you Elijah?

          He said
              I am not

              Are you the Prophet?

          And he answered
              No

22   So they said to him
              Who are you?
              We must give an answer
              To those who sent us
              What do you say about yourself?

23   He declared
              As a voice
              I call in the desert
              Make straight the way of the Lord
              As was said by the prophet Isaiah

24 Now they had been sent out
By the Pharisees

25 And they asked him
  Why are you baptizing
  If you are neither the Christ
  Nor Elijah
  Nor the Prophet?

26 John answered them
  I myself baptize in water
  He stands among you
  Whom indeed you do not know
27   He is the one
  Who comes after me
  And I
  I am not worthy
  To undo the strap of his sandal

28 All this took place in Bethany
Beyond the Jordan
Where John was baptizing

29 The next day
He saw Jesus coming towards him
 And said
  Look on the Lamb of God
  The bearer of the sin of the world
30   This is he
  Of whom I myself said
  One grown to manhood comes after me
  Who existed before me
  Because he preceded me

31 I indeed did not know him
  In order that he should be shown to Israel
  I
  I have come
  Baptizing in water

32 And John bore witness
  Thus I beheld the Spirit
  Descending as a dove from heaven
  And remaining on him

33 I indeed did not know him
But the one who sent me
To baptize in water
Is the one who said to me
He on whom you see the Spirit descending
And remaining on him
He it is
Who will baptize in Holy Spirit

34 And I
I have perceived
And have borne witness
That this is the Son of God

The calling of the first disciples
35 On the next day
John was standing there again
With two of his disciples
36 And watching Jesus where he walked
He said
Look on the Lamb of God

37 The two disciples
Heard him speak
And they followed Jesus

38 Jesus turned
And beheld them following
And said to them
What do you need?

And they said to him
Rabbi
(Which being translated
Means teacher)
Where are you staying?

39 He said to them
Come
And you will see

So they came
And saw where he was staying

And remained with him that day
It was about the tenth hour

40 One of the two
Who heard John speak
And then followed Jesus
Was Simon Peter's brother Andrew
41 Who first found his own brother Simon
    Then said to him
        We have found the Messiah
        (Which being translated
        Means Christ)

42 He brought him to Jesus

    Gazing into him
    Jesus said
        You are Simon the son of John
        You shall be called Cephas
        (Which is translated
        Peter)

43 On the next day
He intended to go into Galilee

    Jesus found Philip
    And said to him
        Follow me

44 Now Philip came from Bethsaida
The same town as Andrew and Peter

45 Philip found Nathanael
And told him
    We have found the one
    Of whom Moses wrote in the Law
    And of whom the prophets wrote also
    Jesus from Nazareth
    The son of Joseph

46 And Nathanael said to him
    From Nazareth?
    Is it possible for anything that is good
    To be from there?

Philip said to him
>Come and see

47 Jesus saw Nathanael
Coming to him
And said
>Look on a true Israelite
>In whom is no deceit

48 Nathanael said to him
>How is it that you
>Recognize me?

Jesus replied
>Before Philip called you
>When you were under the fig tree
>I saw you

49 Nathanael answered him
>Rabbi
>You are the Son of God
>You are the King of Israel

50 Jesus answered
>Do you believe
>Because I said to you
>That I saw you under the fig tree?
>You shall have sight
>Of greater things than these

51 And he said to him
>Of a certainty I say to you all
>You shall have sight of heaven opened
>And the angels of God
>Ascending and descending
>On the Son of Man

2 *The wedding at Cana*

1 On the third day
A wedding took place
At Cana in Galilee
And the mother of Jesus was there

JOHN 2

2   Jesus and his disciples
    Were invited to the wedding

3   When there was no more wine
        His mother said to Jesus
            They have no wine

4   And Jesus said to her
            This is between me and you
            Woman
            My hour has still not come

5   His mother said to those who were serving
            Do whatever he tells you

6   Now six stone water-jars
    Were standing there
    Intended for the Jewish rites of purification
    Each contained two or three measures

7   Jesus said to them
            Fill the water-jars with water

    And they filled them
    To the brim

8   Then he said to them
            Draw some out now
            And take it to the master of the feast

    So they took it

9   When the master of the feast
    Had tasted the water
    Which had now become wine
    And did not know
    Where it had come from
    (But those who were serving knew
    Because they had drawn the water)
        The master of the feast called the bridegroom
10   And said to him
            Every man
            Serves the best wine first
            Then a poorer soft

After all have drunk deeply
But you
You have kept the best wine
Until now

11 It was at Cana in Galilee
That Jesus performed this sign
The beginning
And manifested the glory of his being
And his disciples believed in him

12 After this
He went down to Capernaum
With his mother
And his brothers
And his disciples
They only remained there
For a few days

Traders expelled from the Temple in Jerusalem
13 It was near the Passover of the Jews
Jesus went up to Jerusalem
14 And found in the Temple
Those who sold oxen
And sheep
And doves
And coin-dealers sitting there

15 He made a lash out of cords
And drove them all out of the Temple
With the sheep
And the oxen
He poured out the money-changers' coins
And overturned their tables

16 Then he said to the ones who sold doves
Take them all away from here
Do not make my Father's house
Into a house for trade

17 The disciples remembered
That it is written

The zeal of thy house
Will eat me up

18   So the Jews replied to him
         What sign will you show us
         Now that you do such things?

19   Jesus answered
         Break down this temple
         And I will raise it up
         In three days

20   Then the Jews said to him
         It took forty-six years
         To build this temple
         And you
         Will you raise it up
         In three days?

21   But he spoke
     About the temple of his body

22   When he was raised from the dead
     His disciples remembered
     That he had said this
     And they believed the Scripture
     And the words
     Which Jesus had spoken

23   Now when he was in Jerusalem
     At the Passover festival
     Many believed in his name
     Because they perceived the signs
     Which he did

24   But Jesus did not trust himself to them
25   Because he understood them all
     And did not need anyone
     To witness
     On behalf of humanity
     Because he knew
     What was in humanity

3 *The conversation with Nicodemus*

1 Now there was a man of the Pharisees
Whose name was Nicodemus
He was a leader among the Jews

2   He came to Jesus at night
    And said to him
        Rabbi
        We know
        That you have come from God
        As a teacher
        For no one has power to do the signs
        Which you are doing
        Unless God is with him

3   Jesus answered him
        Of a certainty I say to you
        Unless someone is born again
        He is powerless to see
        The kingdom of God

4   Nicodemus said to him
        What power has a man
        To be born
        When he is old?
        Has he power to enter his mother's womb
        For the second time
        And be born?

5   Jesus answered
        Of a certainty I say to you
        Unless someone is born
        Out of water and spirit
        He is powerless to enter
        The kingdom of God
6   Born out of the flesh is flesh
        Born out of the spirit is spirit

7   Do not be astonished
        Because I said to you
        You all must be born again
8   The wind
        Blows where it wills
        And you hear the sound it makes

But you do not know
Where it comes from
Or where it is going
It is the same with everyone
Born out of the spirit

9   Nicodemus answered
        How has this the power
        To come about?

10 Jesus answered him
        You yourself are the teacher of Israel
        And yet you do not understand this?

11   Of a certainty I say to you
        It is of what we know
        That we speak
        And to what we have seen
        We bear witness
        And you all
        Do not receive our witness

12   If I have spoken to you all
        About the concerns of earth
        And you do not believe
        If I speak to you all
        About the concerns of heaven
        Will you believe?

13   No-one
        Has gone up into heaven
        Except the one
        Who has come down out of heaven
        The Son of Man
        [Who is in heaven]

14   Just as Moses
        Lifted up the serpent in the desert
        The Son of Man
        Must be lifted up
15   So that everyone who believes in him
        May live
        Throughout the ages

16 Because God so loved the world
That he gave the Son
Born the only one
So that everyone who believes in him
Should not be destroyed
But live
Throughout the ages

17 Because God did not send the Son
Out into the world
To pass sentence on the world
But so that the world
Might be saved through him

18 If anyone believes in him
He is not brought to judgment
If anyone does not believe
He has been condemned already
Because he did not believe
In the name
Of the only one
Born Son of God

19 And this is the judgment
That the light
Has come into the world
And men loved darkness
Rather than light
Because their deeds were evil

20 All those who practise meanness
Hate the light
And do not come to the light
So that their deeds are not shamed
21 All those who do what is true
Come to the light
So that their deeds may be shown
To be performed in God

The confession of John the Baptist
22 After these events
Jesus and his disciples
Came into the land of Judea

And he stayed there with them
And baptized

23 John was also baptizing
In Ainon near Salem
Where water was plentiful
The people came there
And were baptized
24 Because John
Had not yet been thrown into prison

25 Now there was a discussion
Between John's disciples
And a Jew
About purification

26   They came to John
    And said to him
        Rabbi
        The one who was with you
        Beyond the Jordan
        And to whom you bore witness
        Look how he is baptizing
        And everyone comes to him

27   John answered
        A man has no power to receive anything
        Unless it is given to him from heaven
28   You yourselves bear me witness
        That I said
        I
        I am not the Christ
        But I have been sent out before him

29   The one who has the bride
        Is the bridegroom
        But the bridegroom's friend
        Who stands and hears him
        Is filled with joy
        And rejoices
        Because of the bridegroom's voice
        So now
        My joy is complete

30	He must wax
	But I must wane
31	The one who comes from above
	Is over all
	He who is earthly
	Belongs to the earth
	And speaks about the earth
	The one who comes from heaven
	Is over all
32	He bears witness
	To what he has seen
	And to what he has heard
	And no-one accepts his witness
33	Whoever accepts his witness
	Puts his seal
	To the truth of God
34	He whom God has sent out
	Speaks God's words
	Because it is not only in verse metre
	That the Spirit is given
35	The Father loves the Son
	And has given everything
	Into his hand
36	He who believes in the Son
	Has life
	Throughout the ages
	He who does not obey the Son
	Will not have sight of life
	But the anger of God
	Remains upon him

4 *The conversation with a Samaritan woman*

1	Now when the Lord knew
	That the Pharisees had heard
	That Jesus
	Is making more disciples than John
	And is baptizing them
2	Although Jesus himself
	Did not baptize

But his disciples did so
3 He left Judea
And returned to Galilee

4 He had to pass through Samaria
5 And came to a Samaritan town
Called Sychar
Near the land given by Jacob
To his son Joseph

6 Jacob's spring was there
As Jesus was tired from the journey
He sat straight down by the spring
It was about the sixth hour

7 A Samaritan woman
Came to draw water

> Jesus said to her
>> Give me a drink

8 His disciples
Had gone away into the town
To buy food

9 > The Samaritan woman said to him
>> As you are a Jew
>> How can you ask me
>> For a drink
>> As I am a woman
>> And a Samaritan?

Because Jews handle nothing
In common with Samaritans

10 > Jesus answered her
>> If you knew the gift of God
>> And who it is
>> That is saying to you
>> Give me a drink
>> You would have asked him
>> And he would have given to you
>> Living water

11 She said to him
>Sir
>You have no water-bucket
>And the well is deep
>From where do you have
>The living water?
12 >Surely you are not greater
>Than our father Jacob
>Who gave us the well
>And drank from it himself
>As did his sons
>And his cattle?

13 Jesus answered her
>Everyone who drinks this water
>Will be thirsty again
14 >But whoever drinks the water
>Which I myself will give him
>Will never be thirsty again
>Because the water
>Which I will give him
>Will become in him
>A spring of water
>Welling up as a source of life
>Throughout the ages

15 The woman said to him
>Sir
>Give me this water
>So that I am not thirsty
>And need not come here
>To draw it

16 He said to her
>Go and call your husband
>And come here

17 The woman answered
>I have no husband

Jesus said to her
>It is right when you say
>I have no husband

18   Because you have had five husbands
       And he whom you have now
       Is not your husband
       In this you spoke the truth

19   The woman said to him
           Sir
           I perceive that you are a prophet
20   Our fathers worshipped
           In this mountain
           And you all say
           That in Jerusalem
           Is the place where there should be worship

21   Jesus said to her
           Believe me
           Woman
           The hour is coming
           When neither in this mountain
           Nor in Jerusalem
           Will you all worship the Father

22   What you worship
           You do not know
           What we worship
           We know
           Because salvation
           Comes from the Jews

23   But the hour is coming
           And has come now
           When the true worshippers
           Will worship the Father
           In spirit and in truth
           For indeed the Father
           Seeks such people to worship him

24   God is spirit
           And those who worship
           In spirit and in truth
           Must they worship

25   The woman said to him
           I know

>
> That Messiah is coming
> He who is called Christ
> When he comes
> He will make everything clear to us

26 Jesus said to her
> I
> I AM
> The one who is speaking to you

27 And at this
His disciples came
And were astonished
That he was talking to a woman
But no one said
What do you need?
Or
Why are you talking to her?

28 Then the woman
Left her water-jar
And went into the town
> And said to the men
29 > > Come and see a man
> > Who told me everything
> > That I have done
> > Is not this the Christ?

30 They went out of the town
And came to him

31 In the meantime
> His disciples said to him
> > Rabbi
> > Eat

32 But he said to them
> I myself have food to eat
> > About which you know nothing

33 So the disciples said to one another
> Has anyone
> > Brought him something to eat?

34   Jesus said to them
          My food
          Is to do the will
          Of the one who sent me
          And to complete his work

35   Do you not have a saying
          There are still four months
          And then comes the harvest?
          I tell you to look
          And lift up your eyes
          And behold the fields
          Because they are white
          Ready for the harvest

36   Already the reaper receives wages
          And gathers fruit
          For life
          Throughout the ages
          So that sower and reaper
          May rejoice together

37   For in this
          The saying is true
          That one sows and another reaps
38   I myself sent you out to reap
          Where indeed you did not toil
          Others have toiled
          And you
          You have entered into their toil

39 Many Samaritans
From that town
Believed in him
Because of the woman's words
Which bore witness
He told me
All that I had done

40 So when the Samaritans
Came to him
They asked him to remain with them
And he remained with them
For two days

41 And many more believed
    Because of his word

42   And they said to the woman
            We no longer believe
            Because of what you said
            But we believe
            Because we have heard for ourselves
            And we know
            That this is truly
            The Saviour of the world

    The healing of a courtier's son
43 After two days
    He left there
    And went into Galilee

44 For Jesus
    Had himself borne witness
    That a prophet has no honour
    In his own native place

45 So when he came into Galilee
    The Galileans welcomed him
    Because they had seen
    All that he had done
    At the festival in Jerusalem
    They had also been to the festival

46 Then he came to Cana in Galilee again
    Where he had made the water wine

    When a courtier
    Whose son was ill in Capernaum
47 Heard that Jesus
    Had come to Galilee from Judea
    He went to him
    And asked him to come down
    And heal his son
    Who was about to die

48   Jesus said to him
            Unless you all see signs and portents
            You will not believe

49   The courtier said to him
     Sir
     Come down
     Before my little child dies

50   Jesus said to him
     Go
     Your son lives

   The man believed the word
   Which Jesus had said to him
   And he went

51   As he was returning
   His servants met him
   And told him that his boy lives
52   So he asked them
   At what time he began to improve
    They said to him
     Yesterday
     At the seventh hour
     The fever left him

53   Then the father became aware
   That it was at the very hour
   In which Jesus had said to him
   Your son lives
   And he believed
   As did his whole household

54   Now this was the second sign
   Performed by Jesus
   When he had come to Galilee from Judea

5

The healing at the Pool of Bethesda

1   After this there was a Jewish festival
   And Jesus went up to Jerusalem

2   Now in Jerusalem
   There is a pool which has five colonnades
   It is near the Sheep Gate
   And in Hebrew it is called Bethesda

3   Many disabled people were lying there
    The blind
    The lame
    And the paralysed

    [They were waiting for the water to be moved
4   Because at certain times
    An angel went down into the pool
    And stirred up the water
    Whoever stepped in first
    After the water was disturbed
    Was made whole from his disability]

5   There was one man
    Who had been disabled
    For thirty-eight years

6   When Jesus saw him
    And became aware
    That he had been lying there
    For a long time
        He said to him
            Is it your will
            To become whole?

7   The one who was disabled
        Answered him
            Sir
            I do not have a man
            To drop me into the pool
            When the water is disturbed
            But while I
            I am coming
            Someone else goes down before me

8   Jesus said to him
            Rise
            Take up your mat
            And walk

9   At once
    The man became whole
    Took up his mat
    And walked

    And that day was the sabbath

10   Therefore the Jews
        Said to the one who was cured
            It is the sabbath
            You are not allowed
            To carry your mat

11   But he answered them
            He who made me whole
            Said to me
            Take up your mat
            And walk

12   They asked him
            Who is the man
            Who said to you
            Take it up and walk?

13 But the one who had been healed
    Did not know who it was
    As Jesus had withdrawn
    In that crowded place
14   Afterwards Jesus found him in the Temple
        And said to him
            See
            You have become whole
            Do not sin any more
            Or something worse may befall you

15 The man went away
    And told the Jews
    That it was Jesus
    Who had made him whole
16   Therefore the Jews persecuted Jesus
        Because he did such things
        On a sabbath

17	But he answered them
	My Father is still working now
	And I myself am working

18	For this reason the Jews
	Were all the more anxious to kill him
	Because he not only broke the sabbath
	But called God his own Father
	Making himself equal with God

Jesus answers the Jews

19	So Jesus said to them
	Of a certainty I say to you
	The son has no power
	To do anything out of himself
	Except what he sees
	The Father doing
	For whatever he does
	The Son does also
20	Because the Father
	Cares for the Son
	And shows him everything
	That he is doing
	And he will show him
	Greater deeds than these
	So that even you
	May be astonished
21	Just as the Father
	Raises the dead
	And gives them life
	So the Son also gives life
	To those to whom he will
22	The Father judges no one
	But has given all judgment to the Son
23	So that everyone should reverence the Son
	As much as they reverence the Father
	He who does not reverence the Son
	Lacks reverence for the Father
	Who sent him

24   Of a certainty I say to you
Whoever hears my words
And believes in the one who sent me
Will live
Throughout the ages
And will not come to the parting of the ways
But has passed out of death
Into life

25   Of a certainty I say to you
The hour has now come
When the dead
Will hear the voice of the Son of God
And those who hear will live

26   Just as the Father
Bears life within himself
He has given to the Son
To bear life within himself
27   And he has given him authority
To make a division
Because he is Son of Man

28   Do not be astonished at this
Because the hour is coming
When all those who are in the graves
Will hear his voice
29   And will come out
Those who have done good
To a resurrection of life
Those who have practised meanness
To a resurrection of condemnation

30   For I
I have no power
To do anything out of myself
As I hear I judge
And my judgment is just
Because it is not my aim
To carry out my own will
But the will
Of the one who sent me

31   If I
     I bear witness to myself
     Then my evidence
     Is not accepted as the truth
32   There is someone else
     Who gives evidence about me
     And I know
     That the evidence which he gives about me
     Is the truth
33   You yourselves sent out to John
     And he bore witness
     To the truth

34   Indeed I
     I do not receive the testimony of men
     But I say this
     So that you yourselves may be saved
35   He was a lamp
     Burning and shining
     And for a while
     Even you were willing
     To rejoice in his light

36   But I
     I have a greater witness
     Than that of John
     As the deeds which the Father
     Gave me to complete
     These deeds which I am doing
     Are evidence that the Father
     Has sent me out

37   And the Father who sent me
     Has borne witness to me
     You have never heard his voice
     You have not perceived his form
38   And his word does not remain in you
     Because you
     You do not believe
     The one whom he has sent out

39   You study the Scriptures
     Which bear witness to me
     Because you think that in them

40	You have the life Which endures throughout the ages But you will not come to me So that you may have life
41	I do not accept the esteem of men
42	But I know That you do not have within you The love of God
43	I I have come in my Father's name And you do not accept me If someone else comes in his own name You will accept him
44	How indeed have you the power to believe Who accept the esteem of one another And do not aim for the esteem of the only God?
45	Do not think that I I will accuse you to the Father There is someone else who accuses you And that is Moses In whom you hoped
46	Because if you had believed Moses You would have believed me For he wrote about me
47	But if you do not believe what he has written How will you believe my words?

6

The feeding of the five thousand

1 After these events
Jesus went away
Across the Sea of Galilee
Which is the Sea of Tiberias

2 And a great crowd followed him
Because they saw the signs
Which he had done
For those who were disabled

3 Jesus went up on to the mountain
And sat there with his disciples

4   It was near the Passover
A festival of the Jews

5   Jesus lifted up his eyes
And beholding the crowds
Coming towards him
    He said to Philip
        Where should we buy bread
        For these people to eat?

6   He said this to test him
Because he knew
What he was going to do

7   Philip answered him
        Two hundred denarii
        Would not buy enough bread
        For each one to take a little

8   Andrew
Simon Peter's brother
Who was one of his disciples
Said to him
9   There is a child here
        He has five barley loaves
        And two little fishes
        But what is this
        Among so many?

10   Jesus said
        Make the people sit down

Now there was plenty of grass there
So the men sat down
They numbered about five thousand

11   Then Jesus took the loaves
And when he had given thanks
He passed them over
To those sitting down
And the same with the fish
As much as they wished

JOHN 6

12 When they were satisfied
    He said to his disciples
        Collect the pieces left over
        So that nothing is destroyed

13 They gathered them up
And filled twelve baskets
With pieces of the five barley loaves
Which had been left over
By those who had eaten

14 When the people
Saw the sign which he had done
    They said
        This is in truth the prophet
        The one coming into the world

15 Then Jesus was aware
That they were about to come
And carry him off
To make him a king
So he went away again
On to the mountain
Himself alone

The disciples see Jesus walking on the water

16 When it grew late
His disciples went down to the sea
17 They embarked in a boat
And set out across the sea
Towards Capernaum

Although it was now dark
Jesus had not yet come to them
18 And the sea became rough
Because a strong wind was blowing

19 So when they had rowed
About twenty-five or thirty stadia
They perceived Jesus
Walking on the sea
And drawing near the boat
And they were afraid

20   But he said to them
         I
         I AM
         Do not be afraid

21   Then they were willing
     To take him into the boat
     And immediately the boat
     Was at the land to which they were going

The sermon in Capernaum on the bread of life
22   The next day
     The crowd which had remained
     Over the sea
     Discovered that only one small boat
     Had been there
     And that Jesus
     Had not entered the boat with his disciples
     But that his disciples
     Had gone away alone
23   Although other small boats from Tiberias
     Came near the place
     Where they had eaten bread
     After the Lord had given thanks

24   So when the crowd
     Saw that Jesus was not there
     Neither were his disciples
     Then they also embarked in the boats
     And came to Capernaum
     Looking for Jesus

25   When they found him
     Over the sea
         They said to him
             Rabbi
             When did you come here?

26   Jesus answered them
             Of a certainty I say to you
             It is not because you saw signs
             That you are looking for me
             But because you ate the bread
             And were satisfied

27   Do not labour
          For the food which perishes
          But for the food which remains
          As life
          Throughout the ages
          Which the Son of Man
          Will give to you
          Because he is the one
          Sealed by the Father God

28   Then they said to him
          What must we do
          So that our deeds
          May be God's work?

29   Jesus said to them
          This is God's work
          That you believe in the one
          Whom he has sent out

30   So they said to him
          What sign will you perform
          So that we can see it
          And believe you?
          What are you doing?
31   Our fathers ate manna
          In the desert
          As it is written
          He gave them bread from heaven to eat

32   Therefore Jesus said to them
          Of a certainty I say to you
          It is not Moses
          Who has given you bread from heaven
          But my Father
          Gives you the true bread from heaven
33   Because the bread of God
          Is coming down from heaven
          And giving life to the world

34   Then they said to him
          Sir
          Always give us this bread

35   Jesus said to them
I
I AM the bread of life
He who comes to me
Will not hunger
He who believes in me
Will never thirst

36   But as I told you
You have seen me
And do not believe

37   All that the Father gives to me
Will come to me
And he who comes to me
I will not cast out
38   Because I have not come down from heaven
To do my own will
But the will
Of the one who sent me

39   And this is the will
Of the one who sent me
That I should lose nothing
Of all that he has given to me
But should raise it up
At the ending of time

40   For this is the will of my Father
That everyone who looks on the Son
And believes in him
May have life
Throughout the ages
And I myself will raise him up
At the ending of time

41 For this reason
The Jews murmured about him
Because he said
I
I AM the bread
Which has come down from heaven

42   And they said
>> Is not this Jesus
>> The son of Joseph
>> Of whom indeed we know
>> The father and the mother?
>> How can he now say
>> I have come down from heaven?

43   Jesus answered them
>> Do not murmur among yourselves

44
>> No one can come to me
>> Unless he is drawn by the Father
>> Who sent me
>> And I myself
>> Will raise him up
>> At the ending of time

45
>> It is written in the prophets
>> *And they shall all be taught by God*
>>
>> Everyone who hears
>> And learns from the Father
>> Comes to me

46
>> Not that anyone has seen the Father
>> Except the one who is with God
>> He has seen the Father

47
>> Of a certainty I say to you
>> He who believes
>> Has life
>> Throughout the ages

48
>> I
>> I AM the bread of life

49
>> Your fathers ate manna
>> In the desert
>> And they have died

50
>> This is the bread
>> Which comes down from heaven
>> So that anyone may eat it
>> And not die

51 I
   I AM the living bread
   Which has come down from heaven
   If anyone eats this bread
   He will live
   Throughout the ages
   And the bread
   Which I will give
   For the life of the world
   Is my flesh

52 Then the Jews
   Argued with one another and said
      How can this man
      Give us his flesh to eat?

53 So Jesus said to them
      Of a certainty I say to you
      Unless you eat the flesh
      Of the Son of Man
      And drink his blood
      You have no life in you
54   He who partakes of my flesh
      And drinks my blood
      Has life
      Throughout the ages
      And I myself
      Will raise him up
      At the ending of time

55   For my flesh is true food
      And my blood is true drink
56   He who partakes of my flesh
      And drinks my blood
      Remains in me
      And I
      I remain in him

57   As the living Father
      Has sent me out
      And I myself live
      Because of the Father
      He who partakes of me

     Will also live
     Because of me

58   This is the bread
    Which has come down from heaven
    Unlike the fathers
    Who ate and died
    He who partakes of this bread
    Will live
    Throughout the ages

59   He said this in synagogue
    Teaching in Capernaum

The difficulties of the disciples
60   When they heard this
    Many of his disciples said
     These are difficult words
     Who can accept them?

61   But within himself Jesus knew
    That his disciples murmured about this
     And he said to them
      Does this offend you?
62   What then if you perceive the Son of Man
     Ascending to where he was before?

63   It is the spirit that gives life
    The flesh is of no benefit
    The words
    Which I myself have spoken to you
    They are spirit
    And are life
64   And some of you
    Do not believe

From the beginning
Jesus knew
Who did not believe
And who would betray him

65   And he said
     Therefore I have told you

That no one can come to me
Unless it is given to him
By the Father

66 After this
Many of his disciples turned back
And no longer went about with him

67 So Jesus said to the twelve
Do not you
You also wish to go?

68 Simon Peter answered him
Lord
To whom should we go?
You have the words of life
Which endure throughout the ages
69 And we have come to believe
And to know
That you are indeed
The Holy One of God

70 Jesus answered them
Did not I myself choose you
The twelve?
And one of you is a devil

71 Now he spoke of Judas
Son of Simon Iscariot
One of the twelve
Who was going to betray him

7 *The feast of Tabernacles*
1 And after these events
Jesus walked in Galilee
He would not go about in Judea
Because the Jews
Were looking for an opportunity to kill him

2 It was near the feast of Tabernacles
A festival of the Jews

3   So his brothers said to him
        Leave here
        And go into Judea
        Then your disciples
        Will be able to see
        The deeds which you perform
4   Because no one
        Does anything in secret
        Who wishes to come into the open
        If you do these things
        Show yourself to the world

5   For even his brothers
    Did not believe in him

6   Therefore Jesus said to them
        For me
        The right moment has not yet arrived
        But for you
        It is always the right moment

7   The world
        Has no power to hate you
        But it hates me
        Because I
        I bear witness
        That its deeds are evil

8   Go up yourselves to the festival
        I am not going up myself to this festival
        Because for me
        The moment is not ripe

9   After saying this to them
    He remained in Galilee
10 But when his brothers
    Had gone up to the festival
    Then he went up also
    Not showing himself
    But as if in secret

11   This was the reason why the Jews
        Searched for him at the festival

And said
>> Where is he?

12 And among the crowds
There was a great deal of murmuring about him

>> Some said
>>> He is a good man
>> But others said
>>> No
>>> He misleads the people

13 But no one spoke about him openly
Because they were afraid of the Jews

Jesus teaches the crowds in the Temple
14 About half-way through the festival
Jesus went up into the Temple
And taught

15 >> The Jews were astonished
>> And said
>>> How can he understand
>>> What is written
>>> As he has never studied?

16 >> So Jesus answered them
>>> My teaching is not mine
>>> But is from the one who sent me
17 >>> If anyone
>>> Desires to do his will
>>> He will know
>>> Whether the teaching comes from God
>>> Or whether I
>>> I speak out of myself

18 >> He who speaks out of himself
>> Is looking for his own glory
>> But he who would give glory
>> To the one who sent him
>> He is true
>> And there is no falsehood in him

19   Did not Moses
     Give you the Law?
     Yet not one of you keeps the Law
     Why do you intend to kill me?

20   The crowd answered
     You have a demon
     Who is intending to kill you?

21   Jesus answered
     I performed one deed
     And you are all astonished?

22   Because Moses
     Has given you circumcision
     (Not that it comes from Moses
     But from the Fathers)
     You circumcise a man
     On a sabbath
23   If a man receives circumcision
     On a sabbath
     So that the Law of Moses
     Is not broken
     Why are you angry with me
     Because I made the whole of a man well
     On a sabbath?
24   Do not judge by appearances
     But come to a just judgment

25   Then some of the people of Jerusalem said
     Is not this the one
     Whom they plan to kill?
26   But see how he speaks openly
     And they say nothing to him
     Surely the rulers have not decided
     That he is the Christ?
27   Because we know
     From where he is
     But when the Christ comes
     No one will understand
     From where he is

28   Jesus was then teaching in the Temple
     And he cried out

You know me
And you also know
From where I am
I have not come of myself
But the one who has sent me
Is true
Whom you yourselves
Do not know

29   But I
I know him
Because it is from him
That I AM
And he is the one
Who sent me out

30   Then they tried to arrest him
But no one laid hands on him
Because his hour
Had not yet come

31   But many of the crowd
Believed in him
And said
When the Christ comes
Surely he will not perform more signs
Than this one has done?

The attempt to arrest Jesus

32   The Pharisees heard the crowd
Murmuring such things about him
And the chief priests and the Pharisees
Sent out attendants to arrest him

33   Then Jesus said
For a short time
I shall still be with you
Then I am going
To the one who sent me
34   You will search for me
And will not find me
And where I
I am

                    You yourselves
                    Have no power to come

35   So then the Jews said to one another
                    Where is he about to go
                    That we shall not find him?
                    Surely he is not going
                    To those dispersed among the Greeks
                    Or to teach the Greeks?

36   What is the meaning
                    Of the words which he said
                    You will search for me
                    And will not find me
                    And where I
                    I am
                    You yourselves
                    Have no power to come?

37   Now on the last day
            The great day of the festival
                    Jesus stood and cried out
                            If any one is thirsty
                            Let him come to me
                            And he who believes in me
                            Let him drink
38   As the Scripture has said
                            Out of his body
                            Shall flow rivers of living water

39   But he said this
            Concerning the Spirit
            Whom those who believed in him
            Were to receive
            For not yet was the Spirit present
            Because Jesus was not yet glorified

40   On hearing these words
                    Some of the crowd said
                            This is in truth the prophet

41   Others said
                            This is the Christ

>> Yet others said
>>> Surely Christ
>>> Will not come from Galilee
42 >>> Has not the Scripture said
>>> That Christ will come
>>> From the descendants of David
>>> And from Bethlehem
>>> The town of David?

43 > Because of him
> The crowd was divided
44 > And some wanted to arrest him
> But no one laid hands on him

> *The Pharisees and Nicodemus*
45 > Then the attendants
> Came to the chief priests
> And to the Pharisees
>> Who said to them
>>> Why have you not brought him?

46 >> The attendants answered
>>> No man has ever spoken
>>> In the way this man speaks

47 >> So the Pharisees replied to them
>>> Surely you yourselves
>>> Have not also been deceived?
48 >>> Have any of the rulers
>>> Or of the Pharisees
>>> Believed in him?
49 >>> But these people are under a curse
>>> Who do not understand the Law

50 >> One of them was that same Nicodemus
>> Who had come to Jesus before
>> And he said to them
51 >>> Does our Law judge a man
>>> Without hearing him first
>>> And understanding what he is doing?

52 >> They answered him
>>> Surely you yourself

JOHN 7

        Are not also from Galilee?
        Search and you will see
        That no prophet
        Arises out of Galilee

The adulterous woman

53   [And each one went to his own house
8   But Jesus went to the Mount of Olives

2   At dawn
    He returned to the Temple again
    And all the people came to him
    And sitting down
    He taught them

3   Then the scribes and Pharisees
    Led in a woman
    Who had been taken in adultery
    And standing her in the centre
4   They said to him
         Teacher
         This woman has been caught
         In the act of adultery
5   In the Law
         Moses commanded us
         To stone such a person
         What do you say?

6   They said this
    In order to test him
    So that they might have something
    With which to accuse him

    But Jesus bent down
    And wrote with his finger
    In the earth
7   Then as they continued to question him
    He stood up

        And said to them
          The one among you
          Who is without sin

        Let him be the first
        To cast a stone at her

8   And stooping down again
    He wrote in the earth

9   When they heard this
    They went out one by one
    Beginning with the older ones
    And he was left alone
    With the woman remaining in the centre

10   Standing erect
      Jesus said to her
          Where are they?
          Has no one condemned you?

11   And she said
        No one
        Sir

    Jesus said
        Neither do I myself
        Condemn you
        Go
        And from now on
        Sin no more]

The light of the world

12   Jesus said to them again
        I
        I AM the light of the world
        He who follows me
        Will not walk in darkness
        But will have the light of life

13   So the Pharisees said to him
        You testimony
        Is about yourself
        Your evidence
        Cannot be accepted as the truth

14   Jesus answered
        Even if I
        I bear witness about myself
        My evidence is true
        Because I know
        Where I come from
        And where I am going
        But you
        You do not know
        Either where I come from
        Or where I am going

15   You indeed
    Judge according to the flesh
    I bring no one to trial
16   But if I
    I make a division
    My judgment is true
    Because I am not alone
    But with me is the Father
    Who sent me

17   And even in your Law
    It is written
    That the evidence of two men
    Can be accepted as the truth

18   I
    I am the one
    Who bears witness about myself
    And testimony concerning me
    Gives the Father
    Who sent me

19   Then they said to him
        Where is your Father?

    Jesus answered them
        You neither know me
        Nor my Father
        If you had known me
        You would also have known my Father

20   He spoke these words in the treasury
Teaching in the Temple
But no one laid hold of him
Because his hour
Had not yet come

A warning to the Jews
21   Then he said to them again
        Indeed I am going away
        And you will search for me
        And in your sin you will die
        Where I
        I am going
        You yourselves
        Have not the power to come

22   So then the Jews said
        Surely he will not kill himself
        Because he says
        Where I
        I am going
        You yourselves
        Have not the power to come

23   And he said to them
        You
        You are from below
        I
        I am from above
        You
        You are of this world
        I
        I am not of this world
24   Therefore I said to you
        That you will die in your sins
        For if you do not believe
        That I
        I AM
        You will die in your sins

25   Then they said to him
        Who are you?

Jesus said to them
THE BEGINNING

26
But why am I speaking to you?
About you I have much to say
And to judge
But the one who sent me is true
And what I myself heard from him
All this I say into the world

27 They did not understand
That he was speaking to them
About the Father

28 So Jesus said
When you have lifted up
The Son of Man
Then you will know
That I
I AM

I do nothing out of myself
But I speak
As the Father taught me
29
And the one who sent me
Is with me
He has not left me alone
Because I
I always do what pleases him

30 As he said all this
Many believed in him

Jesus and Abraham

31 Then Jesus said to those Jews
Who had believed in him
If you yourselves continue in my word
You are truly my disciples
32
And you will know the truth
And the truth will set you free

33 They answered him
We are descendants of Abraham

And have never been the slaves of anyone
Then how can you say
You will be set free?

34 Jesus answered
Of a certainty I say to you
That every one who sins
Is the slave of sin
35 But the slave
Does not remain in the house
Throughout the ages
The Son remains throughout the ages
36 Therefore if the Son
Sets you free
Free you will be indeed

37 I know
That you are descendants of Abraham
But you want to kill me
Because my word
Finds no space in you

38 What I
I have seen with my Father
I say
What you
You have heard from your father
You do

39 They answered him
Abraham is our father

Jesus said to them
If you were Abraham's children
You would do as Abraham did
40 But now you want to kill me
A man who has told you the truth
Which I have heard from God
This Abraham did not do
41 You
You do as your father did

They said to him
> We were not born outside the Law
> We have only one father
> And that is God

42 Jesus said to them
> If God was your father
> You would have loved me
> Because I
> I came forth
> And have come from God
> I have not come of myself
> But he has sent me

43 > Why do you not understand
> My way of speaking?
> It is because you are powerless
> To hear my words

44 > You belong to your father
> The devil
> And wish to carry out
> The desires of your father
> He was a murderer
> From the beginning
> And was not grounded in the truth
> Because in him there is no truth
> When he tells a lie
> He speaks out of his own being
> Because he is a liar
> And the father of it

45 > But because I myself tell the truth
> You do not believe me
46 > Which of you convicts me of sin?
> If I tell the truth
> Why indeed do you not believe me?

47 > A man of God
> Hears the words of God
> Therefore you yourselves do not hear
> Because you are not men of God

48 The Jews answered him
      Do not we indeed say rightly
      That you
      You are a Samaritan
      And have a demon?

49 Jesus answered
      I
      I do not have a demon
      But I honour my Father
      And you
      You dishonour me
50   I
      I do not look for my own glory
      There is one who seeks for it
      And who judges of it

51   Of a certainty I say to you
      If anyone keeps my word
      He will not encounter death
      Throughout the ages

52 The Jews said to him
      Now it is clear to us
      That you have a demon
      Abraham died
      And the prophets
      And yet you are saying
      If any one keeps my word
      He will not taste death
      Throughout the ages
53   Surely you are not greater
      Than our father Abraham
      Who died
      And the prophets who died?
      Whom do you make yourself?

54 Jesus answered
      But if I
      I reveal my being
      My revelation is worth nothing
      It is my Father
      Who reveals my being

JOHN 8

Of whom you yourselves say
He is our God

55 You have not understood him
But I
I know him
If I say that I do not know him
I shall be a liar like yourselves
But I know him
And I keep his word

56 Your father Abraham
Rejoiced that he would see my day
And he saw it and was glad

57 Then the Jews said to him
You are not yet fifty years old
And have you seen Abraham?

58 Jesus said to them
Of a certainty I say to you
Before Abraham was
I
I AM

59 Then they took up stones to throw at him
But Jesus hid himself
And went out of the Temple

9 *The healing of the man born blind*
1 And as he passed by
He saw a man
Who had been blind from his birth

2 And his disciples asked him
Rabbi
Was it he or his parents who sinned
Causing him to be born blind?

3 Jesus answered
Neither he nor his parents have sinned
It is so

That the deeds of God within him
May appear outwardly

4   While it is day
We must do the deeds
Of the one who sent me
The night is coming
When no one has the power to work
5   As long as I am in the world
I am the light of the world

6 Having said this
He spat on the ground
And made clay of the spittle
And spread the clay on his eyes
7   And said to him
Go and wash in the Pool of Siloam
(Which means
Having been sent)

So he went and washed
And came back seeing

8 Then the neighbours
And those people
Who were used to noticing him as a beggar
Said
Surely this is not the one
Who sat and begged?

9 Some said
It is the one

Others said
No
But he is like him

He said
I
I am

10 So they said to him
How were your eyes opened?

JOHN 9

11   He answered them
           The man named Jesus
           Made clay
           And spread it on my eyes
           And said to me
           Go to Siloam and wash
           So I went and washed
           And I could see

12   And they said to him
           Where is he?

      He said
           I do not know

13   Then they led the one who had been blind
      To the Pharisees

14   The day on which Jesus made clay
      And opened his eyes
      Was a sabbath

15   Then the Pharisees
      Asked him again
      How it was that he could see

      And he said to them
           He spread clay on my eyes
           And I washed
           And I can see

16   Then some of the Pharisees said
           This man has not come from God
           Because he does not keep the sabbath

      But others said
           How has a sinful man
           The power to perform such signs?

And they were divided
Among themselves

17   Again they said
      To the one who was blind

JOHN 9

    What do you say about him
    Because he has opened your eyes?

And he said
    He is a prophet

18 But the Jews did not believe
That he had been blind
And now could see
Until they called the parents
Of the one who now had sight
19   And asked them
        Is this your son
        Whom you say was born blind?
        Then how can he see now?

20   So his parents answered
    We know
    That this is our son
    And that he was born blind
21   But we do not know
    Why he can see now
    Or who opened his eyes
    Ask him
    He is of age
    He will speak for himself

22 His parents said this
Because they were afraid of the Jews
For the Jews had already agreed
That if anyone
Acknowledged him to be Christ
He should be expelled from synagogue
23 Therefore his parents said
He is of age
Question him

24 Then they called
The man who had been blind
For the second time
    And said to him
        Give glory to God
        We know
        That this man is sinful

25   But he answered
            I do not know
            Whether he is sinful
            But one thing I know
            That having been blind
            Now I can see

26   Then they said to him
            What did he do to you?
            How did he open your eyes?

27   He answered them
            I already told you
            And you did not hear
            Why do you wish to hear it again?
            Surely you yourselves have no desire
            To become his disciples?

28   And they abused him
        And said
            You are his disciple
            But we
            We are disciples of Moses
29   For indeed we know
            That God has spoken through Moses
            As for this fellow
            We do not know
            Where he comes from

30   The man answered them
            It is remarkable
            That you do not know
            Where he comes from
            And yet he opened my eyes

31   We know
            That God does not hear the sinful
            But that he hears
            Those who are worshippers of God
            And do his will

32   Throughout the ages
            It has never been heard

JOHN 9

        That anyone opened the eyes
        Of one born blind
33   If he did not come from God
        He could do nothing

34   They answered him
        You
        You were entirely born in sin
        And you
        You teach us?

And they threw him out

35 Jesus heard
That they had thrown him out
And when he found him
    He said
        Do you
        In yourself
        Believe in the Son of Man?

36   He answered
        And who is he
        Sir
        So that I could believe in him?

37   Jesus said to him
        You have seen him
        And he is speaking to you

38   Then he declared
        Lord
        I believe

And he worshipped him

39   And Jesus said
        To make a division
        I came myself into this world
        So that those who do not see
        Should see
        And those who see
        Should become blind

40   Some of the Pharisees who were with him
        Heard this
        And said to him
            Surely we
            We are not blind also?

41   Jesus said to them
            If you were blind
            You would not have been at fault
            But now you say
            We see
            So your sin remains

10   *The shepherd of the sheep*
1   Of a certainty I say to you
            Anyone
            Who does not come through the door
            Into the sheepfold
            Is a thief and a plunderer

2   But the shepherd of the sheep
            Comes in through the door
3   For him
            It is opened by the gatekeeper
            He calls his own sheep
            By their names
            And the sheep hear his voice
            And he leads them out

4   When he has brought out
            All those who are his own
            He goes in front of them
            And the sheep follow him
            Because they know his voice
5   They will not follow a stranger
            But will flee from him
            Because a stranger's voice
            They do not know

6   This was the parable
        Which Jesus told them
        But they did not understand
        What he was saying to them

7   Then Jesus said to them again
         I
         I AM the door for the sheep
8   All those who came before me
         Are thieves and plunderers
         But the sheep did not hear them

9   I
         I AM the door
         Anyone who comes in through me
         Will be saved
         And will go in
         And will go out
         And find pasture

10   The thief only comes
         To steal
         And to kill
         And to destroy
         I myself have come
         So that they may have life
         And have it all the more

11   I
         I AM the shepherd
         The rightful one
         The real shepherd
         Who lays down his soul-bearing life
         For the sheep

12   The hired-man
         Who is not a shepherd
         And where the sheep
         Are not his own
         Perceives the wolf coming
         And leaves the sheep
         And flees
         And the wolf
         Seizes and scatters them
13   He flees
         Because he is a hired-man
         And the sheep
         Are not in his care

JOHN 10

14   I
            I AM the shepherd
            The real one
            I am aware of my own
            And those who are mine
            Are aware of me
15   As the Father is aware of me
            And I myself am aware of the Father
            And I lay down my soul-bearing life
            For the sheep

16   And I have other sheep
            Which are not of this fold
            I must bring them also
            And they will hear my voice
            And become one flock
            With one shepherd

17   Therefore the Father loves me
            Because I
            I lay down my soul-bearing life
            So that I may take it again
18   No one takes it from me
            I lay it down myself
            I have the authority
            To lay it down
            And I have the authority
            To take it again
            This commandment I received
            From my Father

19   Because of these words
        The Jews were again divided
20   And many of them said
                He has a demon
                And he raves
                Why do you hear him?

21   Others said
                These are not the words
                Of one possessed by a demon
                Surely a demon
                Cannot open the eyes of the blind

The feast of the Dedication of the Temple

22 In Jerusalem
It was the festival of the Dedication
23 And it was winter

Jesus walked in the Temple
In Solomon's colonnade

24 There the Jews surrounded him
And said
For how long
Will you keep our souls in suspense?
If you are the Christ
Tell us so openly

25 Jesus answered them
I have told you
And you do not believe
The deeds that I myself am doing
In my Father's name
Bear witness to me
26 But you
You do not believe
Because you are not among my sheep

27 My sheep hear my voice
And I myself am aware of them
And they follow me
28 And I
I give them life
Throughout the ages
And throughout the ages
They shall not be destroyed
And no one shall seize them
Out of my hand

29 My Father
Who has given them to me
Is greater than all
And no one has power to seize them
Out of my Father's hand
30 I and my Father are one

JOHN 10

31 The Jews took up stones again
In order to stone him

32 Jesus answered them
   I showed you
   Many of the Father's noble deeds
   For which deed
   Do you stone me?

33 The Jews replied
   It is not for a noble deed
   That we stone you
   But for blasphemy
   And because you
   Who are a man
   Make yourself God

34 Jesus answered
   Is it not written in your Law
   I
   I said
   You are gods?

35   If he called those gods
   With whom was the word of God
   And the Scripture
   Cannot be put aside
36   Do you yourselves say
   To the one whom the Father has consecrated
   And sent into the world
   You are blaspheming
   Because I said
   I am the Son of God?

37   If I were not doing my Father's deeds
   You should not believe me
38   But if I am doing them
   Even if you do not believe me
   Believe in the deeds
   So that you may understand
   And continue understanding
   That the Father is in me
   And I
   I am in the Father

39 Again they tried to arrest him
   But he went away
   From out of their hands

   Jesus returns to the Jordan Valley
40 Then he departed again
   Across the Jordan
   To the place where John
   Had been baptizing at first
   And he remained there

41   Many people came to him
      And they said
         John did not perform any signs
         But all that John said about this one
         Was true

42 And many of those who were there
   Believed in him

11 *The raising of Lazarus*
1 Now there was one who was sick
  Lazarus of Bethany
  The village of Mary
  And her sister Martha
2 It was the same Mary
  Who anointed the Lord with ointment
  And wiped his feet with her hair
  Whose brother Lazarus was sick

3   So the sisters sent to Jesus
      And said
         Lord
         You should know
         That he who is your friend
         Is sick

4   When he heard it
      Jesus said
         This sickness
         Does not lead to death
         But is to reveal the glory of God

That by this means
The glory of the Son of God may be revealed

5 Now Jesus loved Martha
And her sister
And Lazarus
6 But when he heard that he was sick
He remained where he was
For two days
7 Then he said to the disciples
Let us go to Judea again

8 The disciples said to him
Rabbi
Just recently
The Jews were trying to stone you
And now
Will you go there again?

9 Jesus answered
Are there not twelve hours of the day?
If anyone walks in the day
He does not stumble
Because he sees the light of this world
10 But if anyone walks in the night
He stumbles
Because the light is not in him

11 After saying this
He then said to them
Our friend Lazarus
Has fallen asleep
But I am going so that I may awaken him

12 So the disciples said to him
Lord
If he has fallen asleep
He will be saved

13 Now Jesus had spoken of his death
But they thought
That he spoke of the sleep of rest

14   Therefore Jesus told them plainly
        Lazarus has died
15   And for your sakes
        I rejoice that I was not there
        So that you may believe
        But let us go to him

16   Then Thomas
    Called the Twin
    Said to his fellow disciples
        Let us go
        So that we may also die with him

17 When he came
Jesus found that Lazarus
Had already been in the tomb
Four days

18 Now Bethany
Was near Jerusalem
At a distance of about fifteen stadia
19 And many of the Jews
Had come to Martha and Mary
To console them about their brother

20 When Martha heard
That Jesus was coming
She went to meet him
But Mary still sat in the house

21   Then Martha said to Jesus
        Lord
        If you had been here
        This brother of mine
        Would not have died
22   And even now I know
        That whatever you ask from God
        Will be given to you by God

23   Jesus said to her
        Your brother will rise

24   Martha said to him
        I know that he will rise

In the resurrection
At the most distant day

25 Jesus said to her
I
I AM the Resurrection
And the life
He who believes in me
Will live
Even if he dies
26 And all those who live
And believe in me
They will not die
Not unto the ending of the age
Do you believe this?

27 She said to him
Yes Lord
I
I have believed
That you are the Christ
The Son of God
Who is coming into the world

28 After having said this
She went away
And called her sister Mary
Saying secretly
The Teacher has arrived
And is asking for you

29 When she heard that
She got up quickly
And came to him

30 Now Jesus
Had not come as far as the village
But was still in the place
Where Martha had met him

31 Then the Jews
Who were consoling Mary in the house
When they saw that she got up quickly
And went out

JOHN 11

    Followed her
    Because they thought
    She is going to the tomb
    To weep there

32   So when Mary
    Came to where Jesus was
    And saw him
    She fell at his feet
        Saying to him
            Lord
            If you had been here
            My brother
            Would not have died

33   Then Jesus
    When he saw her weeping
    And the Jews weeping
    Who had come with her
    Groaned in the spirit
    And was troubled in himself
34   And said
        Where have you laid him?

    They said to him
        Lord
        Come and see

35   Jesus shed tears
36   Therefore the Jews said
            See how he cared for his friend
37   As he had power to open the eyes
            Of a person who was blind
            Could he not have prevented
            This one from dying?

38   Then Jesus
    Again groaning in himself
    Came to the tomb
    It was a cave
    And a stone was lying on it

39   Jesus said
            Take up the stone

>
> Martha
> Sister of the one who had died
> Said to him
>> Lord
>> By now he stinks
>> Because it is the fourth day
>
> 40 Jesus said to her
>> Did I not tell you
>> That if you believe
>> You will have sight
>> Of the glory of God

41 Then they took up the stone

> Jesus lifted up his eyes
> And said
>> Father
>> I thank thee
>> That thou hast heard me
> 42 Because I
>> I know that thou hearest me always
>> But I said this
>> For the sake of the crowd standing round
>> So that they may believe
>> That thou didst send me

43 When he had said this
> He cried with a loud voice
>> Lazarus
>> Come out

44 He who had died
Came out
His feet and his hands
Bound with bandages
And his face
Bound round with a cloth

> Jesus said to them
>> Unbind him
>> And let him go

The chief priests and Pharisees hold a council

45 Many of the Jews
Who had come to Mary
And who beheld what he did
Believed in him
46 But some of them went to the Pharisees
And told them
What it was that Jesus was doing

47 Then the chief priests and the Pharisees
Assembled a council
And said
What shall we do?
Because this man performs many signs
48 If we leave him alone
Everyone will believe in him
And the Romans will come
And will take away
Both our land
And our nation

49 But Caiaphas
Who was one of them
And high priest that year
Said to them
You
You know nothing
50 Nor do you consider
That it is better for us
That one man
Should die for the people
And not all the nation perish

51 He did not say this out of himself
But being high priest that year
He prophesied that Jesus
Was about to die for the nation
52 And not only for the nation
But to gather into one
The scattered children of God

53 Therefore from that day onwards
They discussed
How they could bring about his death

54   It was for this reason that Jesus
No longer went about openly
Among the Jews
But went away
Into the country on the edge of the desert
To a town called Ephraim
And stayed there
With his disciples

The last Passover is near
55   Now the Jewish Passover was near
And many people out of the country
Went up to Jerusalem before the Passover
To purify themselves

56   There they looked for Jesus
    And said to one another
    As they stood in the Temple
        What do you think?
        Is it certain
        That he will not come to the festival?

57   For the chief priests and the Pharisees
Had given orders
That anyone who knew where he was
Should inform them
So that they could arrest him

12

The anointing at Bethany
1   Then six days before the Passover
Jesus came to Bethany
The home of Lazarus
Whom Jesus
Had raised from the dead

2   There they made a supper for him
And Martha served
But Lazarus
Was one of those
Who sat at the table with him

3   Then Mary
Took a pound of costly ointment
It was pure nard
And she anointed Jesus' feet
And with her hair
She wiped his feet
And the house was filled
With the sweet smell of the ointment

4   But one of his disciples said
       (It was Judas Iscariot
       Who was about to betray him)
5   Why was this ointment not sold
           For three hundred denarii
           And given to the poor?

6   He did not say this
Because the poor mattered to him
But because he was a thief
And took what went into the purse
Which he carried

7   Therefore Jesus said
           Leave her
           So that she may keep it
           For the day of my burial
8   You always have the poor with you
           But you do not always have me

9   When they discovered where he was
Many of the Jews came there
And not only because of Jesus
But also to see Lazarus
Whom he had raised from the dead

10   Then the chief priests in council
Decided to kill Lazarus also
11   Because for his sake
Many of the Jews left
And believed in Jesus

The entry into Jerusalem

12 The next day
The crowds coming to the festival
Heard that Jesus
Was on his way to Jerusalem
13 And they took branches
From the palm trees
And went out to meet him
    And they called out
        Blessed is the King of Israel
        Who comes in the name of the Lord

14 Then Jesus found a young ass
And sat upon it
As it is written
15 *Do not be afraid*
Daughter of Zion
Look how your king is coming
Sitting on the foal of an ass

16 At first
His disciples did not understand
But when Jesus' glory was revealed
Then they remembered
How everything
That had been written about him
Had indeed been done to him

17 The people bore witness
Because they had been with him
When he called Lazarus
Out of the tomb
And raised him from the dead
18 And the crowd met him
Because they had heard
How he had performed this sign

19   Then the Pharisees
    Said to one another
        See how helpless you are
        Look how the world
        Has gone after him

Jesus foretells his death

20 Now among those
Who were going up
To worship at the festival
There were some Greeks

21 They came to Philip
Who was from Bethsaida in Galilee
    And said to him
        Sir
        We wish to see Jesus

22 Philip went and told Andrew
And Andrew and Philip
Went and told Jesus

23   Jesus answered them
        The hour has come
        When the glory of the Son of Man
        Is revealed

24   Of a certainty I say to you
        Unless the grain of wheat
        Which falls into the earth
        Dies
        It remains alone
        But if it dies
        It bears fruit in plenty

25   He who cares
        About his soul-bearing life
        Loses it
        And he who hates
        His soul-bearing life
        In this world
        Will keep it living
        Throughout the ages

26   If anyone serves me
        Let him follow me
        And where I
        I am
        There he who serves me
        Will be also

JOHN 12

      If any one serves me
      The Father
      Will honour him

27   Now the life of my soul
      Has been troubled
      And what shall I say?
      Father
      Save me from this hour?
      But therefore I came to this hour
28   Father
      Reveal the glory of thy name

    Then a voice came from heaven
      I have revealed it
      And I will reveal it again

29 When the crowd standing there
Heard it
    They said
        It thundered

    Others said
        An angel has spoken to him

30   Jesus answered them
        This voice was not heard
        For my sake
        But for yours

31   Now crisis
      Has come upon this world
      Now the ruler of this world
      Will be cast right out
32   And if I
      I am lifted up from the earth
      I will draw every one to me

33 He said this
To give a sign
As to the way he would die

34   Then the crowd answered him
        We have heard from the Law

>
>
> That the Christ
> Remains until the end of the age
> How can you say
> That the Son of Man
> Must be lifted up?
> Who is this Son of Man?

35
>
> Then Jesus said to them
> > For a short time
> > The light will still be with you
> > Walk while you have the light
> > So that darkness
> > Does not overtake you
> > Because whoever walks in darkness
> > Does not know where he is going

36
> > While you have the light
> > Believe in the light
> > So that you may become sons of light

Jesus said this
And going away
He hid himself from them

The Jews are unable to believe

37 Even though he had performed many signs
In their presence
They did not believe in him

38 This was to fulfil the word
Of Isaiah the prophet
When he said
Lord
Who has believed our report?
And to whom has the arm of the Lord
Been made plain?

39 They were not able to believe
Because again Isaiah said
40 *He has blinded their eyes*
And hardened their heart
So that they should not see with the eyes
And comprehend with the heart
And turn
And I will heal them

41 This was said by Isaiah
Because he saw the glory of his revelation
And spoke of him

42 Nevertheless
Even among the rulers
There were many who believed in him
But they did not acknowledge it
Because of the Pharisees
Who might exclude them from the synagogue

43 For indeed
They loved the respect of men
More than the glory of God

44   But Jesus cried out
      Whoever believes in me
      Does not believe in me
      But in the one who sent me
45   And whoever looks on me
      Looks on the one who sent me

46   I
   I have come
   As light into the world
   So that all who believe in me
   May not remain in darkness

47   If any one hears my words
   And does not keep them
   I myself do not act as his judge
   Because I did not come
   To condemn the world
   But to save the world
48   Whoever rejects me
   And does not receive my words
   Has a judge already
   For at the end of time
   He will be judged
   By the word which I have spoken

49   Because I
   I did not speak out of myself
   But the Father

Who has sent me
Has given me commandment
As to what I may say
And how I may speak

50   And I know
That his commandment
Is life
Throughout the ages
Therefore what I
I say
I speak as the Father
Has told me

13 *Jesus washes his disciples' feet*

1   Before the festival of the Passover
When Jesus knew
That the hour had come
When he should pass from this world
To the Father
He loved those who were his own
In the world
And he loved them to the last

2   During supper
When already the devil
Had put the intention to betray him
Into the heart of Judas Iscariot
The son of Simon

3   And when Jesus knew
That everything had been given into his hands
By the Father
And that he came forth from God
And was going to God

4   He rose from supper
And when he had taken off his clothes
He took a towel
And tied it round his waist

5   Then he poured water into a basin
And began to wash the feet
Of the disciples
And to wipe them with the towel
Which he had tied round him

6   He came to Simon Peter
             Who said to him
                 Lord
                 Are you going to wash my feet?

7   Jesus answered him
             Now you do not know
             What I
             I am doing
             But after this you will understand

8   Peter said to him
             As long as this age shall last
             You shall not wash my feet

         Jesus answered him
             Unless I wash you
             You have no part with me

9   Simon Peter said to him
             Lord
             Not only my feet
             But also my hands
             And my head

10   Jesus said to him
             Anyone who has taken a bath
             Has no need to wash
             [Except for his feet]
             You are clean
             But not all of you

11   He said
Not all of you are clean
Because he knew
Who was going to betray him

12   When he had washed their feet
And had put on his clothes
He sat down again
             And said to them
                 Do you understand
                 What I have done to you?
13   You call me

The Teacher and the Lord
And that is right
For so I am

14 If I have myself washed your feet
Who am Lord and Teacher
You too should wash one another's feet
15 Because I have given you an example
That as I
I have done to you
You yourselves should do also

16 Of a certainty I say to you
A servant
Is not greater than his master
Nor a messenger
Greater than the one who has sent him
17 If you know this
Blessings will be yours
If you do it

18 I am not speaking about you all
Myself I know
Whom I have chosen
In order that the Scripture may be fulfilled
Which says
He who eats my bread
Has lifted up his heel against me

19 From now on I shall be telling you
Before it takes place
So that when it does take place
You may believe that
I
I AM

20 Of a certainty I say to you
He who receives whomever I may send
Receives me
And he who receives me
Receives the one who sent me

Judas leaves the upper room

21 When he had said this
Jesus was disturbed in his spirit
    And declared
        Of a certainty I say to you
        One of you will betray me

22 The disciples looked at one another
At a loss as to whom he meant

23 One of the disciples
The one whom Jesus loved
Was leaning on his breast
24   So Simon Peter beckoned to him and said
        Tell us whom he means

25 So leaning back on the breast of Jesus
    He said to him
        Lord
        Who is it?

26   Jesus answered
        It is the one
        Where I shall myself dip the portion in the dish
        And shall give it to him

Then he dipped the portion
And took it
And gave it to Judas
Son of Simon Iscariot

27 After the portion
Satan entered into him
    Therefore Jesus said to him
        What you intend to do
        Do quickly

28 But no one sitting there
Understood what he said to him
29 For some thought
Because Judas had the purse
That Jesus had said to him
Buy what we need for the festival
Or that he should give something to the poor

30 Having taken the portion
He went out immediately
And it was night

Jesus begins his farewell talks
31 When he had gone out
　　Jesus said
　　　　Now the glory of the Son of Man
　　　　Was revealed
　　　　And the glory of God
　　　　Was revealed in him
32 　　　If the glory of God
　　　　Was revealed in him
　　　　God will both reveal his glory in him
　　　　And will reveal his glory immediately

33 　　　Children
　　　　I shall still be with you
　　　　For a little while
　　　　Then you will search for me
　　　　And as I said to the Jews
　　　　Where I
　　　　I am going
　　　　You yourselves have not the power to come
　　　　So now I am also saying it to you

34 　　　I am giving you a new commandment
　　　　That you love one another
　　　　Just as I have loved you
　　　　You also love one another
35 　　　And because you love one another
　　　　Everyone will recognize you
　　　　As my disciples

36 　　Simon Peter said to him
　　　　Lord
　　　　Where are you going?

　　Jesus answered
　　　　Where I am going
　　　　You have no power to follow me now
　　　　But you will follow me later

37   Peter said to him
>Lord
>Why am I powerless to follow you just now?
>For you
>I will lay down my soul-bearing life

38   Jesus answered
>Will you lay down your soul-bearing life
>For me?

>Of a certainty I say to you
>>A cock will not crow
>>Before you have denied me
>>Three times

14 *The way, the truth, and the life*

1   Do not let your hearts be troubled
>You believe in God
>You also believe in me

2   There are many rooms
>In my Father's house

>If it were not so
>Would I have told you
>That I am going
>To prepare a place for you?

3   And if I go
>And prepare a place for you
>I will come again
>And will take you to myself
>So that where I
>I am
>You indeed may be also
>And where I
>I am going
>You know the way

5   Thomas said to him
>Lord
>We do not know
>Where you are going
>How do we know the way?

6 Jesus said to him
> I
> I AM the way
> And the truth
> And the life
>
> No one comes to the Father
> Except through me
7
> If you had recognized me
> You would also have known my Father
> From now on you recognize him
> And have seen him

8 Philip said to him
> Lord
> Show us the Father
> And it is enough for us

9 Jesus said to him
> Have I been with you all
> For such a long time
> And you have not recognized me
> Philip?
> He who has seen me
> Has seen the Father
> How can you say
> Show us the Father?
10
> Do you not believe
> That I am in the Father
> And that the Father
> Is in me?
>
> Indeed the words which I say to you
> I do not speak out of myself
> But the Father
> Who remains in me
> Does his deeds
11
> Believe me
> I in the Father
> And the Father in me
> Or believe
> For the sake of the deeds themselves

JOHN 14

12   Of a certainty I say to you
        He who believes in me
        Will also do the deeds which I do myself
        And he will do even greater things
        Because I
        I am going to the Father

13   Whatever you ask in my name
        This I will do
        So that the glory of the Father
        May be revealed in the Son
14   If you ask anything in my name
        I myself will do it

15   If you love me
        You will keep my commandments
16   And I myself will ask the Father
        And he will give you another counsellor
        To be with you
        Throughout the ages

17   The Spirit of Truth
        Whom the world has no power to receive
        Because it neither perceives him
        Nor recognizes him
        You recognize him
        Because he remains with you
        And will be in you

18   I will not leave you orphans
        I will come to you

19   There is still a little while
        Then the world
        Will lose sight of me
        But you will not lose sight of me
        And because I
        I live
        You yourselves will live also

20   In that day
        It will become clear to you
        I in my Father

And you in me
And I in you

21 He who has my commandments
And keeps them
Is the one who loves me
And he who loves me
Will be loved by my Father
And I
I will love him
And will make myself visible to him

22 Judas (not Iscariot) said to him
Lord
What has taken place
So that you will make yourself visible to us
And not to the world?

23 Jesus answered him
If anyone loves me
He will keep my word
And my Father will love him
And we will come to him
And make our dwelling with him
24 Anyone who does not love me
Does not keep my words
And the word which you hear
Is not mine
But is from the Father
Who sent me

25 I have said this to you
While remaining with you
26 But the Counsellor
The Holy Spirit
Whom the Father
Will send in my name
Will teach you everything
And recall to you everything
Which I myself have told you

27 Peace I leave with you
My peace I give to you

Not as the world makes a gift
I
I give to you

Do not let your hearts be troubled
Nor let them be fearful
You heard what I told you myself
I am going away
But I will come back to you
If you loved me
You would have rejoiced
Because I am going to the Father
For the Father
Is greater than I

And now I have told you
Before it takes place
So that when it takes place
You may believe

I will no longer say much to you
Because the ruler of this world
Is coming
And he has no part in me
For the world's understanding
Of my love for the Father
Whatever the Father has commanded me
That is what I do

Rise
Let us go from here

15 *The true vine*

I
I AM the true vine
And my Father cultivates the ground
He takes away every branch of mine
That bears no fruit
And cleans every fruit-bearing branch
To make it bear more fruit
You are clean already
Because of the word
Which I have spoken to you

JOHN 15

4 Remain in me
   And I in you
   As the branch has no power
   To bear fruit by itself
   Unless it remains in the vine
   Neither have you
   Unless you remain in me

5 I
   I AM the vine
   You are the branches
   He who remains in me
   And I in him
   Bears plentiful fruit
   Because separated from me
   You have no power to do anything

6 Those who do not remain in me
   Are like branches which dry up
   They are gathered together
   Thrown into the fire
   And burnt

7 If you remain in me
   And my words remain in you
   Ask whatever you will
   And it shall come about for you

8 My Father's glory is revealed
   When you bear plentiful fruit
   And so become my disciples

9 As the Father has loved me
   I
   I have also loved you
   Remain in my love

10 If you keep my commandments
   You will remain in my love
   As I
   I have kept my Father's commandments
   And remain in his love

11 I have said this to you
   So that my joy may be in you
   And that your joy may be complete

12	This is my commandment That you love one another As I have loved you
13	No one can have greater love Than to lay down his soul-bearing life For his friends
14	You are my friends If you do What I myself command you
15	I no longer call you servants Because the servant Does not know What his master is doing But I have proclaimed you friends Because all that I heard from my Father I have passed on to you
16	You did not choose me But I I have chosen you and appointed you So that you yourselves should go and bear fruit And your fruit should remain Then whatever you ask the Father In my name He will give you
17	This is what I command you To love one another

Hatred and persecution

18	If the world hates you You are aware That it has hated me before you
19	If you belonged to the world The world would have cared for its own But because you do not belong to the world I I chose you out of the world Therefore the world hates you

JOHN 15

20 Remember what I myself said to you
The servant is not greater than his master
If they persecuted me
They will also persecute you
If they kept my word
They will also keep yours
21 But they will do all this to you
Because of my name
As they do not know
The one who sent me

22 If I had not come
And spoken to them
They would not have been to blame
But now they have no excuse for their sin
23 Anyone who hates me
Hates my Father also

24 If I had not done deeds among them
Which no one else has done
They would not have been to blame
But now they have seen and have hated
Both me and my Father
25 So that the word
Which is written in their Law
Might be fulfilled
They hated me
Without a cause

26 But when the Counsellor comes
Whom I myself will send to you
From the Father
The Spirit of Truth
Who proceeds from the Father
He will be my witness
27 You also are witnesses
Because you have been with me
From the beginning

16 This I have told you
So that you should not be shaken
2 They will exclude you from synagogue
Indeed the hour is coming

                When anyone who kills you
                Will think that he is offering a service to God
3   And they will do all this because
                They neither recognize the Father
                Nor me

4   But this I have said to you
                So that when the hour comes
                You may remember that I told you myself

The sending of the Holy Spirit
                I did not say this to you
                From the beginning
                Because I was with you
5   Now I am going away
                To the one who sent me
                Yet none of you asks me
                Where are you going?
6   But because of what I have told you
                Sorrow has filled your hearts

7   But I
                I am telling you the truth
                It is better for you
                That I myself should go away
                Because if I do not go away
                Surely the Counsellor
                Will not come to you
                But if I go
                I will send him to you
8   And when he comes
                He will make clear to the world
                What is sin
                What is right
                And what is the judgment

9   What is sin
                Because they do not believe in me
10   What is right
                Because I am going to the Father
                And you will lose sight of me
11   What is the judgment
                Because the ruler of this world
                Has been condemned

JOHN 16

12 I still have much to say to you
　　But you cannot bear it now

13 When the Spirit of Truth comes
　　He will guide you into all the truth
　　He will not speak out of himself
　　But he will say what he has heard
　　And will proclaim to you
　　The things that are to come

14 He will reveal my glory
　　Because what he receives from me
　　He will proclaim to you
15 Everything that the Father has
　　Is mine
　　Therefore I said
　　What he receives from me
　　He will proclaim to you

16 After a little while
　　You will lose sight of me
　　Then after a little while
　　You will see me again

17 Some of his disciples
　　Said to one another
　　　　What is he saying to us?
　　　　After a little while
　　　　You will lose sight of me
　　　　Then after a little while
　　　　You will see me again
　　　　And
　　　　Because I am going to the Father?

18 And so they said
　　　　What is he saying?
　　　　After a little while?
　　　　We do not know
　　　　What he is saying

19 Jesus understood that they wished to question him
　　And he said to them
　　　　Do you consult one another about this
　　　　Because I said

After a little while
You will lose sight of me
Then after a little while
You will see me again?

20   Of a certainty I say to you
That you will weep
And will mourn
But the world will rejoice
You will be filled with sorrow
But your sorrow will turn into joy

21   A woman in childbirth has suffering
Because her hour has come
But once the child is born
She forgets the distress
In her joy
That a man has been born into the world

22   It is now that you have sorrow
But I will see you again
And your hearts will rejoice
And no one
Will take your joy from you
23   And in that day
You will not put any question to me

Of a certainty I say to you
Whatever you ask of the Father
He will give it to you in my name
24   Until now
You did not ask anything in my name
Ask and you will receive
So that your joy may be complete

25   I have told you all this in parables
The hour is coming
When I will no longer speak to you in parables
But quite openly
Will proclaim to you the Father

26   In that day
You will ask in my name
And I do not say to you

>
> That I
> I will request the Father for you

27
> Because the Father is himself a friend to you
> As indeed you have been friends to me
> And have believed
> That I
> I came forth from God

28
> I came forth out of the Father
> And have come into the world
> Now I leave the world again
> And go to the Father

29 His disciples said to him
> We see that you are speaking quite openly
> And not in parables

30
> Now we understand
> That you know everything
> And do not need anyone to question you
> Because of this we believe
> That you came forth from God

31 Jesus answered them
> Do you now believe?

32
> See how the hour is coming
> Indeed it has come already
> When you will be scattered
> Each one on his own
> And will leave me alone
> Yet I am not alone
> Because the Father is with me

33
> I have told you all this
> So that in me
> You may have peace
> In the world
> You will have trouble
> But have confidence
> I
> I have won the victory
> Over the world

17 *The high priestly prayer of Christ*
1
  When Jesus had spoken
  He lifted up his eyes to heaven
  Saying
     Father
     The hour has come
     Reveal the glory of thy Son
     So that the Son
     May reveal thy glory

2
     As thou gavest him authority
     Over all flesh
     So that he may give life
     Throughout the ages
     To everyone whom thou gavest to him
3
     And this is life
     Throughout the ages
     That they may become aware of thee
     The only true God
     And the one
     Whom thou hast sent out
     Jesus Christ

4
     I myself revealed thy glory
     On the earth
     And finished the work
     Which thou gavest me to do
5
     And now Father
     Glorify me with thy self
     With the glory which I had with thee
     Before the world came into being

6
     I showed forth thy name
     To the men whom thou gavest me
     Out of the world
     They belonged to thee
     And thou gavest them to me
     And they have kept thy word

7
     Now it has become clear to them
     That all those things
     Which thou gavest me
     Are from thee
8
     Because the teaching

Which thou gavest to me
I have given to them
And they have received it
And are aware
That in truth
I came forth from thee
And they have believed
That thou has sent me out

9 I
I pray for them
I do not pray for the world
But for those whom thou gavest to me
Because they belong to thee
10 All those who are mine
Belong to thee
All those who belong to thee
Are mine
And my glory has been revealed in them

11 I am no longer in the world
But they are in the world
And I
I come to thee

Holy Father
Keep in thy name
Those whom thou gavest to me
So that they may be one
As we are

12 When I was with them
I kept in thy name
Those whom thou gavest to me
I guarded them
And none of them was destroyed
Except the son of destruction
That the Scripture
Might be fulfilled

13 But now I come to thee
And I have said all this
In the world
So that in themselves

They may have my joy
To the full

14 I myself gave thy word to them
And the world
Has hated them
Because they do not belong to the world
Just as I
I do not belong to the world

15 I do not pray
That thou shouldst take them
Out of the world
But that thou shouldst protect them
From the evil one

16 They do not belong to the world
Just as I
I do not belong to the world
17 Consecrate them in the truth
Thy word is truth
18 As thou hast sent me
Into the world
Even so I
I send them into the world
19 And for them I consecrate myself
So that they also
May be consecrated in truth

20 It is not for these only
That I pray
But also for those
Who will believe in me
Through their word

21 So that they all may be one
As thou
Father
Art in me
And I
I in thee
They also may be in us
And the world may believe
That thou hast sent me out

JOHN 17

22   The revelation which thou gavest me
I myself gave to them
So that they may be one
As we are one

23   I in them
And thou in me
So that they may be completely one
And the world may be aware
That thou hast sent me out
And hast loved them
As thou hast loved me

24   Father
I will that those whom thou gavest to me
May also be with me
Where I
I am
So that they may perceive my glory
Which thou hast given to me
Because thou hast loved me
Before the foundation of the world

25   Righteous Father
The world was not aware of thee
But I
I was aware of thee
And these were aware
That thou hast sent me out

26   And I have declared to them thy name
And will declare it
So that the love
With which thou hast loved me
May be in them
And I
I in them

18 *Jesus is arrested*

1   Having said this
Jesus went forth with his disciples
Across the winter-stream of the Kidron
Where there was a garden
Into which he entered with his disciples

2   Now Judas
Who was betraying him
Knew the place
Because Jesus and his disciples
Often met there

3   So then Judas
Came from the chief priests and the Pharisees
With a band of soldiers and officials
Carrying torches and lamps and weapons

4   Then as Jesus knew everything
That was coming to him
He went forward
    And said to them
        Who are you searching for?

5   They answered him
        Jesus
        The Nazarene

        He said to them
            I
            I AM

Now Judas
Who was betraying him
Stood with them

6   When Jesus said to them
I
I AM
They moved backwards
And fell to the ground

7   Then he questioned them again
            Who are you searching for?

        And they said
            Jesus
            The Nazarene

8   Jesus answered them
        I said to you
        That I
        I AM
        So if you are searching for me
        Allow these men to go

9   This was to fulfil the words
    Which he had spoken
    Of those whom thou gavest me
    I have not lost one

10   Then Simon Peter
    Who had a sword
    Drew it
    And struck the high priest's servant
    Cutting off his right ear
    The servant's name was Malchus

11   So Jesus said to Peter
        Put your sword
        Into the sheath
        Shall I not drink the cup
        Which the Father
        Has given to me?

Jesus before Annas and Caiaphas

12   Then the band of soldiers
    With their captain
    And the Jewish officials
    Took Jesus
    And bound him

13   They led him first to Annas
    The father-in-law of Caiaphas
    Who was high priest that year

14   Now it was Caiaphas
    Who had advised the Jews
    That it was better
    For one man to die
    On behalf of the people

15   Simon Peter
And another disciple
Followed Jesus
That disciple was known to the high priest
And he went with Jesus
Into the high priest's court

16   But Peter
Stood outside at the door
So the other disciple
Who was known to the high priest
Went out
And spoke to the doorkeeper
And brought in Peter

17   But the maidservant
        Who kept the door
        Said
            Are you not
            Also one of this man's disciples?

        He said
            I am not

18   The servants and the officials
Having made a charcoal fire
Stood and warmed themselves
Because it was cold
Peter also stood with them
And warmed himself

19   Then the high priest
Questioned Jesus
About his disciples
And about his teaching

20   Jesus answered him
            I myself have spoken openly
            To the world
            Indeed I always taught
            In a synagogue
            Or in the Temple
            Where all the Jews meet together
            And I have said nothing in secret

21   Why do you ask me?
             Ask the people
             Who heard what I said to them
             For they are the ones who know
             What I
             I have said

22   When he had said this
      One of the officials
      Who stood near by
      Gave Jesus a slap on the face
          Saying
                Is this how you answer
                The high priest?

23   But Jesus replied to him
          If what I said was wrong
          Bear witness to the wrong
          But if it was rightly said
          Why do you strike me?

24   Then Annas had him bound
      And sent him to Caiaphas
      The high priest

25   Now Simon Peter
      Was standing there warming himself

          So they said to him
              Are not you
              Also one of his disciples?

          He denied it
          And said
             I am not

26   One of the high priest's servants
      Was related to the one
      Whose ear Peter had cut off
          And he said
              Did I not see you myself
              In the garden with him?

27 Then Peter denied it again
And immediately a cock crowed

Jesus before Pilate
28 They led Jesus
From Caiaphas
To the praetorium
It was early
And they did not go into the praetorium
So that they should not be defiled
But be able to eat the passover

29   Therefore Pilate
    Went outside to speak to them
    And said
        What accusation
        Do you bring against this man?

30   They answered him
        We would not have handed him over to you
        If he had not been doing wrong

31   Pilate said to them
        Take him yourselves
        And judge him according to your Law

    The Jews replied
        It is not lawful for us
        To condemn anyone to death

32 This was to fulfil the word of Jesus
Which he had spoken
Telling of the death
Which he was about to die

33 Then Pilate
Entered the praetorium again
    And calling Jesus
    He said to him
        Are you
        The King of the Jews?

34 Jesus answered
>> Do you say this yourself
>> Or have others
>> Said this about me?

35 Pilate replied
>> Am I myself a Jew?
>> Your own countrymen
>> And the chief priests
>> Handed you over to me
>> What have you done?

36 Jesus answered
>> My kingdom
>> Is not of this world
>> If my kingdom
>> Was of this world
>> My followers would have fought
>> So that I should not have been handed over
>> To the Jews
>> But my kingdom
>> Is not from here

37 Pilate said to him
>> Then you are not really a king?

Jesus answered
>> You say
>> That I am a king
>> I myself was born for this
>> And for this
>> I have come into the world
>> To bear witness to the truth
>> Everyone who belongs to the truth
>> Hears my voice

38 Pilate said to him
>> What is truth?

And having said this
He went out again to the Jews
>> And said to them
>>> I
>>> I do not find him guilty

39   But you have a custom
           That at the Passover
           One prisoner should be released
           Do you choose
           That I should release to you
           The King of the Jews?

40   Then they cried out again
             Not this one
             But Barabbas

Now Barabbas
Was a bandit

19 Then Pilate
Had Jesus taken away
And scourged

2   The soldiers plaited a crown of thorns
And put it on his head
And they threw a purple garment round him

3   They came up to him
           And said
              Hail
              King of the Jews

And they slapped him
On the face

4   Pilate went outside again
        And said to them
           Look how I am bringing him out to you
           So that you may be clear
           That I do not find him guilty

5   Then Jesus came out
Wearing the thorny crown
And the purple garment

        And he said to them
           Look upon the man

6   When the chief priests
And the guards saw him

They cried out
>> Crucify him
>> Crucify him

Pilate said to them
>> You take him yourselves
>> And crucify him
>> Because I
>> I do not find him guilty

7 The Jews answered him
>> We have a law
>> And according to that law
>> He ought to die
>> Because he made himself
>> The Son of God

8 So when Pilate
Heard these words
He was still more afraid
9 And went into the praetorium again
>> And said to Jesus
>>> Where do you come from?

But Jesus
Did not give him any answer

10 Therefore Pilate said to him
>> Will you not speak to me?
>> Do you not know
>> That I have the authority
>> To release you
>> And I have the authority
>> To crucify you?

11 Jesus answered
>> You would have no authority
>> Over me
>> Unless it was given to you
>> From above
>> Therefore he
>> Who handed me over to you
>> Has the greater sin

JOHN 19

Jesus is condemned to death

12 From then on
Pilate tried to release him

    But the Jews cried out
        If you release this one
        You are no friend to Caesar
        Everyone who makes himself a king
        Speaks against Caesar

13 Then Pilate
When he heard these words
Brought Jesus outside
And sat on the judgment seat
In a place called the Pavement
But in Hebrew
Gabbatha

14 Now it was the Preparation of the Passover
At about the sixth hour
    He said to the Jews
        Look upon your king

15   But they shouted
        Take him
        Take him
        Crucify him

    Pilate said to them
        Shall I crucify your king?

    The chief priests answered
        We have no other king
        Except Caesar

16 Then he handed him over to them
To be crucified

The Crucifixion

17 So they took Jesus
And carrying his own cross
He went out
To the place called the Place of a Skull

Or in Hebrew
Golgotha
18 Where they crucified him
And with him two others
One on either side
And Jesus in the centre

19 Pilate wrote an inscription
And had it put on the cross
On it was written
Jesus the Nazarene
The King of the Jews

20 Many of the Jews
Read this inscription
Because the place
Where Jesus was crucified
Was near the city
And it was written
In Hebrew
In Latin
And in Greek

21 Therefore the chief priests of the Jews
Said to Pilate
> Do not write
> The King of the Jews
> But that he said
> I am King of the Jews

22 Pilate answered
> What I have written
> I have written

23 When the soldiers
Had crucified Jesus
They took his clothing
And made four shares
A share for each soldier

There was also the tunic
Now the tunic had no seam
But was woven in one piece

24   So they said to one another
          Do not let us tear it
          But cast lots
          To see who should have it

     This is in order that the Scripture
     Might be fulfilled
     They parted my clothing
     Among themselves
     And over my clothes
     They cast a lot

25   And this
     Is what the soldiers did

     But beside Jesus' cross
     Stood his mother
     And his mother's sister
     Mary the wife of Clopas
     And Mary Magdalene

26   When Jesus saw his mother
     And the disciple whom he loved
     Standing there
        He said to his mother
            Woman
            Here is your son

27   Then he said to the disciple
          Here is your mother

     And from that hour
     The disciple
     Took her into his home

28   After this
     When Jesus knew
     That everything was finished
     In order that the Scripture
     Might be fulfilled
        He said
            I thirst

29   A jar full of vinegar
     Was standing there
     So they put a sponge full of vinegar
     On to hyssop
     And brought it to his mouth

30   When he had taken the vinegar
         Jesus said
             It is finished

     And he bowed his head
     And delivered up his spirit

31   As it was the Preparation
     And the Jews
     Did not want the bodies
     To remain on the cross
     On the sabbath
     Because that sabbath
     Was a great day
     They requested Pilate
     To allow their legs to be broken
     And to allow them to be taken away

The burial

32   So the soldiers came
     And broke the first one's legs
     Then those of the other one
     Who was crucified with him

33   When they came to Jesus
     And saw that he had already died
     They did not break his legs
34   But one of the soldiers
     Pierced his side with a lance
     And blood and water
     Came out immediately

35   He has borne witness
     Who saw this
     And his witness is true
     And he knows

That he speaks the truth
So that you also may believe

36 For all this took place
In order that the Scripture
Might be fulfilled
No bone of him
Shall be broken

37 And again
Another Scripture says
They shall look on him
Whom they pierced

38 Now after all this
Joseph of Arimathea
Who was a disciple of Jesus
But had kept it secret
For fear of the Jews
Asked Pilate
If he might take the body of Jesus
And Pilate gave him leave
So he came
And took away his body

39 Nicodemus
Who had first come to Jesus at night
Came with him
And he brought a mixture of myrrh and aloes
Weighing about a hundred pounds

40 So they took Jesus' body
And bound it in linen sheets
With the spices
According to the burial custom of the Jews

41 In the place where he was crucified
There was a garden
And in the garden
A new tomb
In which no one
Had yet been laid

42 Because for the Jews
It was the Preparation
And because the tomb
Was near by
They laid Jesus there

20

Mary Magdalene and two disciples find the tomb empty

1 On the first day after the sabbath
Mary Magdalene
Came to the tomb
It was early in the morning
And still dark

She saw that the stone
Had been taken from the tomb
2 So she ran
And came to Simon Peter
And to the other disciple
The one dear to Jesus

    And she said to them
        They have taken the Lord
        Out of the tomb
        And we do not know
        Where they have laid him

3 Then Peter
And the other disciple
Went out and came to the tomb

4 Now the two ran together
And the other disciple
Ran faster than Peter
And came to the tomb first
5 When he stooped down
He saw the linen clothes lying there
But he did not go in

6 Simon Peter followed him
And went into the tomb
And he perceived the linen sheets lying there
7 And the napkin
Which was on his head

Not lying with the linen sheets
But rolled up separately
In a place by itself

8 Then the other disciple
The one who had come to the tomb first
Went in
And he saw and believed

9 Because they did not yet know
The Scripture which said
That he should rise from the dead

10 Then the disciples
Went away to their home

Jesus appears to Mary Magdalene
11 But Mary
Stood outside the tomb
She was weeping
And as she wept
She bent down into the tomb
12 And perceived two angels in white
One was sitting at the head
And one at the feet
Where the body of Jesus
Had been lying

13   They said to her
      Woman
      Why are you weeping?

  She said to them
     Because they have taken my Lord
     And I do not know
     Where they have laid him

14 Having said this
She turned back
And perceived Jesus
Standing there
But she did not know
That it was Jesus

15   Jesus said to her
        Woman
        Why are you weeping?
        For whom are you searching?

    She thought he was the gardener
    And she said to him
        Sir
        If you have taken him away
        Tell me where you have laid him
        And I will take him

16   Jesus said to her
        Mary

    She turned
    And said to him in Hebrew
        Rabboni
        Which means teacher

17   Jesus said to her
        Do not touch me
        Because I have not yet ascended
        To the Father

        But go to my brothers
        And tell them
        That I am ascending
        To my Father
        And to your Father
        And to my God
        And to your God

18 Mary Magdalene
Came to the disciples
And brought the news
    Saying to them
        I have seen the Lord

And she told them
What he had said to her

JOHN 20

Jesus appears to the disciples in the upper room

19   On that day
     The first after the sabbath
     In the early evening
     When the disciples were behind closed doors
     For fear of the Jews
     Jesus came
     And stood among them
          And said
               Peace be with you

20   And having said this
     He showed them
     Both his hands
     And his side

     Then the disciples rejoiced
     On seeing the Lord

21   Jesus said to them again
               Peace be with you
               As the Father has sent me
               I also send you

22   And having said this
     He breathed on them
          And said
               Receive Holy Spirit
23   Those whom you free from their sins
               They are freed from them
               Those whom you hold to them
               They are held

24   But Thomas
     One of the twelve
     Called the Twin
     Was not with them when Jesus came

25   So the other disciples
          Said to him
               We have seen the Lord

          But he said to them
               Unless I see in his hands

        The mark of the nails
        And put my finger
        Into the place of the nails
        And put my hand
        Into his side
        I will not believe

26   And after eight days
      His disciples were again inside
      And Thomas was with them
      The doors were closed
      But Jesus came
      And stood among them
          And said
              Peace be with you

27   Then he said to Thomas
        Bring your finger here
        And look on my hands
        And bring your hand
        And put it into my side
        And be not unbelieving
        But believe

28   Thomas answered him
        My Lord and my God

29   Jesus said to him
        Have you believed
        Because you have seen me?
        Blessed are they
        Who do not see
        And yet believe

30   Now Jesus performed many other signs
      In the presence of his disciples
      Which have not been recorded in this book
31   But these have been recorded
      So that you may believe
      That Jesus is the Christ
      The Son of God
      And that in believing
      You may have life
      In his name

21 *The appearance by the Sea of Tiberias*

1   Afterwards
    Jesus showed himself
    To his disciples again
    By the Sea of Tiberias
    And he showed himself
    In this way

2   Simon Peter
    Was together with Thomas
    Called the Twin
    Nathanael from Cana in Galilee
    The sons of Zebedee
    And two other disciples of his

3   Simon Peter said to the others
            I am going fishing

        They said to him
            And we are coming with you

    They went out
    And embarked in the boat
    And during that night
    They caught nothing

4   When dawn came
    Jesus stood on the shore
    Although the disciples
    Did not know
    That it was Jesus

5   Jesus said to them
            Children
            Have you no fish to eat?

        They answered
            No

6   So he said to them
            Cast the net
            On the right side of the boat
            And you will find some

Then they cast it
And were no longer able to haul it in
Because of the full catch of fish

7   Then the disciple whom Jesus loved
       Said to Peter
              It is the Lord

When Simon Peter
Heard it is the Lord
He tied his tunic round him
Because he was naked
And threw himself into the sea
8 But the other disciples
Came in the little boat
Dragging the net with the fish
As they were not far from the land
Only about two hundred cubits

9 When they disembarked
On to the land
They saw a charcoal fire there
With a fish lying on it
And bread

10   Jesus said to them
              Bring some of the fish
              Which you have just caught

11 Simon Peter went on board
And drew the net to the land
It was full of large fish
A hundred and fifty-three
And even with so many
The net was not torn

12   Jesus said to them
              Come
              Make an early meal

None of the disciples
Ventured to ask the question
Who indeed are you?
They knew
It is the Lord

13   Jesus came
     And took bread
     And gave it to them
     And also the fish

14   Now this was the third time
     That Jesus
     Showed himself to his disciples
     After being raised from the dead

The charge to Peter
15   When they had made their meal
         Jesus said to Simon Peter
             Simon
             Son of John
             Do you love me more than these do?

         He replied
             Yes Lord
             You know
             That you are dear to me

         Jesus said to him
             Feed my little lambs

16   Then he said to him again
         The second time
             Simon
             Son of John
             Do you love me?

         He replied
             Yes Lord
             You know
             That you are dear to me

         Jesus said to him
             Shepherd my little sheep

17   Then he said to him
         For the third time
             Simon

> Son of John
> Am I dear to you?

Peter was grieved
That he said to him
The third time
Am I dear to you?

> And he said to him
>> Lord
>> You know everything
>> You are aware
>> That you are dear to me

> Jesus said to him
>> Feed my little sheep

18
> Of a certainty I say to you
> When you were young
> You tied your own belt
> And walked where you wished
> But when you grow old
> You will stretch out your hands
> And someone else will tie you
> And will carry you
> Where you do not wish to go

19 And he said this
To show by what death
He will reveal
The glory of God

> When he had told him this
> He said to him
>> Follow me

20 Peter turned
And he saw that the disciple whom Jesus loved
Was following
He was the one
Who had leaned on his breast at the supper
And had said
Lord
Who will betray you?

21   When he saw him
    Peter said to Jesus
        Lord
            What about this one?

22   Jesus said to him
        If it is my will
        For him to remain until I come
        Does that concern you?
        You follow me

23 Because of this
It was said among the brothers
That this disciple would not die
But Jesus did not say
That he would not die
But said
If it is my will
For him to remain until I come
Does that concern you?

Conclusion

24 This is the disciple
Who bears witness to these events
And who has recorded them
And we know
That what he says is true

25 Jesus also did many other things
Indeed if they were all written down
I expect that the world itself
Would not contain
The books being written

References to the Old Testament

The Gospel of Matthew

1:23	Isa.7:14	11:10	Exod.23:20, Mal.3:1
2:6	Mic.5:2	12:7	Hos.6:6
2:15	Hos.11:1	12:18	Isa.42:1–4
2:18	Jer.31:15	13:14f	Isa.6:9f
2:23	Possibly Isa.11:1	13:35	Ps.78:2
3:3	Isa.40:3	15:4	Exod.20:12, Lev.20:9, Exod.21:17
4:4	Deut.8:3		
4:6	Ps.91:11f	15:8	Isa.29:13
4:7	Deut.6:16	21:5	Zech.9:9
4:10	Deut.6:13	21:9	Ps.118:26
4:15f	Isa.8:23, 9:1	21:13	Isa.56:7, Jer.7:11
5:21	Exod.20:13	21:16	Ps.8:2
5:27	Exod.20:14	21:42	Ps.118:22,23
5:31	Deut.24:1	22:37	Deut.6:5
5:33	Lev.19:12	22:39	Lev.19:18
5:33	Exod.20:7	22:44	Ps.110:1
5:38	Exod.21:24, Lev.24:20, Deut.19:21	23:39	Ps.118:26
		24:15	Dan.9:27
5:43	Lev.19:18	26:31	Zech.13:7
7:23	Ps.6:8	27:9,10	Possibly Zech.11:12, Jer.32:6–15
8:17	Isa.53:4		
9:13	Hos.6:6	27:46	Ps.22:1

The Gospel of Mark

1:2	Mal. 3:1	11:17	Isa. 56:7, Jer. 7:11
1:3	Isa. 40:3	12:10f	Ps. 118:22f
4:12	Isa. 6:9f.	12:26	Exod. 3:6
7:6f	Isa. 29:13	12:29f	Deut. 6:4f.
7:10	Exod. 20:12, 21:17	12:31	Lev. 19:18
8:18	Jer. 5:21, Ezek. 12:2	12:36	Ps. 110:1
9:48	Isa. 66:24	13:14	Dan. 9:27
9:49	Ezek. 43:24, Lev. 2:13	14:27	Zech. 13:7
10:7f	Gen. 2:24	15:28	Isa. 53:12
11:9	Ps. 118:26	15:34	Ps. 22:1

REFERENCES TO THE OLD TESTAMENT

The Gospel of Luke

2:23	Exod.13:12	10:27	Deut.6:5, Lev.19:18
3:4–6	Isa.40:3–5	13:35	Ps.118:26
4:4	Deut.8:3	18:20	Exod.20:12–16, Deut.5:16–20
4:8	Deut.6:13	19:38	Ps.118:26
4:10f	Ps.91:11f	19:46	Isa.56:7, Jer.7:11
4:12	Deut.6:16	20:17	Ps.118:22
4:18f	Isa.61:1f	20:42	Ps.110:1
7:27	Mal.3:1	22:37	Isa.53:12
8:10	Isa.6:9f, (Jer.5:21, Ezek.12:2)		

The Gospel of John

1:23	Isa.40:3	12:38	Isa.53:1
2:17	Ps.69:9	12:40	Isa.6:9-10
6:31	Ps.78:24	13:18	Ps.41:9
6:45	Isa.54:13	15:25	Ps.35:19, 69:4
7:38	Obscure. The words may come from the liturgy of the feast of Tabernacles.	18:9	John 17:12
		19:24	Ps.22:18
		19:28	Ps.69:21
10:34	Ps.82:6	19:36	Exod.12:46, Ps.34:20
12:13	Ps.118:26	19:37	Zech. 12:10
12:15	Zech.9:9		